isco
Fun

DO NOT REMOVE
CARDS FROM POCKET

Also by Carole Terwilliger Meyers:

*Weekend Adventures for City-Weary People:*
*Overnight Trips in Northern California*

*Eating Out with the Kids in San Francisco and the Bay Area*

*How to Organize a Babysitting Cooperative and*
*Get Some Free Time Away From the Kids*

*Getting in the Spirit: Annual Bay Area Christmas Events*

# San Francisco
# Family Fun

## Carole Terwilliger Meyers

**CAROUSEL PRESS**
P.O. Box 6061
Albany, CA 94706
415/527-5849

Library of Congress Cataloging-in-Publication Data

Meyers, Carole Terwilliger.
 San Francisco family fun / Carole Terwilliger Meyers.
  p. cm.
 Rev. ed. of: Eating out with the kids in San Francisco and the Bay Area. c1985.
 ISBN 0-917120-10-8
 1. Restaurants, lunch rooms. etc.—California—San Francisco—Guide-books. 2. Restaurants, lunch room, etc.—California—San Francisco Bay Area—Guide-books. 3. Hotels, taverns, etc.—California—San Francisco—Guide-books. 4. Hotels, taverns, etc.—California—San Francisco Bay Area—Guide-books. 5. San Francisco (Calif.)—Description—Guide-books. 6. San Francisco Bay Area (Calif.)—Description and travel—Guide-books . . . . I. Meyers, Carole Terwilliger. Eating out with the kids in San Francisco and the Bay Area. II. Title.
TX907.3.C22S3664 1990
647.95794'61'083—dc20

90-32917
CIP

Printed in the United States of America

10 9 8 7 6 5 4 3 2 1

*To my babies, David and Suzanne*

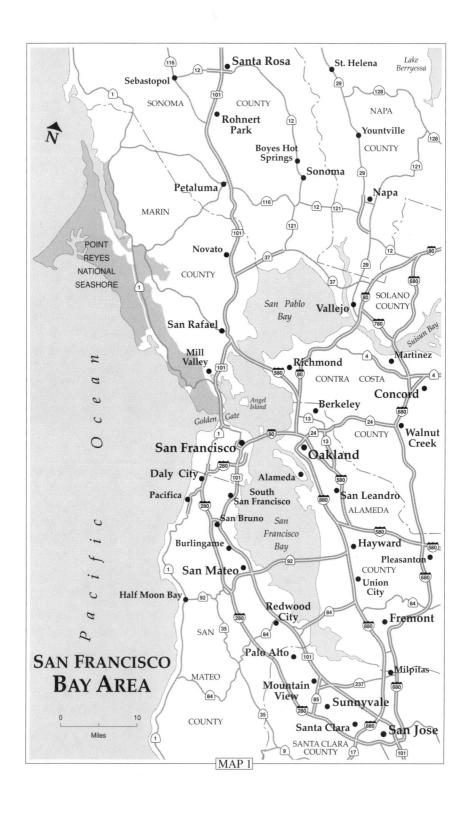

SAN FRANCISCO
BAY AREA

MAP 1

# Table of Contents

INTRODUCTION 1
    On Eating Out With Kids 1
FOOD FOR THOUGHT 3
BASIC INFORMATION FOR VISITORS TO SAN FRANCISCO 4
    Visitor Information 4
    Telephone Area Code 4
    Weather 5
    Transportation 5
    Baby/Child Equipment Rentals 5
    Dial-A-Story 5
HELPFUL HINTS FOR DINING IN RESTAURANTS WITH CHILDREN 6
    Alternative Methods of Seating Children in Restaurants 6
    The Goodie Bag 8
    Ordering for Children 10
    Waiting for the Food to Arrive 10
    Training Children 11
    Cleanup 11
    Tipping 11
    Dining With Teens 11
    Ethnic Restaurants 12
    Family Hours 12
    Sunday Brunch 12
    Money-Saving Idea 12
    An Aside to Restaurant Owners 12
    "Adult" Restaurants 13
    A Final Note 13
MINI-GUIDE TO CHINESE CUISINE 14
    Styles of Cooking 14
    Wo Choy 14
    Tea 14
    Dim Sum 14
    MSG 16
    If Only the Starving Children in China Could Have
        What You've Left on Your Plate 16
    Chinatown Parking 16
MINI-GUIDE TO THAI CUISINE 16
PICNIC HINTS 17
MEAL DELIVERY TO YOUR HOME 18
COOKING CLASSES FOR KIDS 20
GUIDELINES FOR INTERPRETING THIS BOOK 21

# San Francisco 25

**WHERE TO EAT** 25
    Picnic Pick-Ups 65
**WHAT TO DO** 68
    Historic Sites 68
    Performing Arts 78
    Museums 81
        Art 81
        Children's 84
        Floating 84
        Science 89
        Miscellaneous 93
    Outdoors/Parks 95
    Shopping 105
    Tours 112
        Guided Boat 112
        Guided Bus 113
        Guided Walking 113
        Do-It-Yourself 114

**WHERE TO STAY** 116
    Union Square 116
    The Embarcadero 121
    Chinatown/North Beach 123
    Motel Row 123
    Outer Geary 123
    The Beach 124
    Golden Gate Park 124
    Fisherman's Wharf 124
    Miscellaneous 126

# East Bay 131

**WHERE TO EAT** 131
    Picnic Pick-Ups 160
**WHAT TO DO** 163
    Historic Sites 163
    Performing Arts 167
    Museums 171
    Outdoors/Parks 174
    Miscellaneous 184

## South Bay 189

**WHERE TO EAT** 189
 Picnic Pick-Ups 202
**WHAT TO DO** 203
 Performing Arts 203
 Museums 203
 Outdoors/Parks 203
 Miscellaneous 206

## North Bay 211

**WHERE TO EAT** 211
 Picnic Pick-Ups 220
**WHAT TO DO** 223
 Historic Sites 223
 Performing Arts 223
 Museums 223
 Outdoors/Parks 224
 Miscellaneous 229

**CATERED BIRTHDAY PARTIES** 231
 Birthday Programs Minus Catering 234
**ANNUAL EVENTS** 237
**APPENDIXES** 257
 I. The Big Yellow House Meets Suzie 257
 II. A Family Fast: Oxfam Fast for a World Harvest 260
 III. Books for Further Exploration 262
**INDEXES** 267
 Alphabetical 267
 San Francisco Neighborhoods 275
 Categorical 276
**CREDITS** 280
**ABOUT THE AUTHOR** 281
**ORDER FORM** 283
**FEEDBACK** 285

**MAPS**
 1. San Francisco Bay Area (next to Table of Contents)
 2. San Francisco Overview 22
 3. San Francisco Detailed 24
 4. Golden Gate Park 98
 5. East Bay 130
 6. South Bay 188
 7. North Bay 210

Because of inflation, prices keep climbing. Prices are mentioned in this book only to give you assistance in planning your family fun budget. They may change at any time. If accurate cost is important, I recommend calling to check the current situation.

Restaurants are coping with inflation in different ways. Some raise their prices and maintain the same menu with fewer extras. Some keep prices at a standstill by cutting portions or quality. Many do something in between. Most of the restaurants listed in this book have been around for awhile and, though their prices may have gone up, their food quality has generally remained high. But in a business that has a failure rate of 80%, it's a good idea to call before setting out just to make sure the restaurant is still there.

# Introduction

This book has evolved from another entitled *Eating Out With the Kids in San Francisco and the Bay Area*. That it was the only dining guide in the country written exclusively for families is not surprising. San Franciscans—even those with children—take their food seriously. The city is said to have more restaurants per capita than any other in the world. And a plethora of ethnic foods, which seem to be particularly popular with families, are available.

I've changed the format of this new book so that information is included which will help the tourist planning a vacation in San Francisco as well as the local planning a day trip. In addition to a hefty section on restaurants and picnics (which comes first because in this food-obsessed city eating seems to be of primary interest to everyone), there are also large sections on attractions and lodgings. Chapters are also included on the surrounding East, South, and North Bay areas.

## ON EATING OUT WITH KIDS

When my husband and I want a peaceful and restful dinner out, we get a babysitter and go to an adult-oriented restaurant. But on the occasions when we take our children with us, we draw on the tested and true establishments listed in this book. And they've really been put to the test, because we don't have the type of children who make dining out easy.

My firstborn is an extremely active boy. He came into the world a colicky infant, and he has retained and embellished upon that noisy, boisterous personality throughout his life. Until recently he was not at all reliable about being cooperative or quiet or neat when we dined out. Now a teenager, he sometimes just refuses to go with us. This has turned out to be a blessing in disguise.

My second child, a girl, has been a little bit easier, but this has been more than compensated for by the entrance of that horrendous thing known as sibling rivalry. She shrieks and hollers and yells when her brother looks at her cross-eyed and is not at all influenced by what others may think of her behavior (see The Big Yellow House Meets Suzie, p. 257). However, when we dine with her alone, she can be an angel.

There have been times when I have snarled to my husband that I would never again dine with these two children in a restaurant. On those occasions my husband has pointed out that I would then be out of prime subject matter for this book. How true. Fortunately, like most mothers, I have a short memory for pain. I've learned to cope, but I've also grown reluctant to try a new restaurant with my children in tow unless I am fairly sure ahead of time that it is responsive to families.

In this book I provide good leads on where to spend your dining-out-as-a-family dollars. I have purposely eliminated the usual family haunts—hamburger, taco, and pizza chains. These are places that I'm sure you know enough about already. But I do not mean to berate them as they serve a definite purpose. There are times when families want to dine quickly and inexpensively and opt for a chain which has reliably standard food. But there are other occasions when there is more time and money, and a dining experience at one of the Bay Area's many fine restaurants would better be enjoyed by the entire family.

# Food For Thought

*We both know better than to try to work on Sundays. That's why, unless we're careful to plan something as a family, structure the day, we always end up snarling at each other and feeling uncared for. Sundays are terrible because it is clear that there is no one in charge of the world. And this knowledge leaves you drifting around, grappling with unfulfilled expectations and vague yearnings. Sundays reactivate all the memories of your childhood, when things were planned for you and done with you. If you're not careful, if you just sit around, you find yourself waiting for them to happen again; and things begin to disintegrate when you realize it isn't possible. All your own needs for sustenance and nurturing come crawling out like worms on Sunday; it's the day when you're the most aware of the relentlessness of the parenting task, and of your own irreversible adulthood. ("You can't go home again." —Thomas Wolfe.) But of course no one ever quite believes that, not entirely; that's why you've got to be on your toes on Sunday. It can be a real killer.*

— Sheila Ballantyne
*Norma Jean the Termite Queen*

# Basic Information For Visitors To San Francisco

**VISITOR INFORMATION**

Before your visit contact the San Francisco Convention and Visitors Bureau (P.O. Box 6977, San Francisco, CA 94101). For $1 they will send you a copy of *The San Francisco Book*. It is filled with sightseeing, shopping, and dining information. Another booklet, *The Lodging Guide*, will also be included.

Upon arrival, a multi-lingual staff is available to assist you at the **Visitor Information Center** (Hallidie Plaza, Market St./Powell St., one block from the cable car turn-around, 391-2000; M-F 9-5:30, Sat 9-3, Sun 10-2). Plan to make a stop there to get oriented. You can also pick up an assortment of helpful brochures.

For a recorded listing of the day's events, call 391-2001. For the same information in French call 391-2003, German 391-2004, Spanish 391-2122, and Japanese 391-2101.

**TELEPHONE AREA CODE**

Unless otherwise noted, all telephone numbers in this book carry the 415 prefix.

## WEATHER

Surely you've heard the saying attributed to Mark Twain, "The coldest winter I ever spent was a summer in San Francisco." Scholars may dispute that the words were Twain's, but no one who has spent a summer in San Francisco will dispute the claim.

This city is known for its morning and evening fog in summer. Locals coming in from the suburbs have learned to always bring along wraps. In summer it is easy to spot tourists. They are the ones wearing shorts . . . or white shoes, another no-no among locals. Perhaps these visitors are confusing San Francisco with the image of southern California's warm beaches. That is a mistake.

In general the climate is temperate, usually ranging between 40 and 70 degrees.

## TRANSPORTATION

For information on the MUNI—which runs the buses, trolleys, and cable cars—call 673-MUNI. Reduced fares are available for children ages 5 to 12; under 5 ride free.

For information on BART (Bay Area Rapid Transit), the underground rail system operating between San Francisco and the East Bay, call 788-2278.

Ferries are a good way to get to scenic Marin County. Golden Gate Transit ferries board at the Ferry Building located at the foot of Market Street and sail to Sausalito and Larkspur. For schedule and fare information call 332-6600. The Red and White Fleet boards at Pier 41 at Fisherman's Wharf and goes to Sausalito and Tiburon. For information call 546-2896 or 800/445-8880.

Taxis may be hailed if you can find one. Rates are relatively high ($2.90 for the first mile, then $1.50 per mile), and you'll most likely have to telephone for one. The biggest companies include Yellow (626-2345) and Allied (826-9494).

## BABY/CHILD EQUIPMENT RENTALS

If you find that you have forgotten some important piece of equipment, don't despair. Just head on over to Such A Business (see p. 110). They'll take care of everything.

## DIAL-A-STORY

Maintained by the San Francisco Public Library, this story line operates 24 hours a day and is free except for normal toll charges. Stories change each week and run Monday to Monday. For a story in English dial 626-6516, in Spanish 552-0535, in Cantonese 552-0534.

# Helpful Hints For Dining In Restaurants With Children

### ALTERNATIVE METHODS OF SEATING CHILDREN IN RESTAURANTS

Most parents know from experience that restaurants are unpredictable in their seating facilities for children. We know that we must sometimes rely upon our own ingenuity to make a dining experience tolerable. Though I've taken care in this book to mention the availability of highchairs and booster seats at each restaurant listed, there are still bound to be times when you will be forced to improvise. And you must be especially prepared when dining out with an infant. Here are some suggestions for you to consider:

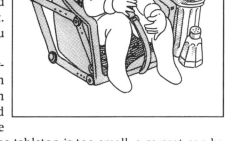

■ Many contemporary carseats can be taken directly from the car into the restaurant, with baby comfortably strapped in and still sleeping. Sometimes it can be placed right on the table. When the tabletop is too small, a carseat can be placed on the seat of a booth or on two chairs pushed together. Don't put

it on the floor unless there is no other alternative. Babies like to be up where they can watch what's going on, and on the floor there is also the danger that someone might accidentally trip or spill something on the child.

■ An **infantseat** may be used with babies under six months. (Older babies often will not stay put in one.) It can be used in the same manner as a carseat (described above).

■ A **fabric cuddler** works well with infants under three months but is less comfortable for the parent. And there is the danger that something might spill on the baby en route to the parent's mouth.

■ The type of **backpack** with a frame that allows it to stand up by itself can be very handy.

■ A **stroller** works well and, when you're out walking anyway, is quite convenient. But know your baby. There are those who will not stay put.

■ A **car bed** is great for an infant or soundly-sleeping toddler. Be aware, though, that car beds are not considered safe to use in the car as a carseat.

■ A **fabric wrap** that converts any chair into a highchair is available in many baby supply stores. They are inexpensive and small enough to carry in a purse.

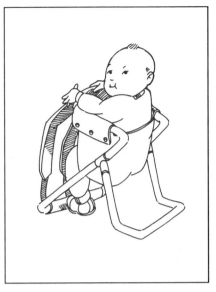

■ For babies who can sit up, a **parent's belt** works well for holding them in a chair. This works only for a short period, as it is restraining.

■ Sit the baby on **your lap**. This always works as a last resort, and children love it. Parents don't always love it as much.

■ Some diehard patrons such as myself have even been known to drag along their own highchair to favorite restaurants which fail to provide this necessity. For those of you who fall into this category, there exists a **portable highchair** that is easy to carry and can be clamped onto the edge of a table. Be careful, though, as the table must either be secured to the floor or have four legs.

■ The novel idea of tying a toddler into a booster seat with a **dish towel** was devised by a clever waiter at Yet Wah. It works very well.

However, after having tried all of the above methods myself, I suggest that when a restaurant doesn't have the needed highchair or booster seat and you can select another place to dine, do so. And make a point of notifying the bypassed restaurant that you are not patronizing them because of their lack of facilities for children. If you feel that you must go to such a restaurant anyway because of its special ambiance or cuisine, make every effort to get a babysitter. Enjoy the experience instead of forcing yourself to contend with the inadequate provisions available for children.

## THE GOODIE BAG

After my first child turned one, I never went to a restaurant with him unless I had first packed him a "goodie bag." Before then he was nursed, and the "goodies" were always available without any preplanning.

The goodie bag seems like such an obvious idea, yet it took me quite a while to come up with it. It occurred to me soon after I engaged in a mad struggle to keep my active toddler in his highchair. At that time he was still too young to be given a portion of my meal or to order for from a children's menu, so I learned to think ahead and bring along his own special food. Even older children can benefit from an "appetizer" to placate them until the restaurant food is served.

The goodie bag was originally packed with finger foods. Favorites were:

| | |
|---|---|
| cheese chunks | bread |
| orange slices | animal cookies |
| crackers | bananas |
| meat sticks | small box of |
| a bottle | dry cereal |
| raisins | apple slices |

As my children grew I varied the contents of this bag appropriately—always making every effort to keep it interesting to them. I could always tell when I had packed the wrong items— the food would be tossed aside, sometimes landing on other diners who were unfortunate enough to be sitting nearby. So I kept on my toes and always had my eyes peeled for new, intriguing items to add to the goodie bag.

For older children the following non-food items are appropriate:

| | |
|---|---|
| pads of paper | scotch tape |
| colored felt pens and pencils | gummed paper shapes or stickers |
| midget cars | pipe cleaners |
| finger puppets | magic slate |
| little people figures | |

For the goodie bag itself you can use an old purse, a backpack, a small basket, a shopping bag, etc. To avoid arguments it is best to have a separate bag for each of your children.

A disposable bib can easily be made by packing a sweater guard (which abound at garage sales and second-hand stores) and using it to hold a napkin around baby's neck. Or keep two large safety pins pinned to the lining of your purse or wallet; use them to secure a napkin to your child's shirt. And don't forget pre-moistened wipes to make after-eating-cleanup almost easy.

I think you'll find the goodie bag so useful that you will begin using it in other ways—on car trips, on rainy days, when your children are sick, or when you leave them with a babysitter.

And if on some occasion you forget to bring along the goodie bag or it just doesn't seem to be working, you can always resort to bribery by offering a special dessert for good behavior. Who knows, it might even work.

"YUCK"

**ORDERING FOR CHILDREN**

Rare is the restaurant which offers that old standby—a peanut butter & jelly sandwich. Fortunately, another favorite—the grilled cheese sandwich—is easier to find. I am particularly fond of these sandwiches because they hold together well and create a minimum of mess. Other favorites with children are, of course, the hot dog and hamburger.

Although messy, cottage cheese provides a nutritious and easily eaten meal. Both jello and scrambled eggs are usually reasonably priced and available on many menus. And, of course, ice cream is very common and makes a good dessert.

Many of the restaurants mentioned in this book serve portions ample enough to permit sharing your meal with a small child. Most will provide extra plates when requested. Always ask, though, to verify whether or not you will be charged for the extra plates—often referred to as an "extra service" or "plate charge." Family-style restaurants generally do charge for an extra place setting. Sometimes, even if your child will be unable to eat it all, it turns out to be more economical to order a child's portion.

It might be worth investing in a baby food grinder. It can be conveniently taken along wherever you go and allows baby to eat whatever you are eating. I have found mine to be useful at home as well. Many parents of infants find that feeding them just before they go out works well, too.

And always try to order one item which will be served right away.

**WAITING FOR THE FOOD TO ARRIVE**

How you pass this time will, of course, depend on your personality, your mood, and the ages of your children. Here are a few ideas which have worked well for my family.

■ Talk to each other. It's surprising how often this simple solution is overlooked.

■ Play a distracting game like Twenty Questions or Ghosts.

■ Suggest that your children shake a sealed container of cream until it turns into butter. (My daughter has proven that this does happen.)

■ Have them count. How many chairs are there in the room? How many light fixtures? How many people? Etc.

■ If you're really desperate, suggest they rub two toothpicks together to make fire. (Neither of my children have been able to prove that this happens.)

## TRAINING CHILDREN

I believe that the best way to teach children to behave well in restaurants is to expose them often to the experience of dining out. Make dining out as a family a regular event.

Should your children get out of control, threaten to leave. Then do it if they don't shape up. You'll probably never have to do it again because they will remember. And you will have the sympathy of every other parent in the restaurant, because we've all been through it.

## CLEANUP

Children are messy! I'll bet you knew that already. Always make an effort to tidy up the mess your children leave. Teach the older ones to pick up after themselves. For babies, pick up the larger droppings from the floor or at least brush them out of the path of foot traffic. If you are leaving behind a big mess and for some reason are unable to clean it up, explain the situation to the server and try to compensate by leaving a generous tip.

## TIPPING

When you dine out as a family, you should expect to leave a good tip. Fifteen to twenty percent is the current rate. I suggest leaving twenty percent when service has been excellent and fifteen percent when service has been adequate. Leave extra if you have made the server's job especially difficult or have asked for many special services.

Everyone must decide for themselves what to do when service has been bad. Do bear in mind, though, that some restaurants are purposely understaffed by the management, and the servers usually get blamed for poor service even though they may be doing everything within their power to serve you well. In this case, tip fairly, and let the management know that the service was terrible and that you realize it is because of their policy of underhiring and overworking their staff.

## DINING WITH TEENS

As a child enters the uncommunicative teens, it often works well for one parent to take that child out alone. Let your teen help choose a restaurant and perhaps a pre- or post-dining activity. Use this valuable undistracted time to talk to your teen, who most likely will really appreciate your complete attention.

### ETHNIC RESTAURANTS

Dining at an ethnic restaurant can be educational if time is taken to prepare for it by learning about the culture behind the food. Visit the library to gather information and a children's book on the culture. The time spent together as a family at the library (or bookstore) is an added bonus to the actual family dining experience.

### FAMILY HOURS

The best dining time for families in most restaurants seems to be before 7 p.m. for dinner, with Sunday being the traditional family night out. Breakfast and lunch are also generally good times, and they also tend to be more casual and less expensive than dinner.

### SUNDAY BRUNCH

Many families have found Sundays to be depressing (see p. 3). Maybe it's because we've been racing along at high speed all week, and when Sunday rolls around, all that potential leisure can be overwhelming. How will we fill the void?

The Sunday paper is one good way. Another is to pack up and head out for a leisurely brunch. Some people have even been known to combine reading the paper with their brunch, but I prefer to encourage interaction with your dining companions.

Sunday brunch tends to be a great family dining experience. In general even the fancier restaurants are set up to accommodate children of all ages and dispositions. You're fairly safe in taking them along almost anywhere.

### MONEY-SAVING IDEA

Be sure to plan into your budget a fund for dining out as a family. A device that might work for you is to put aside a special bank and fill it with money you save at the supermarket using cents-off coupons. What a motivation to clip and use all those coupons we're always seeing.

### AN ASIDE TO RESTAURANT OWNERS

You really should keep a cookie jar filled for cranky babies whose parents forget to bring along a goodie bag. Crackers and extra napkins should be offered as a matter of course. Tattered or dangerously wobbly highchairs and booster seats should be replaced. Drop cloths should be provided when you want to protect the flooring, as is done routinely in Japan. And any of you that are redecorating or building a new restaurant—consider sectioning off a small play area complete with toys for the more restless children who accompany us to restaurants.

## "ADULT" RESTAURANTS

If you have a favorite restaurant which seems amenable to children in every way except the providing of proper seating arrangements, voice your irritation to the management. Or write a letter informing the manager that regrettably you will be unable to patronize the restaurant until conditions improve. There is a good chance that things will change for the better, and then all parents will benefit from your action.

But remember, too, that there are some restaurants with no accommodations for children and where children are not appropriate. They cater exclusively to an adult clientele which seeks them out when wanting a quiet, elegant meal. These are the restaurants to patronize when you are fortunate enough to have a babysitter for the evening.

## A FINAL NOTE

Notice that I offer no advice on how to make your child actually eat. There is a reason for this. It is that I am waiting for someone to tell me how to make my fussy, picky youngest eat what I consider to be a balanced meal. Some say this fussiness is only a "stage." Others suggest it is a gourmet in the making. For what is a gourmet if not a selective (picky) eater?

# Mini-Guide To Chinese Cuisine

**STYLES OF COOKING**

There are basically five types of Chinese cuisine available at restaurants in the Bay Area.

*Cantonese.* This is what most people think of when they head out for Chinese food. This style originates in southern China. Seasonings are subtle though not necessarily bland. Chow mein and sweet and sour dishes are examples, as are the dim sum specialties.

*Hunan.* This style originates in south-central China. Meats are smoked and dishes are spicy-hot. More liberal use of chili peppers makes this style even hotter than Szechwan.

*Mandarin.* This style is a composite of foods and styles of cooking from many areas.

*Northern or Peking.* This style originates in northern China. Steamed breads, noodle dishes, potstickers, sizzling rice soup, hot pots, and other simply seasoned dishes are examples.

*Szechwan.* This style originates in the mountainous Szechwan province. It is appreciated by those who enjoy spicy-hot foods such as kung pao shrimp and hot and sour soup.

**WO CHOY**

Wo choy is worth mentioning to those of you who are on the road to becoming connoisseurs of Chinese cuisine. These are simple, inexpensive dishes which change daily and are usually listed on the menu in Chinese only. If your server speaks English or if you speak Chinese, you may be able to determine ahead of time what you will be getting. Otherwise you must just order by pointing at random and taking what you get.

But ordering in a Chinese restaurant you've never been to before almost always means taking a chance anyway. Their menus rarely itemize the ingredients in each dish. This makes ordering almost any dish a surprise—sometimes pleasant, sometimes not.

**TEA**

There are three kinds of tea you're likely to run into: mild green, semi-fermented oolong, and strong fermented black. Chrysanthemum combines black tea with the dried flowers; jasmine combines oolong with the dried flowers.

When you want more tea, do as the Chinese do. Simply turn over the lid on the tea pot. This signals the server that you need a refill.

**DIM SUM**

Translated variously as meaning "touch of heart," "touch your heart," "heart's desire," and "heart's delight," dim sum items were originally served for breakfast during the Tang Dynasty (618 to 907 A.D.). Nowadays you can enjoy a meal of these appetizers as an interesting change of pace for breakfast or lunch.

The varieties of dim sum are seemingly endless and include steamed buns, fried dumplings, and turnovers. Of the many I have sampled there have been few I didn't care for—mainly delicacies like stewed duck feet. Though I consider it great fun to just pick and choose and take my chances and be surprised, some of you may feel less daring. For you I highly recommend a trip to the library to read two very good magazine articles that describe and illustrate in color various of the "heart's delights": "The Inscrutable Feast," *New West*, February 13, 1978, and "Dim Sum? Deem Soom? Dihm Sohm? . . . ," *Sunset*, February 1980.

Another good introduction for the novice is a visit to **Kow Loon Pastry** (909 Grant Avenue, 362-9888), where many of these items are displayed and identified in English and available for take-out. Though the atmosphere is not nearly as interesting as at the regular "teahouses," as dim sum establishments are referred to, it will give you the opportunity to identify the items which you might most enjoy.

In the teahouses service is usually from carts (Hong Kong-style) or trays brought to your table laden with various delicacies. You may have difficulty in getting a server to describe what a particular item is made of—depending on how crowded the restaurant is and on whether or not they speak English—so you should plan to simply choose whatever looks appetizing. Just flag down the servers as they come around, and take your chances. Carts will continue to circulate throughout your meal.

Tea is brought automatically, and

some teahouses offer a choice of other drinks.

Note that crossed chop sticks are usually an omen of bad luck, except in dim sum houses where they signal the server that you are done.

The bill is determined by how many serving plates are on your table at the meal's end. (This concept reminds me of a little town I once visited in Italy which is filled with belltowers and where a family's wealth is measured by the height of their belltower.) Most teahouses charge about $1.35/plate. To keep a running tab, just make a neat little stack of the serving plates and steamers as you finish with them. This is also a good opportunity to give your children a lesson in math and economics.

## MSG

I understand that people who are sensitive to the flavor enhancer monsodium glutamate (MSG) can experience anything from a buzzing in their head to outbursts of violent behavior. If you ask, most restaurants will omit it when preparing your order.

### IF ONLY THE STARVING CHILDREN IN CHINA COULD HAVE WHAT YOU'VE LEFT ON YOUR PLATE

It seems that in China when children leave rice in their bowl, mothers tell them that their future spouse will have as many pock marks on his or her face as there are grains of rice left uneaten.

### CHINATOWN PARKING

It is nearly impossible to find a parking spot on the street in San Francisco's congested Chinatown. Try the relatively inexpensive city-owned Portsmouth Square Garage at 733 Kearny Street at Clay.

# Mini-Guide To Thai Cuisine

I know many parents take their children to exotic Thai restaurants, because I've seen them. I have also observed some of those kids eating amazing dishes without complaint. (Are these kids *real* kids?) My kids do not do this. My kids are willing to eat only certain totally non-threatening items. (Are my kids *real* kids?)

My daughter is extremely fond of sweet, amber-colored Thai iced tea swirled prettily with half-and-half, milk, or condensed milk—depending on the restaurant. She also likes satay on a stick with peanut dipping sauce and creamy-smooth fried bananas. And she will usually eat a portion of plain steamed rice. My older, more daring son will try most dishes that aren't incredibly spicy-hot or made with fish. Both are disappointed by Thai tapioca pudding, which tends to be hard-jelled and delicately flavored—not creamy and sweet as they prefer.

Since my husband and I are Thai cuisine enthusiasts, we eat at these usually moderately-priced restaurants frequently. We almost always have one or both of our kids in tow. From desperation we've learned what works for them. But mistakes in ordering for the kids have never been a loss. I just have it packed up to take home for my weekday lunch.

# Picnic Hints

Years ago a friend introduced me to what has become my own ideal picnic fare: a bottle of wine, a hunk of cheese, a loaf of french bread, a jar of marinated artichoke hearts, a container of yogurt, and some fresh fruit. Its beauty is its simplicity. No preparation is required. Most of the items are always on hand in my kitchen, and it all goes together deliciously. All that is needed for perfection is a straw picnic basket in which to tote it.

More convenient yet, especially for spur-of-the-moment picnics, is to simply stop at a delicatessen for supplies. (Each Where to Eat section of this book has a subsection devoted to the best places to secure Picnic Pick-Ups.) To help spontaneity along I always keep in my car trunk a picnic blanket, a day pack (for those picnic spots requiring a hike to reach), and a plastic pull-string bag stocked with paper plates, cups, napkins, plastic eating utensils, straws, a can opener, and a corkscrew. To protect the temperature of picnic fare, it's a good idea to also carry an insulated cooler.

Picnics are the perfect outing for families. Just about anywhere you can lay a blanket is acceptable. But some spots are more pleasant than others. My favorites are cross-referenced in the categorical index under Great Picnic Sites.

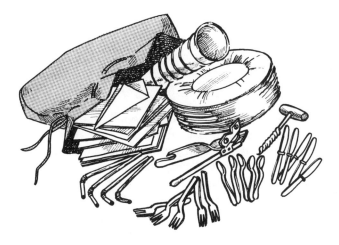

# Meal Delivery To Your Home

There are times when you don't want to cook, don't have the time to cook, or don't have anything in the house to cook—and you also don't want to go out. Or perhaps your attitude toward cooking is like that of Representative Pat Schroeder (D-Colo.) who was quoted in the *San Francisco Chronicle* as saying, "Cooking is not my strong suit. As my children will attest, my favorite recipe is Domino's phone number."

Any of these situations can be made better by the new businesses which deliver prepared meals to your doorstep. Each provides an advance menu. Call for further information.

## HOMEMADE EXPRESS
*420-1787; $7.50/adult, $4.50/child; order by 10am for same-day service; delivery M-F; serves Berkeley, Oakland, Alameda, Albany, Emeryville.*

Homemade Express prepares a different enticing meal each weekday and delivers it to your office, child's school, or home. It is packed so that when you get home, you either pop it in the fridge or oven or just serve it right away at room temperature.

I've tried two of these easy meals and want more. It's kind of like having your own part-time traditional housewife.

The first menu I tried consisted of moist baked Szechwan-spiced chicken pieces and chewy individual bread rounds topped with sweet sauteed onions. An accompanying sesame noodle salad was fragrant with sesame oil, crunchy with bean sprouts, and tangy with a bit of hot spiciness.

The second featured a Mediterranean corkscrew pasta salad tossed with tomato, black olives, artichoke hearts, and creamy cubes of mozzarella cheese. It also included a green salad with a really great vinaigrette dressing, more of that onion bread, and a big chocolate chip cookie made with chocolate dough. My teen licked his plate clean (literally), and my preteen (refusing to try anything) kept her plate squeaky clean . . . causing me to ponder how people actually survive parenthood to become old. The preteen wouldn't even eat the cookies . . . because they had nuts in them. On the other hand the teen ate more than his portion commenting, "These are soooo good."

Servings were generous. My teen could hold his own with an adult portion, but, as you can see, my daughter didn't even need a child's portion. Next time I'll forget her portion and just make her a peanut butter & jelly sandwich to eat while the rest of us feast.

Note that containers are designed to be popped into a microwave and double as storage containers for leftovers. The price is fair and equivalent to a moderately priced restaurant meal. You do have to provide a drink, there is usually no dessert, and you can wind up with dishes to do if you don't have paper plates on hand. But you don't have to tip, and sometimes there is enough left over for a lunch the next day.

And when you tell your friends to mention your name with their first order, you are given a free meal for every three who do. Please tell them I sent you.

## HELP AT HOME
*561-1256; $7.50/person + $2.50 delivery charge; order 24 hours in advance; delivery on Tu & F; serves San Franciso.*

Meals include an entree, rice or potato, and a vegetable. Soup is available at $1.60 per pint, and dessert is an additional $1.25.

This Jewish Family & Children's Services program is licensed by the State of California. It can also help you with childcare, home care, and laundry.

## WAITERS ON WHEELS
*252-1470; call daily 10am-11pm; $5 delivery charge; serves San Francisco.*

Meals from client restaurants are delivered to your door. Call for a catalogue of menus and further details.

## DINNER IS SERVED
*938-9065; call M-Sat 5-9; $5 delivery charge; serves Walnut Creek, Danville, Alamo, Pleasant Hill, Lafayette, Moraga.*

Similar to Waiters on Wheels, this service delivers your meal on a silver platter and provides you with a complimentary red rose to decorate your table.

# Cooking Classes For Kids

### SAN FRANCISCO SCHOOL OF COOKING
*2801 Leavenworth St., in The Cannery, 474-3663; $30/class/parent + 1 child, each additional child + $10; reservations essential.*

My daughter has expressed an interest in cooking since she was very young. In feeding that interest I find that I benefit from outside inspiration. So when I saw this cooking school's Children's Birthday Party class for parents and children, I signed us both up right away.

When we arrived, Chef Lucas Schoemaker of Jil's Restaurant was busy preparing for the lesson. Blues guitar licks drifted up from the street below, providing pleasant background music, and school owner Shirley Cano prepared coffee for us adults to wake up with.

Participants this day included several fathers (one of whom arrived with a Barbie tucked by the legs in his jeans hip pocket), several mothers, and a clutch of eager kids. Chef Lucas charmed us all with his Dutch accent and pleasant manner with children. He managed to get all the kids up to the demonstration table helping with things like stemming strawberries and rolling cookie dough "sausages."

Chef Lucas had prepared enough Birthday Cake Bisquits ahead of time for each pair of us to have one for decorating. So we filled and frosted them with Strawberry Cream Mousse while sampling buttery Sand Cookies we had helped with earlier. When the Strawberry Sherbet failed to freeze, the Chef laughed it off and called it Strawberry Soup—a handy attitude trick all cooks should master.

Past classes have included a Parent/Child Basic Cooking Series. Call for a current class schedule.

### LE MERIDIEN HOTEL
*50 Third St., San Francisco, 974-6400 x7466; $20/child.*

Once a month this refined hotel opens its impressive kitchen to children for cooking classes. Chef Pascal teaches children ages 8 to 14 the basics of pastry. Recipes, chef hats, aprons, and utensils are included in the fee.

### YAN CAN/CHARLOTTE COMBE INTERNATIONAL
### COOKING SCHOOL
*1064-G Shell Blvd., Foster City, 574-7788.*

This school occasionally offers cooking classes for children and teens. In the past they have offered a class in crepe-making for teens. Call for current schedule.

# Guidelines For Interpreting This Book

Most listings in this book include when possible: street address, cross street, city, phone, and whether a fee or free parking lot adjoins.

Information for **attractions** additionally includes when possible: days and hours of operation, admission price for adults and children, whether there are picnic tables or food service, and an indication if strollers are not permitted.

Descriptions for **restaurants** also include: meals served (B=breakfast, L=lunch, D=dinner, SunBr=Sunday brunch) and days open; code for the price range per adult of an average meal exclusive of drinks, tax, and tip ($=inexpensive, under $10; $$=medium priced, $10-$20; $$$=expensive, over $20. Realize that if you are a lover of steak, lobster, alcohol, and/or rich desserts, no restaurant will be inexpensive.); if highchairs, booster seats, or booths are available (If it is important to you to have any of these items, phone ahead and reserve them.); if there are children's portions (Sometimes these special portions are limited to children under a specific age. Also, prices can vary tremendously. It is always wise to ask how much before you go and to ascertain policy regarding children sharing a parent's order.); if it is 100% non-smoking (Most restaurants now have non-smoking sections.); if take-out delivery is available (Most restaurants will prepare food for take-out.); if reservations are accepted (Most restaurants that do not take reservations will reserve space for parties of six or more.); which credit cards are accepted (AE=American Express, DC=Diner's Club, MC=MasterCard, V=Visa/BankAmericard. Many inexpensive restaurants do not accept credit cards. This is often because a low operating overhead doesn't allow absorbing the extra charges which are paid to credit card companies. The fact that a restaurant does not take credit cards usually works out to the diner's advantage in the form of lower menu prices).

Descriptions for **delis and bakeries** also mention: whether pre-packed picnic boxes are available by reservation, whether beer and/or wine is available, and whether sit-down service is available.

Descriptions for **hotels** include: rate range for 2 people, the number of suites and the rate range, if children under a specific age may stay free in their parents' room, if there are refrigerators, if there is room service and if it offers children's items, if there is a dining room and if it is equipped for children (highchairs, booster seats, children's portions), if there is parking available and the rate. In the text mention is made of how many stories high the building is, the year it was built, and the number of rooms it has.

# SAN FRANCISCO OVERVIEW

Golden Gate Bridge
101
Fort Point

Crissy Field

Palace of Fine Arts & Exploratorium

PRESIDIO

Baker Beach

China Beach

Lands End

N

Lincoln Park

Cliff House

Palace of the Legion of Honor

Geary

Blvd

LAUREL HEIGHTS

Masonic

RICHMOND

USF

Fulton St

de Young Museum

Panhandl

Golden Gate Park

California Academy of Sciences

HAIGH

Lincoln Way

UCSF

Judah St

SUNSET

7th Ave

Noriega St

Sunset Res

19th Ave

Twin Peaks

DIAMON HEIGHT

Taraval St

Portola

Mt Davidson Park

Stern Grove

35 Sloat Blvd

Zoo

City College

280

Lake

Harding Park

SF State Univ

Geneva Ave

Fort Funston

35 Merced

Pacific

Ocean

Golden Gate Natl Rec Area

Great Hwy

Sunset Blvd

Park Presidio Blvd

Lincoln Blvd

0    1    2
Miles

MAP 2

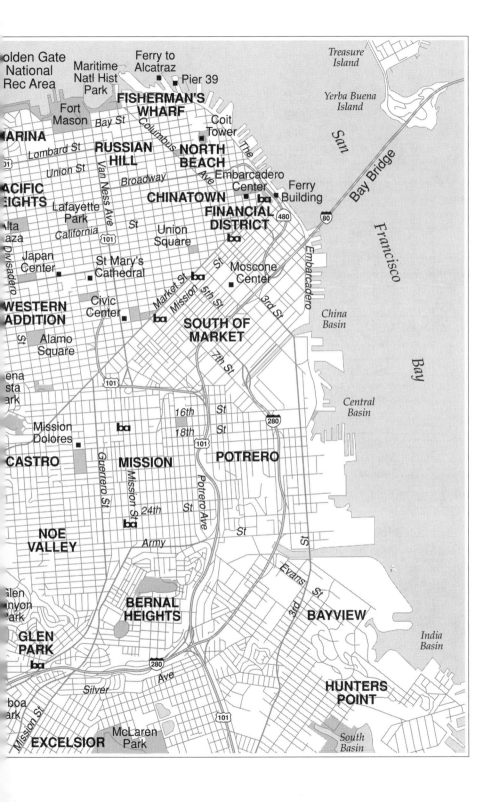

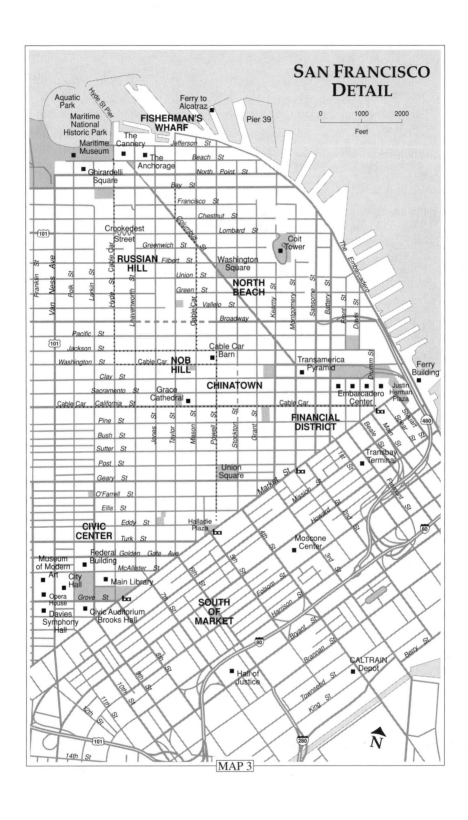

# SAN FRANCISCO DETAIL

0    1000    2000
Feet

Aquatic Park

Maritime National Historic Park

Hyde St Pier

Maritime Museum

The Cannery

Ghirardelli Square

The Anchorage

**FISHERMAN'S WHARF**

Ferry to Alcatraz

Pier 39

Jefferson St

Beach St

North Point St

Bay St

Francisco St

Chestnut St

Crookedest Street

Lombard St

Greenwich St

Coit Tower

**RUSSIAN HILL**

Filbert St

Washington Square

Union St

Green St

**NORTH BEACH**

Vallejo St

Broadway

Columbus Av

Cable Car

Cable Car

Leavenworth St

Hyde St

Larkin St

Polk St

Van Ness Ave

Franklin St

Pacific St

Jackson St

Washington St

Clay St

Cable Car

**NOB HILL**

Cable Car Barn

**CHINATOWN**

Transamerica Pyramid

Ferry Building

Sacramento St

Grace Cathedral

Justin Herman Plaza

Embarcadero Center

Cable Car

California St

Cable Car

**FINANCIAL DISTRICT**

Pine St

Bush St

Sutter St

Post St

Geary St

O'Farrell St

Ellis St

Jones St

Taylor St

Mason St

Powell St

Stockton St

Grant St

Kearny St

Montgomery St

Sansome St

Battery St

Front St

Davis St

Drumm St

Union Square

Transbay Terminal

Market St

Mission St

Howard St

1st St

2nd St

3rd St

Beale St

Main St

Spear St

Stewart St

Fremont St

Eddy St

Halladie Plaza

Turk St

**CIVIC CENTER**

Federal Building

Golden Gate Av

McAllister St

Moscone Center

Museum of Modern Art

City Hall

Main Library

Grove St

Opera House

Davies Symphony Hall

Civic Auditorium
Brooks Hall

**SOUTH OF MARKET**

4th St

5th St

6th St

7th St

8th St

9th St

10th St

11th St

12th St

Folsom St

Harrison St

Bryant St

Brannan St

Townsend St

King St

Berry St

CALTRAIN Depot

Hall of Justice

14th St

The Embarcadero

101

101

480

80

80

101

280

N

MAP 3

# San Francisco

## Where To Eat

### BASQUE HOTEL
*15 Romolo Place/Broadway, 788-9404; D Tu-Sun; $$; highchairs, booster seats; children's portions; no reservations; no cards.*

Back a few years, in the good old days, this was a popular place with starving students. Prices were cheap, portions big, and the atmosphere festive. These qualities led me to believe that it might now be a good spot for frugal families. A visit confirmed my hopes.

On a Saturday night, we parents sipped a pleasantly-bitter Picon Punch aperitif while selecting from the day's five entree choices. Meanwhile, our daughter gulped down a sweet Shirley Temple.

My first entree was a beautifully prepared filet of red snapper topped with a delicate lemon sauce; the second—tender slices of roast beef—was served with crisp french fries which arrived still sizzling. My husband chose a more full-flavored ox-tail stew and succulent roast chicken.

Vegetable soup began the meal. An iceberg lettuce salad accompanied it. A choice of rich, creamy vanilla, chocolate, or spumoni ice cream and a cup of coffee ended it. Nowadays wine is extra.

The fixed-price dinner is offered in smaller, less-expensive portions for children. For an even smaller fee my daughter, who is mostly a vegetarian, was permitted to share our portions and was served her own bowl of ice cream.

### BILL'S PLACE
*2315 Clement St./25th Ave., 221-5262; L & D daily; $; highchairs, booster seats; children's portions; reservations accepted; no cards.*

A large variety of hamburgers (most named after local celebrities), hot dogs, and sandwiches (including grilled cheese and peanut butter & jelly) share the menu here with giant french fries made from fresh potatoes, milkshakes made with Dreyer's ice cream and served in old-fashioned metal cannisters, and made-from-scratch soups, potato salad, and coleslaw. Choice shoulder chuck is ground in the kitchen daily for the exceptionally tasty hamburgers, which are grilled medium-rare and served on a sesame bun. For a small extra charge they can be ordered on an English muffin, french roll, or in pita bread.

Seating is at an assortment of tables or at a long counter with swivel stools. In mild weather a pleasant outdoor patio, landscaped with a Japanese garden complete with waterfall and living orchids, is open. At prime dining times expect a short wait, as this popular spot is usually full to overflowing.

### THE BREAD & HONEY TEA ROOM
*334 Mason St./Geary St., in The King George Hotel, 781-5050; tea M-Sat 3-6:30; $; no reservations; AE, DC, MC, V.*

Reached via either a narrow, winding marble stairwell or a vintage elevator, this second-floor balcony tea room offers a cozy respite. Menu items include simple teas consisting of choice of tea (ten kinds) and either a crumpet, a giant homemade muffin, a raisin scone, fruit and custard tarts, or traditional finger sandwiches. A larger tea service includes several of these items plus such extra goodies as a quail egg and preserved kumquat on a pick or a blackberry trifle infused with sherry. A rich chocolate layer cake and glasses of sherry and port are also available.

Soothing background music is provided by a classical pianist.

### CADILLAC BAR
*1 Holland Ct./4th St., 543-8226; L & D daily; $$; highchairs, booster seats; take-out delivery; reservations suggested; AE, DC, MC, V.*

Located south-of-Market near Moscone Center, this wonderful Mexican cantina sports an atmosphere that feels authentically south-of-the-border.

Margaritas and sunrises are available from a massive bar, helping to ease any wait. Once seated, service is uniformly pleasant and reasonably fast.

Appetizers include delicious beef panchos (a relative of nachos prepared with nicely seasoned beef) and queso flameado (a baked cheese tortilla dip flavored with chorizo and chiles). A mesquite grill produces fresh fish (available with assorted herb butters and salsas) and marvelous fajitas (a make-your-own-taco dish consisting of marinated strips of steak, fresh spicy-hot salsa, and flour tortillas). Many more interesting fish entrees, cabrito (milk-fed kid), and carnitas (seasoned pork) are also on the creative menu.

Loud thumps are heard throughout a visit here. They are "slammers": glasses of tequila and 7-Up which are slammed on the table and then swallowed macho-style in one gulp.

## CAFFE ROMA

*414 Columbus Ave./Green St., 391-8584; B, L, & D daily; $; highchairs; no reservations; DC, MC, V.*

Winged cherubs dance on the tall, Florentine-blue walls of this very Italian and very popular North Beach coffeehouse. Tables in the front allow diners to view the sidewalk traffic; a large patio in back is pleasant on warmer days.

A full menu is available to accompany the extensive selection of coffee and drink concoctions. For breakfast there are a variety of omelettes (even a create-your-own-omelette) as well as eggs cooked in various styles and french toast. All are served with fried potatoes.

For the rest of the day, pizza is the premier item. (A create-your-own-pizza is also available.) Using an old family recipe, the dough for the crust is made up fresh in the kitchen each day. Soups, salads, sandwiches, and homemade pastas are also available.

And for dessert there is a showcase full of magnificent selections, among them white chocolate cheesecake and homemade cannoli.

## CALZONE'S

*430 Columbus Ave./Green St., 397-3600; L & D daily; $-$$; booster seats, booths; no reservations; AE, MC, V.*

The new kid on the pizza block, this noisy place feels European. Walls reaching to high ceilings are painted dark green and lined with colorful Italian cooking ingredients—reflecting the colors of the Italian flag. Small formica tables detract from comfort, but diners seated at them downstairs enjoy superb views of sidewalk traffic; some upstairs diners are entertained by overviews of the downstairs diners. All the while soft rock plays loudly, cranking up the overall noise level and making eating here with the kids less obtrusive.

Meals begin with a crusty hunk of Italian bread. For appetizers I am particularly fond of the sauteed prawns wrapped in radicchio and stuffed with fresh basil. I also like the light and crunchy—not chewy—deep-fried calamari served with a tangy basil pomodoro sauce. (My kids find both disgusting.) The house salad, however, is quite uninteresting.

The crisp-bottomed pizza is prepared in a wood-fired brick oven.

Because the pizzas are only ten inches (six slices), we usually get two for our family. We adults favor the #6 topped with prosciutto, roasted garlic, fresh tomato, marinated artichoke hearts, fresh herbs, and melted mozzarella. The kids favor the #2 topped with pepperoni, fresh tomato, a dash of basil, and both Parmesan and mozzarella cheeses.

Once when my daughter had one of these pizzas all to herself, she ate two-thirds of a slice and then proceeded to pick off and discard all the tomato slices and pick off and consume all the pepperoni. About the pepperoni she inquired suspiciously, "What kind of animal is this?" We were evasive. Maybe that's why she ate every last bit of it. Additional fresh Parmesan is grated onto the pizzas at the table.

Contrary to what one would expect given this restaurant's name, only a few calzones (sort of like a pizza turnover) are available. However, they are unusual and delicious. One we particularly like, but which is not always on the menu, is a salami with sweet onions, jalapeno Jack cheese, and basil vinaigrette. Sometimes the menu offers an unusual BBQ chicken-cilantro-roasted garlic-onion-oregano-mozzarella version which I'm looking forward to trying.

Fresh fettuccine, linguine, and angel hair pastas are served with a variety of interesting toppings, and homemade lasagna and tortellini are also available. The restaurant does not prepare half-portions for children.

An assortment of varietal wines are available by the glass. Sometimes children are served milk in a wine glass, adding to the festive ambiance.

For dessert, my husband and I enjoy prolonging the pleasure with a decaf cappuccino followed by a family stroll to **Cookies North Beach** (318 Columbus Ave., 397-4997) for a sweet.

### CAPP'S CORNER
*1600 Powell St./Green St., 989-2589; L M-F, D daily; $$; highchairs, boosters seats, booths; children's portions; ask about parking validation; reservations suggested; MC, V.*

The fun begins here as soon as you walk through the saloon-style swinging doors. Reputed to be the liveliest and noisiest of the North Beach family-style restaurants, this popular spot is usually crowded. If you must wait for a table, there are often seats at the Victorian-era bar, where drinks are inexpensive and strong and kids don't seem to cramp your style.

In the cozy, friendly interior dining room, photos of prior happy diners decorate the walls, and noisy family groups rub elbows with swinging singles while enjoying the hearty Italian food. After you are seated, a server starts bringing the bountiful five-course lunch or six-course dinner. Dinner courses include minestrone soup, a green salad, pasta, sauteed vegetables, an entree (steak, roast duck, chicken breast picatta, osso buco, lasagne, seafood cannelloni, etc.), and spumoni ice cream.

## CELIA'S #1
*4019 Judah St./46th Ave., 564-3192; L Tu-Sat, D Tu-Sun; $; highchairs, booster seats, booths; reservations suggested; AE, MC, V.*

I remember the good old days when Celia's used to be a noisy, unpretentious cafe. Although it has followed the path of many successful restaurants and revamped the decor, costumed the waitresses, and opened many branches, Celia's #1 still manages to serve delicious Mexican food.

House specialties include crab enchiladas and enchiladas en mole, but the avocado tostada and chicken enchilada verde are still my favorites. Most entrees come with rice, beans, a tangy coleslaw, and corn tortillas. Side orders are a good choice for young children. A hamburger and steak are also on the menu.

One advantage to the isolated location is that a parking space can easily be found.

Branches are in Berkeley (see p. 135), Palo Alto and San Mateo (see p. 191), and San Rafael (see p. 212).

## CHEVYS
*150 Fourth St., 543-8060.*

For description see page 136.

## COMPADRES MEXICAN BAR & GRILL
*900 North Point St., Ghirardelli Square, 2nd floor of Mustard Building, 885-2266; Sat & SunBr; $$; highchairs, booster seats; no reservations; AE, DC, MC, V.*

This attractive restaurant features gorgeous views of the bay from its Sun Room and outdoor patio areas. While we waited to be seated for brunch, my children visited with two bright red, green-winged macaws known as Sid and Caesar.

For starters, the kids both ordered creamy strawberry-banana smoothies. They declared them delicious. My husband and I each had a pretty Mimosa made from fresh-squeezed orange juice and champagne. We declared them relaxing. With our drinks we munched on a basket of complimentary crisp, freshly-fried tortilla chips served with a mild dipping salsa.

My entree was Chorizo con Huevos, a tasty dish in which the spicy Mexican sausage was scrambled with eggs, tomatoes, and onions. It was served with flavorful potatoes fried with chiles and onion. My husband had a heaping plate of traditional Huevos Rancheros. Our easy-to-please teen ordered Dos Eggs Benedict Olé, in which the poached eggs are placed on top of chopped ham in a fried flour tortilla shell and topped with hollandaise.

Our hard-to-please preteen ordered San Francisco French Toast, made with three huge slices of sourdough. As Murphy would have it, her order arrived after everyone else's and without syrup, yet! The kitchen apparently had run out. I credit them with sending someone out right away to buy more, but still service overall was mañana-style. A dessert order of Mexican hot chocolate took fifteen minutes, though it was explained that this was because the special chocolate had to be tediously shaved and melted down.

Gringo-style eggs are also available, as are an assortment of omelettes. Lunch and dinner menus include many traditional Mexican dishes as well as great fajitas and all-American hamburgers. Olé.

A branch is in Palo Alto (see p. 191).

## THE COMPASS ROSE
*335 Powell St./Geary St., in the Westin St. Francis, 774-0167; tea served M-Sat 3-4:45; complete service $12.50; highchairs, booster seats; reservations suggested; AE, DC, MC, V.*

What better way to catch your collective breath after a hectic Union Square shopping excursion than over tea in the elegant St. Francis?

Seated among the staid, plush, Old World splendor of this room, tired families may choose from nine flavors of revitalizing tea plus two relaxing herbals.

The complete tea service includes a scone and crumpet, several delicate tea sandwiches sans crust (the way most kids like them), fresh berries topped with Devonshire cream, and an assortment of petit fours. These items may also be ordered a la carte—a good idea for children with small appetites or strong preferences.

On our visit my daughter rejected everything from her plate except the crumpet and accompanying tiny jar of strawberry jam, both of which she adored. She drank her entire miniature pot of Russian Caravan tea, blended by our server to my specification of weak, and requested another crumpet, which was served to her gratis.

But nothing was wasted. It seems our duty as the parents of a picky child to finish the kid's rejects. And so we did while relaxing to the musical strains of a violin-bass-grand piano trio.

More goodies are available from a tempting dessert cart: cheesecake, a delicious moist German chocolate cake, etc.

## DOIDGE'S KITCHEN
*2217 Union St./Fillmore St., 921-2149; B & L daily; $$; booster seats; reservations suggested; MC, V.*

Breakfast here is a winner, and it's available all day. Eggs are cooked to order and served with toast and a side of either cottage fries or sliced tomato. My fussy daughter ate everything on her plate plus some on mine. Eggs Benedict, omelettes, pancakes, homemade granola, and french toast made from a choice of six different breads are among the other items available. Don't miss the Motherlode bacon, a flavorful honey-cured variety made without preservatives. Though the bacon's source is a well-kept secret, it is available for take-out. And then there's the fresh-squeezed orange and grapefruit juices, brewed decaf, and hot chocolate made with milk. For lunch it's a variety of hamburgers, sandwiches (a grilled cheese is among them), homemade soups, and a stunningly beautiful fresh fruit salad.

Without reservations expect a long wait for seating in the cozy dining room. If there are just two of you, consider sitting at the counter, where seating is first-come, first-served and a bonus is getting to watch the busy cooks.

### EAGLE CAFE
*Pier 39, 433-3689; B & L daily; $; booster seats; ask about parking validation; no reservations; no cards.*

When Pier 39 opened, the Eagle was moved intact from its location across the street (where it had been in business since 1920) to its present location. Patrons are a cross-section of informality. They get in line to place orders at the kitchen window and then hustle back later to pick them up when their number is called.

Seating is a choice of several long, crowded communal tables, a few smaller tables, and a few outside tables used in mild weather. Surprisingly, considering the downright cheap prices and unimpressive furnishings, the view is great.

The hearty breakfasts are especially good and include nicely seasoned grilled hash and fried potatoes, omelettes, and gigantic buttermilk pancakes. At lunch, when sandwiches dominate the menu, the homemade meatloaf is a standout. The gigantic burgers and clam chowder are pretty good, too.

Strong drinks are always available from the antique bar.

### EL MANSOUR
*3123 Clement St./32nd Ave., 751-2312; D daily; $$; children's portions; free parking lot adjoins; reservations suggested; AE, DC, MC, V.*

From the outside this Moroccan restaurant promises little. But once you enter its double doors, you become encased in another world. Cloth is draped from the ceiling of the intimate dining room, giving occupants the illusion of being inside a tent. Adding to the sensuous feeling are pink walls, floors covered with plush oriental carpets, and seating on hassocks at low tables of inlaid wood.

After choosing an entree from the prix fixe menu, a waiter dressed in a long caftan appears to perform the ritual handwashing. Diners gather their hands over a large brass pot, placed in the middle of the table, to be splashed with warm water.

Then the first course, a tasty lentil soup, arrives. Since no eating utensils are provided in this restaurant, you drink it right from the bowl. A bland Arabic bread is offered to accompany it. Next a salad plate arrives bearing spicy marinated rounds of carrots and cucumbers and a wonderful mixture of tomatoes and green peppers—to be scooped up with the bread. Then comes a bastilla, a fragrant pie containing a sweet chicken and nut mixture wrapped in filo pastry and sprinkled with powdered sugar. Children seem especially fond of this.

Next, the entree. Choices include Moroccan seafood, squab, rabbit, couscous, and a flamboyantly served shish kabob. Both succulent roasted chicken and tender stewed lamb are offered with a choice of toppings such as almonds, honey, or prunes. Then comes the dessert of fried bananas with honey and a repeat of the hand-bathing ritual. And finally the waiter pours mint tea, skillfully and carefully, from up high.

If you time your visit right, somewhere during your dinner a belly dancer will perform. Inquire about the schedule when you make your reservation.

Children are welcome, but I recommend bringing none younger than 4. Children tend to be impressed with the many unusual customs and to enjoy the basically sweet foods, but it doesn't hurt to prepare them ahead of time for the exotic sights they will see. Young children may share their parents' dinners, but older, hungrier children should order a child's portion.

## EL SOMBRERO
*5800 Geary Blvd./22nd Ave., 221-2382; L & D Tu-Sat; $-$$; highchairs, booster seats, booths; children's portions; no reservations; MC, V.*

If you should have to wait to be seated, time passes quickly in the comfortable bar—especially if your order a tangy Margarita made with fresh lime juice (a strawberry version is also available).

Hot peppers, salsa, and tortilla chips are on the table for nibbling on while consulting the menu. Choices include several kinds of enchilada, chicken or beef tamales, chile colorado, and light-as-air chile relleños. More unusual dishes include chalupas (on Fridays and Saturdays only), steak picado, and chicken in a spicy chocolate mole sauce. I am partial to the green chile enchilada which is stuffed with chicken and topped with a tangy green tomatillo sauce and a mound of sour cream.

Dinners come with a side of delicious corn tortillas. On Friday and Saturday nights customers can watch them being prepared by hand in a corner of the front dining room. My young daughter was entranced, and the busy señora, dressed like the waitresses in a bright red-orange dress whose hem swept the floor, gave her one hot off the grill to eat. She also gave her a wad of dough with which to pit-pat out her own tortilla.

For dessert there is flan and authentic Mexican hot chocolate. Attractive Mexican-rancho decor adds to the whole experience.

## FANTASIA
*3465 California St./Laurel St., 752-0825; Tu-Sat 7:30-6:45, Sun & M 8:30-6; sit-down area, no table service; free parking lot adjoins; MC, V.*

This well-known bakery has been owned and operated by the same family since 1948. It is famous for its huge assortment of baked goodies including cakes, pastries, tortes, petit fours, cookies, muffins, and teacakes. Specialty cakes include an almondine, charlotte mandarin, and Grand Marnier. My personal favorite is the Black Forest cake. Very special decorated birthday cakes are also available.

If you're from out of town, don't forget a box of milk chocolate cable cars to take home as a delicious souvenir.

Especially wonderful items are available around Christmas. Then you can enjoy gingerbread, marzipan, fruit cakes, mincemeat and pumpkin pies, several buche de noels, and elaborate gingerbread houses.

Call for details on the free children's cookie-decorating parties held four times each year near Valentine's Day, Easter, Halloween, and Christmas.

## FAR EAST CAFE
*631 Grant Ave./Sacramento St., 982-3245; L & D daily; $$; highchairs, booster seats; reservations suggested; AE, DC, MC, V.*

This intriguing, well-maintained restaurant looks now much as it did when it opened in 1920. My family especially enjoys dining at a table inside one of the 30 spacious private wooden booths that have curtains for a door. These wonderful enclosures provide the ultimate in privacy and are especially handy for those times when your children's behavior is unpredictable. Here you can avoid hostile glares from other diners and possibly still enjoy yourselves. All this and high ceilings, carved screens, and ornate Chinese lanterns, too.

For service, which can be slow, you press an old-fashioned buzzer. (I've been told by the management that these buzzers work, but I remain unconvinced.)

Family-style dinners are a popular way to order from the Cantonese menu. One we have enjoyed includes a bland winter melon soup, an appetizer of crispy deep-fried prawns and sweet barbecued spareribs, excellent sweet and sour pork, snow pea beef, barbecued pork chow mein, tea, and fortune cookies. Ordering this for two should adequately serve a family of two adults and two young children. If you have older children, you'll want to order supplementary dishes.

The extensive a la carte menu also includes sizzling rice soup, fried won tons, pot stickers, lemon chicken, cashew chicken, deep-fried squab, mu shu pork, lobster with black bean sauce, and a variety of chow meins and chop sueys. If the kids are being naughty, you can promise and deliver a shark's fin, bird's nest, or seaweed soup.

## FRENCH ROOM
*495 Geary St./Taylor St., in the Four Seasons Clift Hotel, 775-4700; B, L, & D daily, SunBr; $$$; highchairs, booster seats; separate children's menu; reservations suggested; DC, MC, V.*

Sometimes a family has need of a fine restaurant. One where the adults can enjoy sophisticated fare while the children enjoy kid's stuff. One where they can celebrate together a special occasion, whether because they desire to be in each other's company or because they can't get a sitter.

The elegantly appointed Louis XV-style French Room in the Clift Hotel fills the bill. During a plush pre-matinee lunch there with our daughter, my husband and I started with a delicious Caesar salad topped with melt-in-the-mouth croutons and fresh Dungeness crab. Our daughter, dressed in black velvet, carefully drank a thick chocolate shake. Seated comfortably under crystal chandeliers and beside tall palms, we made pleasant conversation—reacting in reserved kind to our refined surroundings.

The attractively designed, enticing, and moderately-priced children's menu offers staples such as a peanut butter & jelly sandwich, hot dog, and hamburger. My daughter selected macaroni and cheese—a creamy, cheesy made-from-scratch version she liked. From the more sophisticated adult menu, I chose a beautifully presented entree of tender peppered veal with lemon-sauced angel hair pasta. My husband's choice of grilled sea bass with delicate Chardonnay sauce was served with roasted peppers and was equally beautiful.

For dessert mother and daughter agreed to share a rich chocolate mousse cake. Father ordered an almond tart colorfully topped with rows of perfect raspberries. All through the meal our attentive waiter had been treating our daughter like a queen. Now he placed an extra raspberry tart and a pot of hot chocolate in front of her. "It's on me," he whispered.

## GHIRARDELLI CHOCOLATE MANUFACTORY
*900 North Point St./Larken St., in Ghirardelli Square, 771-4903; Sun-Thur 10:30am-11pm, F & Sat to midnight; $; booster seats, booths; no reservations; MC, V.*

Imagine visiting a real chocolate factory—just like Willie Wonka's! Well, almost. This ice cream parlor does have a small working chocolate factory in the back.

After reading the mouth-watering menu (which may be kept as a souvenir), each ice cream-lover fills out an order slip at a table located at the entrance to the restaurant, hands the order to a clerk, and then sits down to await the fulfillment of an ice cream fantasy. Special concoctions include The Alcatraz Rock (a rocky road and vanilla ice cream island set in a bay of whipped cream and armored with a shell of Ghirardelli chocolate, nut rocks, and a cherry) and The Emperor Norton (two scoops of vanilla ice cream in hot fudge sauce with bananas, whipped cream, nuts, and cherries). Sodas and milkshakes are also available.

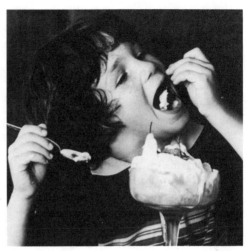

After eating you can purchase Ghirardelli chocolate goodies, including a five-pound chocolate bar, at the candy counter near the entrance.

## GOLDEN TURTLE
*308 5th Ave./Clement St., 221-5285; L & D Tu-Sun; $$; booster seats; reservations suggested; AE, MC, V.*

At first sight the tranquil appearance of this Vietnamese restaurant, with fresh flowers and cloth napkins folded with a florish sitting prettily on dark green tablecloths, might make a parent think twice about entering en famille. However happy diners and background music combine to provide a noisy atmosphere into which families fit fine. Do, however, make a reservation. The wait without one can be a bit much with kids in tow.

The menu offers a number of items which children may enjoy, and the subtle dishes, a cross between Cantonese and Szechwan Chinese, are served family-style.

We like to start with an appetizer of imperial rolls (crisp-fried rolls filled with a mixture of minced pork, prawn, and crab). They are sliced small and served on a bed of thin, slippery rice noodles and lettuce leaves with a mild dipping sauce and a garnish of bright orange carrot "flowers." My son once said he was sure there must be something in them he didn't like, but he ate them anyway because they were so good. More dramatic beginning courses include barbecued quails flambé and sizzling rice soup.

A dish our whole family enjoys is grilled beef kabob. A dish only adults seem to favor is the fragrant, saucy, and spicy lemon-grass curry prawns mixed with onion, mushrooms, and summer squash. Listed as "hot," in reality it is quite mild. Promising menu items include steamed whole red snapper in a ginger sauce with mushrooms, fresh catfish in a clay pot, and mixed vegetables and mushrooms sauteed in black bean sauce. Seven jewel beef is a dinner consisting of seven special beef dishes served in a specific order. Each dish is also available as a separate entree.

The tangy fresh-squeezed lemonade is sweet enough to please children's palates. Tea comes with the meal. For dessert, don't miss the spectacular presentation of the bananas flambé. Two bananas per order are deep-fried and then, at the table, doused with alcohol and lit. Kids are quite impressed. The delicious bananas are crisp on the outside and buttery smooth on the inside.

A branch is at 2211 Van Ness Avenue at Broadway (441-4419).

## GREENS
*Fort Mason Center, Bldg. A, Laguna St./Marina Blvd., 771-6222; L & D Tu-Sat, SunBr; $$; highchairs, booster seats; 100% non-smoking; free parking lot adjoins; reservations suggested; MC, V.*

Reservations are almost essential for this trendy all-vegetarian restaurant. Some unreserved seating is available at a counter, but this is not the best arrangement for families.

The modern interior features high ceilings and large windows with dramatic views of the Golden Gate Bridge. Colorful modern art hangs on the walls. The overall effect is stunning, yet the atmosphere at lunch and brunch is cheerful and noisy, and children fit in fine.

Lunch begins with a basket of delicious breads and sweet butter. Starter choices might include fragrant and flavorful Mexican black bean chile (mixed with cheese and topped with crème frâiche and a sprig of cilantro) or watercress salad (a delicate mixture of watercress, pears, walnuts, and croutons with Roquefort vinaigrette dressing). Entrees change regularly and include unusual items such as pasticcio (an individual Italian casserole of mushrooms, carrots, fennel, cauliflower, and tomatoes layered with pasta, Parmesan cheese, and ricotta cheese custard), tofu brochettes (marinated tofu, mushrooms, tomatoes, peppers, and other vegetables skewered and cooked over mesquite), spinach salad (spinach tossed with hot olive oil and sherry vinegar, kalamata olives, bermuda onions, feta cheese, garlic, and croutons), and a refined pizza.

Varietal wines are available by the glass, and a dessert tray holds temptations such as triple chocolate and poppyseed cakes and chocolate macaroons.

The always-changing la carte brunch menu might include the likes of a blueberry muffin, corn bread with peppers and cheddar cheese, a three-egg omelette stuffed with guacamole and several cheeses, and buttermilk pancakes. Adults can look forward to flavorful coffee served in oversize mugs, and kids can choose from four styles of milk: cold, steamed, cold chocolate, and hot chocolate!

The Friday and Saturday night prix fixe dinner consists of five courses and is not recommended for young children; weeknights the menu is a la carte and similar to lunch.

Greens is run by the San Francisco Zen Center, and many of the herbs and potatoes are grown at the center's West Marin farm. The delicious breads may be purchased to take home.

## HARBIN MANCHURIAN

*327 Balboa St./4th Ave., 387-0274; L & D daily; $$; highchairs, booster seats; reservations suggested; AE, DC, MC, V.*

If you've never experienced a Mongolian firepot dinner, this is definitely the place to discover it. The firepot consists of a large bowl of boiling chicken broth filled with cellophane noodles and vegetables. Using small wire baskets and fondue forks, the raw items (beef, pork, chicken, shrimp, fish, bean curd, meatballs, and vegetables) are cooked by each person in a broth bowl placed in the center of the table. Once cooked, the items may be spiced with a fragrant hot sauce (made with chili peppers, sesame oil, and soy sauce) and eaten with rice. When everyone has finished cooking, the broth is spooned into bowls and eaten as soup. My young child's comment on the procedure was, "This is fun." (To avoid a very long wait while the cooks prepare the multi-dish spread, reservations are suggested.)

There is also an extensive menu of northern Chinese dishes.

Children enjoy standing on the bridge over a koi-populated pond in the center dining room. Be sure to provide them with a coin to toss and make a wish upon.

## HARD ROCK CAFE

*1699 Van Ness Ave./Sacramento St., 885-1699; L & D daily; $-$$; highchairs, booster seats, booths; children's portions; no reservations; AE, MC, V.*

This trendy spot opened a few years ago not just to long waits for tables—but to actual lines of people waiting out front just to get inside to put their names on the waiting list! Now the wait isn't as bad, but for a minimal one it's a good idea to arrive before 7 p.m. If you are later than that, take heart. The public relations person confided to me that families can look forward to being seated quickly because "they can't do us any good at the bar." (The huge oval bar in the center attracts a youngish, singles crowd for drinks.) And sitting in one of the roomy booths, which are positioned on raised platforms around the perimeter of the cavernous room, you can observe plenty.

Formerly a showroom for new cars, the dining room now sports bizarre decorations on its walls: half a Cadillac convertible, Elvis's rhinestone-bedecked white cape, the leather jacket worn by Harrison Ford when he played the role of Indiana Jones.

As might be expected from the name, rock & roll blasts out at ear-splitting levels. In fact, the Hard Rock was reported by the *San Francisco Examiner* to be, perhaps, the noisiest restaurant in town. This has its plus side for families. If you visit on an evening when interacting is causing problems, it can provide a welcome relief.

Considering the sensory overload and the fact that many people come here to look and to be seen, it is impressive that the American-style food is quite good, the service attentive, and the prices reasonable. The house

salad is made of crisp, cold romaine lettuce. Homemade Thousand Island dressing is tangy with fresh onion. Hamburgers are served on whole wheat sesame buns and are just plain good. Ribs, basted with a sweet watermelon sauce, are tender. French fries are made from scratch but are, unfortunately, limp. Moist chocolate cake is served in big hunks. The menu also offers an assortment of sandwiches, homemade chile, grilled fresh fish, steak, and a selection of rich, old-fashioned desserts.

And don't forget the souvenir counter. The logo sweatshirts and t-shirts make super status souvenirs. In fact, the line to buy souvenirs is usually longer than the line to get in. It seems many people come just to get a t-shirt and they don't stay to eat.

### HONG KONG TEA HOUSE
*835 Pacific Ave., 391-6365; dim sum daily 8:30-3; $; highchairs, booster seats; no reservations; no cards.*

The atmosphere and dim sum are very similar to that of New Asia (see p. 53).

## HORNBLOWER DINING YACHTS

*Pier 33/Bay St., 394-8900; Sat & Sun Br; $$; booster seats, children under 12 half-price; 100% non-smoking; reservations required; AE, MC, V.*

Next time you're celebrating a special family occasion, consider a brunch cruise aboard the *City of San Francisco*. Cruises board at 11 a.m. and return at 1 p.m. I think it would be an especially nice indulgence when the grandparents are in town. Not only do you get a groaning board of tasty brunch buffet items, but you also get magnificent views of San Francisco and the bay. While my family munched on brunch and imbibed o.j. and champagne, our boat went out under the Golden Gate Bridge, past Sausalito and Angel Island, and beside Alcatraz.

And you can relax. Everything is orderly. There is no need to elbow anyone. Tables are assigned, and the maitre d' announces to each table when it is their turn to visit the buffet.

Diners are seated on three decks at tables covered elegantly with white nappery. Live piano music plays in the background, and the Captain himself makes the rounds to meet everyone. After dining, you can tour the ship and let the often gusty bay winds refresh you for the return to shore.

You can also look forward to picking up a nice souvenir family portrait: Photos are snapped by professionals as each group prepares to board (see p. 281).

Special events are often scheduled. Lunch cruises depart on Fridays; dinner cruises are scheduled daily.

## HOUSE OF PRIME RIB

*1906 Van Ness Ave./Washington St., 885-4605; D daily; $$$; highchairs, booster seats, booths; children's portion; ask about parking validation; reservations suggested; AE, DC, MC, V.*

The posh booths and carpeting in this dark, busy restaurant help absorb family noise and make everyone comfortable. The specialty of the house is the finest aged prime rib, served right from the cart and carved to order at your table. (In fact, the only other entree on the menu is fresh fish.) Choices are limited to a regular cut, an English cut (thinner slices),

or, for those with king-size appetites, a Henry VIII cut. The complete dinner includes a chilled green salad prepared at your table and served with a delicious house dressing and *chilled* forks, bread and butter, either mashed potatoes and gravy or a baked potato, fresh horseradish sauce, creamed fresh spinach, and Yorkshire pudding. And then there are the desserts . . .

Most people leave carrying a doggie bag, as the prime rib is just too good to leave uneaten, and very few manage to finish their generous serving. Come here hungry.

### HUNAN
*924 Sansome St./Broadway, 956-7727; L & D daily; $$; booster seats; reservations suggested; AE, DC, MC, V.*

This used to be a tiny, obscure restaurant located in Chinatown. It seated 29 people. Then it was described in *The New Yorker* as "the best Chinese restaurant in the world." You can imagine what happened. It was no longer possible to just saunter in and sit down at one of the few tables or at the counter—where half the pleasure was watching the cooks in action. Lines formed, and I, for one, avoided satisfying my cravings for the fiery, spicy Hunan cuisine.

A commercial success, the restaurant opened a branch in a huge warehouse. Graced by murals on the walls and little else, it is still "hot," but the fiery dishes seem a little tamer. The restaurant now seats 314, and you can no longer easily view the cooks frantically preparing the orders. But there is a bar now where the overflow can drown their impatience.

Tables are covered with plastic cloths, and seating is on folding chairs. Tea cups are ordinary coffee mugs, and water glasses look like old-time service station premiums. This frugal approach to decorating has not kept the prices as low as one would hope. But the restaurant does add to its kitchen costs by using unsaturated oils, lean meats, and skinned chicken. Also, no MSG or sugar is used, and salt-free dishes are available.

I would never have taken children to the original location (still there, by the way, at 853 Kearny) due to the lack of space and facilities and the fact that a waiter there informed me, "Kids hate this food—too hot." Even though his advice still holds, children are seen at the new Hunan. And so are highchairs even though the restaurant provides none: People bring their own.

To feed children here, I recommend trying rice topped with some soy sauce and samplings of the milder adult orders. The mild deep-fried green onion cakes are also a good choice. Kids may also appreciate that soft drinks come in a can and are served with lots of ice.

To feed adults, start with a soup such as the hot and sour. Appetizer dumplings are just like pot stickers only spicy hot. Harvest pork (a traditional dish fed to farm workers and pallbearers to give them strength), hot and sour chicken, and bean sprout salad are all especially good, as is the famous cold chicken salad mixed with shredded cucumbers and shiny noodles and tossed with a peanut dressing. Specialties include the excellent fresh seafood dishes and the unusual house-smoked ham, chicken, and duck—all of which are smoked over hickory wood, tea leaves, and orange peels. And do try the unusual and popular Diana's Special consisting of meat sauce and lettuce between two deep-fried flour pancakes.

The distinctive hot bean sauce—a combination of fermented black beans, powdered red peppers, garlic, oil, and vinegar—is available to take out. With some of this sauce and a copy of owner Henry Chung's book, *Henry Chung's Hunan Style Chinese Cookbook* (available at the register), you'll be ready to try out some of these dishes at home in your own wok.

## JUST DESSERTS
*248 Church St./15th St., 626-5774; daily 8:30am-11pm; $; booths; no reservations; MC, V.*

Here you get just what the name indicates: just desserts. The hard-surfaced decor isn't the most comfortable, but the bakery cases are filled with goodies like almond croissants, blackbottom cupcakes, chocolate chip cookies, and a variety of danish, muffins, cheesecakes, and pies. My favorites are the cakes, which include such wonders as carrot cake with cream cheese frosting, chocolate fudge cake with a rich fudge frosting, lemon cake topped with a choice of lemon or bittersweet chocolate glaze, and an exquisite German chocolate cake. And on and on. And you needn't feel too guilty. Though they may be fattening, the desserts here aren't bad for you: No preservatives or artificial colorings or flavorings are used.

Branches are at Three Embarcadero Center (421-1609), 3735 Buchanan Street at Marina Boulevard (922-8675), and 836 Irving Street at 10th Avenue (681-1277).

## KHAN TOKE THAI HOUSE
*5937 Geary Blvd./24th Ave., 668-6654; D daily; $$; booster seats (double cushions on the floor); reservations suggested; AE, MC, V.*

Mind the state of your socks before a visit here. Diners remove their shoes in the entryway for the walk into a maze of lushly decorated small dining rooms. Most diners sit on floor pillows at richly embellished tables, but some tables are also available with wells in the floor underneath, into which legs may dangle. Pleasant, unobtrusive Thai background music soothes during the wait between courses—also a good time to observe the fine Indonesian artworks located throughout the restaurant.

My kids find this exotic atmosphere impressive. I am even more impressed with the fact that many of the unusual Thai herbs used in preparing dishes for the extensive menu are grown in a courtyard behind the restaurant.

If you're unsure what to order, consider the all-inclusive complete dinner. The decisions are made for you! Add an extra drink per kid and perhaps another dish you know they'll eat, and you're set. The complete dinner includes an appetizer of fried fish cakes, spicy and sour shrimp soup, a green salad, a choice of two entrees, either a pudding or fried banana, and hot tea or coffee.

The lightly battered fried banana is memorable. It comes with a smiling face on top made with nuts. My daughter, after carefully removing each nut (she hates nuts), said, "Yum."

See also page 16.

### KING OF CHINA RESTAURANT

*939 Clement St./11th Ave., 668-2618; dim sum daily 9-3; $; highchairs, booster seats; no reservations; AE, MC, V.*

Brunch in a dim sum palace has long been a favorite outing with my family. Children fit in well with the casual atmosphere and overall din exhibited in these lively places. But we have never been fond of the wait usually associated with these meals in Chinatown.

Located out on Clement, this dim sum palace offers the same high caliber of food associated with Chinatown without the wait. On a Sunday, almost at high noon, our party of four was seated immediately.

In a gigantic dining room on the second floor, with an entire wall mirrored to make it appear even larger, we picked and chose among the delicacies parading by on carts. My favorites—deep-fried taro balls and delicate steamed shrimp dumplings—were there along with succulent roasted duck and a finger-licking-good foil-wrapped chicken. The kids favored the familiar potstickers, custard tarts, and shimmering squares of bland almond jello.

Though we found attracting a waiter similar to hailing a cab in New York City, we were fully-fed and out of there in 45 minutes. And we had only a short walk to our car: We had found a *free* parking place on the street *within two blocks.*

Another dim sum spot, the **Tong Palace** (668-3988), is located right next door.

See also page 14.

### KIRIN

*6135 Geary Blvd./26th Ave., 752-2412; L & D Tu-Sun; $; highchairs, booster seats; no reservations; MC, V.*

This unpretentious restaurant is yet another example of the axiom that some of the best Chinese restaurants in San Francisco are not in Chinatown. The authentic Mandarin and Szechwan dishes served here are complex combinations of spices and ingredients and a pleasure both to the eye and palate.

Meals begin with a pot of tea and a complimentary appetizer bowl of bok choy marinated in hot oil. Menu items include a fragrant and tasty shredded pork with fish flavor and garlic sauce (a combination of tender pork bits, woodear, hot red peppers, bits of crunchy water chestnut, and green onion), chewy dry-fried beef (batter-dipped pieces of meat, deep-fried and served with a delicious thick sauce) and crunchy, tasty dry-sauteed string beans.

Children may be unimpressed with hot braised fish a la kirin—a specialty. It consists of a crispy-fried whole rock fish in a dark sauce of ginger, green onions, and garlic.

Children do seem, however, to particularly like the chef's handmade noodles with plum sauce. (My children appreciate that the "things" they are mixed with are easy to pick out.) These noodles are also available fried chow mein-style with pork, chicken, or shrimp. My children also appreciate that both potstickers and steamed baos are on the menu.

Ask the server about off-menu dishes such as sweet cherry meat items and house-made chow fun noodles.

### LA CUCHINA
*2136 Union St./Fillmore St., 921-4500; B & L daily, SunBr; $-$$; highchairs, booster seats; no reservations; AE, MC, V.*

It's not easy to find a restaurant on upscale Union Street where children are welcome. But here children are given crayons and paper when they arrive. When they have finished an art piece, they are allowed to put it up in the front window. And the cook likes kids so much that he makes special Mickey Mouse-shaped pancakes for them.

At breakfast the menu includes comfortingly standard renditions of traditional breakfast items plus three-egg omelettes and french toast made with either cinnamon or raisin bread and optionally topped with fruit and cream. On Sunday the menu adds brunch items such as the proverbial eggs Benedict, eggs scrambled with chorizo and bell peppers, and buttermilk pancakes topped with a ladle of blueberries and sprinkled with powdered sugar. All egg dishes are served with toast and either cottage fries (during the week) or homefries (on the weekend). On Sundays all adults are treated to a complimentary glass of champagne.

At lunch the menu offers homemade soup, several salads (including a classic Greek salad with Feta cheese), and several kinds of hamburgers as well a hot dog, assorted sandwiches, and the specialty of the house— gyros, a Greek marinated beef dish served with homemade pita bread.

There is often a wait to get in, but the management pays attention and the line moves quickly.

### LA RONDALLA
*901 Valencia St./20th St., 647-7474; L & D Tu-Sun; $; highchairs, booster seats, booths; no reservations; no cards.*

For some reason they never get around to taking down the Christmas decorations here. But the tinsel and blinking tree lights help entertain everyone when there is a wait, as does the jukebox filled with lovely Mexican melodies and tunes from the '50s. There are also stuffed animal trophies and black velvet paintings galore decorating the walls. Those over 21 can entertain themselves with a tangy Margarita from the bar as well, and late at night mariachis perform.

Once seated at a formica-topped table in one of three unpretentious but cozy dining rooms, diners are presented with warm fresh-fried tortilla chips. Service then is quite fast.

Kids might like a quesadilla (a flour or corn tortilla folded over melted cheese). They may also order a la carte from the generic Mexican menu.

Everyone else chooses from complete dinners which come with refried beans, Mexican rice, salad, and two corn tortillas. Especially good entrees include asado (grilled beef topped with a tomato-onion-potato combination), adobada (a pork version of asado), and lomo saltado (beef sauteed with green peppers, onions, and potatoes and topped with a spicy tomato sauce).

The restaurant is known for goat meat items such as birria de chivo (a spicy stew). Gallina en mole (chicken in a chocolate sauce), huge enchiladas, and outstanding chile verde are also on the menu.

A cooling flan makes the perfect finale.

## LA TAQUERIA
*2889 Mission St./25th St., 285-7117; L & D daily; $; highchairs; no reservations; no cards.*

To experience fast-food Mexican-style, step through one of the two arches and up to the counter to place your order. Pick a table, and then sit back and relax until your number is called. Entertain yourself by studying the colorful folk mural decorating one wall, by watching the cooks in the open kitchen busily preparing your order, or by depositing a coin in the jukebox featuring Mexican music.

The menu is simple. Choose between tacos made with two steamed corn tortillas and burritos made with chewy flour tortillas. Fillings are a choice of superb pork (carnitas), beef (carne asada), sausage (chorizo), chicken (pollo), or cheese (queso). Each is filled out with wonderful homemade pinto beans and a fresh tomato salsa accented with cilantro. Avocado and sour cream cost a little extra. The Mexican answer to a grilled cheese sandwich—a quesadilla (corn tortilla stuffed with melted Jack cheese)—is a good choice for children with small appetites.

For drinks try the homemade fresh fruit juices. Depending on the season choices include strawberry, cantaloupe, orange, banana, and pineapple.

My whole family is particularly fond of this place. My son is hooked on the cheese burritos, my food-finicky daughter loves the quesadillas, and I will go out of my way to stop here for what I consider to be the town's best chorizo and pork burritos.

A branch **(Taqueria Vera Cruz)** is at 635 Clay Street (989-4456).

If you have room for a sweet, stop in next door at **Dianda's Italian-American Pastry** (647-5469). This wonderful bakery makes an assortment of pastries, cakes, bread, and cookies and even has candies. Not to be missed is the colorful St. Honoré cake—a beautifully decorated concoction of rum custard and cream puffs which is best taken home to eat. The cannolis are filled with ricotta cheese, chocolate chips, and glazed fruits and are great for a walk-away dessert. Everything here is made the old-fashioned way—from scratch.

## LEON'S BAR-B-Q
*2800 Sloat Blvd./46th Ave., 681-3071; L & D daily; $; highchairs, booster seats, booths; no reservations; no cards.*

After a visit to the zoo, what better place to revive yourself than here? Located right across the street, this tiny and extremely casual spot is known for delicious, messy pork ribs slathered with a tangy sweet sauce. Good beef ribs, hot links, and barbecued chicken are also available. Meals come with a corn muffin and choice of baked beans, spaghetti, potato salad, or coleslaw. The menu is rounded out with a half-pound hamburger, homemade chile, and tiny homemade pecan or sweet potato pies.

All orders can be prepared to go, and the picnic area in the zoo or the nearby beach are good places to take them.

Branches are at 1913 Fillmore Street (922-2436) and 3600 Taraval Street (759-1523).

## LITTLE JOE'S
*523 Broadway/Columbus Ave., 982-7639; L & D daily; $$; highchair, booster seats; parking validated at 425 Broadway; no reservations; no cards.*

The t-shirt sold in this restaurant reads "Rain or shine, there's always a line." How true. And it's usually quite long. Fortunately, there is bar service available to those standing in the winding, snake-like queue, and people-watching provides free entertainment.

If your party is two or less, the counter seats are the best in the house—allowing you to watch the cooks rushing to fill orders—and are usually available more quickly than a table. Wall murals provide decoration. The ambiance is lively and fun, and there is no way a child could make too much noise.

People come here for the low prices and large portions of good Italian food. Simpler dishes tend to be best. Huge and delicious hamburgers are served on french bread. Veal dishes include piccata, saltimbocca (layered with prosciutto and Jack cheese), a saucy version of parmigiana, and scaloppine smothered with mushrooms. Calamari is sauteed in white wine, tomato sauce, and garlic. Prawns napoli (butterflied and sauteed in a sauce

LITTLE JOE

of tomatoes, onions, and garlic) and caciucco (a flavorful tomato-based seafood stew combining rockfish and shellfish) are also available. Juicy roast chicken and gnocchi are served only on Thursdays.

Meat dishes come with a choice of rigatoni, beans, spaghetti topped with the excellent house meat sauce, or chunky unseasoned vegetables cooked al dente.

For younger children, stick to side orders or share.

If you still have room for dessert, head over to **Victoria Pastry** (1362 Stockton St., 781-2015). It has been in business since 1914. You can get a fresh Italian confection, such as a cannoli, to eat while you stroll—or something bigger, like a cream-filled zuccotto cake (unique to this bakery) or zuppa inglese (said to be the best in town), to take home.

## THE MAGIC PAN
*900 North Point, in Ghirardelli Square, 3rd floor of Mustard Bldg., 474-6733; L & D daily, Sat & SunBr, dessert any time; $$; highchairs, booster seats; separate children's menu; validated parking in Ghirardelli Square garage; reservations suggested; MC, V.*

This long-time Ghirardelli restaurant, known for both its superb bay view and its creative crepes, was among the first in a chain that now numbers 50.

Entree crepes include stuffings of spinach souffle and fajita steak strips, but items such as fettuccine Alfredo, fresh salmon picatta, and Cobb salad are also on the menu. There is an additional charge for salad (crisp lettuce tossed with almond slivers and a tasty oriental-style dressing) and bread (a toasted baguette with herb butter).

The inexpensive children's menu features a deep-fried Monte Carlo sandwich and crispy cheese dog, but my youngest prefers a cheese blintz with fresh strawberries from the regular menu.

Desserts are a high point. Among them are Taste of Heaven, a house specialty consisting of a thin crepe stuffed with both Ghirardelli chocolate mousse and fresh strawberries and then topped with whipped cream, and an Apple Delight, a crepe sprinkled with cinnamon sugar and toasted pecans and filled with a hot spiced-apple mixture.

A branch is at 341 Sutter Street (788-7397). Branches are also located in San Mateo and San Jose (see p. 196).

## MAI'S VIETNAMESE RESTAURANT
*316 Clement St./4th Ave., 221-3046; L & D daily; $; highchairs, booster seats; reservations accepted for 4+; AE, MC, V.*

Vietnamese food is prepared similarly to Chinese, with shredded and chopped vegetables and some stir-frying. What makes it different is its unusual and subtle spices such as lemon-grass, anise, and fish sauce. This informal restaurant provides a good introduction to this exotic cuisine.

Subtly spiced shrimp-pork rolls (a springroll-like appetizer consisting of uncooked rice paper filled with shrimp, pork, rice noodles, and lettuce) are served cold with a dipping sauce. Imperial rolls are the same thing, only deep-fried. Beef salad consists of thinly sliced beef and shredded carrots, cucumbers, and celery served with a vinegar-sugar dressing and fried shrimp chips. Fragrant and tasty lemon-grass chicken (tender chicken pieces stir-fried in a spicy sauce) and sauteed beef with coconut sauce (delicately seasoned beef stir-fried with whole mushrooms and slices of onion) both stretch nicely with a side order of rice. Promising menu items include chicken salad, la lot beef (spiced ground beef wrapped in a leaf and charcoal-broiled), coconut chicken, five-spice barbecued beef, and Vietnamese shabu—a cook-it-yourself dish prepared at the table on a hotplate.

Drinks include a wide selection of beers and fresh lemonade. Deep-fried bananas, crispy on the outside and velvety smooth on the inside, make a nice, light dessert.

A branch is at 1838 Union Street (921-2861).

If you prefer a richer dessert, stop a few doors down at the **Blue Danube Coffee House** (306 Clement St., 221-9041). This casual open-air cafe is a good spot to enjoy dessert and coffee. An authentic New York egg cream is also on the menu.

## MAMA'S
*1701 Stockton St./Filbert St., 362-6421; B & L daily; $$; highchairs, booster seats; no reservations; no cards.*

Located on a corner of Washington Square in North Beach, this cozy, cheery restaurant is a weekend breakfast favorite of locals. It gets very crowded at peak dining times, and there can be a long wait for a table. Service is modified cafeteria-style: You order at the counter, and your meal is brought to you when ready.

The breakfast menu features blueberry pancakes, thick french toast made from a choice of breads, wonderful eggs Bentley scrambled with sauteed onions, and a variety of omelettes with crab, fruit, spinach, or mushroom fillings. Orange and grapefruit juices are fresh-squeezed, and many items are served with a toasted baguette and homefries on the side.

There is a large selection of salads, and sandwiches are available on a variety of breads with a generous choice of fillings. Hamburgers, hot dogs, and grilled cheese are also available. If you're around when the zucchini and cheese frittata is removed from the oven, it will be hard to resist the heavenly aroma, so save room.

Mama's is known for deliciously fattening desserts and for fresh strawberry creations—even out of season.

Though child-size portions are not on the menu, the kitchen is flexible about preparing them. The "children's favorite" omelette is filled with mushrooms, green onions, tomatoes, and Jack cheese—which sounds good to me but is shunned by my children.

A branch is at 398 Geary Street at Mason Street (788-1004).

## MAX'S DINER

*311 3rd St./Folsom St., 546-MAXS; L & D daily; $$; booster seats, booths; take-out delivery; reservations suggested (taken for D only); AE, MC, V.*

Located near Moscone Center, Max's specializes in large portions of '50s food.

The clean-lined decor features deco light fixtures, lots of chrome and formica, miniature tabletop jukeboxes filled with '50s selections, and oversize vinyl booths which are wonderfully private for families. Waitresses dressed in black and white uniforms and bobby socks look *almost* like they used to in coffee shops. One who served us quickly and pleasantly brought us back to the present with an ear laden with *four* pierced earrings.

The clientele tends toward the singles and "child-free," with a definite artsy bent. But don't let that stop you.

An extensive menu offers crispy-coated chicken-fried steak, a gigantic hamburger with bacon and cheese, and a blue plate special of nicely-seasoned, moist meatloaf served with made-from-scratch mashed potatoes indented with a gravy crater. If you want to save room for one of Max's famous gargantuan desserts, consider a meal of appetizers—country-style ribs, sliders (baby burgers), spicy chicken wings with blue cheese dip, deliciously greasy giant onion rings—and side dishes—a salad (a wedge of iceberg lettuce topped with homemade dressing), slaw, boiled or mashed potatoes, cottage cheese, tasty homemade chile. For fussy kids, hot dogs and grilled cheese sandwiches are available.

Now for those desserts. Choose a tapioca pudding layered with strawberries and topped with whipped cream, bread pudding with vanilla sauce, an excellent seven-layer cookie topped with hot fudge and ice cream, or perhaps something from the large selection of ice cream concoctions.

To top it all off, each diner receives a three-cent piece of Bazooka bubble gum with the check.

A branch is located in San Ramon (see p. 150).

## MAX'S OPERA CAFE

*601 Van Ness Ave./Golden Gate Ave., 771-7300; L & D daily; $$; booster seats, booths; no reservations; AE, DC, MC, V.*

The extensive menu at this glossy, yet comfortable spot offers fare to please any stage of hunger. There are huge New York-style deli sandwiches served with an assortment of mustards and a house-made potato salad or coleslaw made interesting with the tang of horseradish.

Among the many salads is a wonderful fresh spinach, tossed with a warm honey-mustard dressing and sprinkled with bits of honeyed ham, fresh mushrooms, and boiled egg. Dinner entrees include smoked chicken, mesquite-grilled fresh fish, and succulent, messy hickory-smoked ribs.

And there are BIG desserts—a variety of creamy cheesecakes, a devilish chocolate Niagara Falls cake with vanilla buttercream frosting, and design-your-own sundaes made with toppings imported from the Big Apple.

As an added bonus, the talented servers not only wait tables—they take turns between 7 and 11 p.m. serving entertaining stints singing at the mike as well.

If you have a child that still isn't impressed, note that a McDonald's is just across the street.

Branches are in Walnut Creek (see p. 150) as well as in Burlingame and Palo Alto (see p. 197).

## MELS DRIVE-IN

*2165 Lombard St./Fillmore St., 921-2867; B, L, & D daily; $; highchairs, booster seats, booths; separate children's menu; free parking lot adjoins; no reservations; no cards.*

Mels used to be a *real* drive-in. One where the carhops came out to the cars with trays so that you could actually eat in your car. Now you can drive in off one of the city's busiest streets, which is convenient, but the eating goes on in the restaurant.

You want casual, we've got casual. You can sit at a long counter, in booths, or at tables with chairs. Most seats are within reach of a computerized mini-jukebox where you can select an oldie but goodie for a quarter. (Did you know that jukeboxes were invented in San Francisco in 1888?) Note that the sound system is best at the Geary location. The Lombard location gets so noisy that the music is often drowned out. My preteen daughter likes this. She especially likes making selections from the full-size ornate jukebox. She calls the place "cool."

Families and kids are everywhere. Dress is just-off-the-jogging-trail casual. My teen likes Mel's enough to have actually requested return visits. Like mother, like son, it seems. I liked it back when, he likes it now. And I love telling him stories about The Old Days when we used to hang out at the drive-in on Saturday night.

Though prices are a bit high for fast food, this food isn't really all that fast, and it is pretty good. The Famous Melburger, made with 1/3 pound of ground chuck and served on a sesame bun with all the trimmings—even mayo—is my favorite. A side of fries, made with the skins still on, are only a pittance more. I usually also need an order of the crisp, heavy onion rings.

And there are sandwiches galore: grilled cheese, BLT, fried egg—all served with a very good potato salad or coleslaw.

If your appetite is more substantial, try the chicken pot pie served with a salad and roll, the meat loaf served with lumpy mashed potatoes and gravy, or the day's blue plate special. Salads, soups, and homemade chile round out the menu.

Drinks include flavored cokes (cherry, chocolate, vanilla, and lemon) and thick old-fashioned milk shakes made with Carnation deluxe ice cream and served in the tin. The only item marring this solid '50s/'60s menu is the Calistoga water with a twist of lemon.

Desserts include homemade berry pie, chocolate fudge cake, banana or chocolate cream pie, a banana split, and hot apple pie with cinnamon sauce.

The color-in kid's menu is served with a cup of crayons. (My daughter was given a helium-filled balloon, too, and kept herself busy tying sugar packets to the string to keep it from getting away.) It offers a hot dog, 1/4-pound hamburger, and grilled cheese sandwich as well as several dinner plates and an assortment of breakfast items and kid-sized beverages. My daughter was impressed that she could order scrambled eggs at dinner time (Mels serves breakfast all day long) and commented enthusiastically, "These eggs are great!"

A branch is at 3355 Geary Boulevard (387-2244)—the exact location of one of the three original Mels.

## MIFUNE
*1737 Post St., 922-0337; L & D daily; $; booster seats, booths; children's portions; parking validated in Japan Center garage; no reservations; AE, DC, MC, V.*

Located in the restaurant mall inside the Kintetsu Building of the Japan Center (see p. 106), this is a most unusual Japanese restaurant. Specializing in serving only two types of easily digested and low-calorie homemade noodles (udon—fat white flour noodles, and soba—thin, brown buckwheat noodles), it is part of a well-established chain of similar restaurants in Japan.

Before you walk through the noren (slit curtain) into the noisy, well-lit interior, take a look at the plastic food on display in the exterior windows. This will help you visualize the uncommon dishes you will be choosing from on the menu. Approximately eighteen topping choices are available for either noodle type. They include chicken, beef, and shrimp tempura as well as more exotic raw egg, sweet herring, and seaweed. (Because it is put on top of a fish-broth soup, the tempura is soggy. If you like it crisp, ask for it to be served on the side.) The menu is rounded out with some cold noodles dishes, a few rice dishes, and green salads. Sesame spice salt is on each table for pepping up the basically bland dishes.

The children's plate is called the Bullet Train. It consists of cold noodles with shrimp and vegetable tempura and is served in a ceramic replica of the famous Japanese train.

Portions are generous, making this fantasy trip to Japan easy on the pocketbook.

More unusual restaurants are scattered throughout the Japan Center complex. Each will open exotic avenues of food exploration for you and your family. The following are within a few steps of Mifune:

**Benihana of Tokyo** (563-4844) is a good choice to experience with older children, who are sure to enjoy the drama accompanying the meal. Diners are seated at a community table in the middle of which is imbedded a large grill. When the communal table has filled with diners, the chef dramatically begins to prepare each order as everyone watches. I expected karate yells from the chefs, who are adept performers with their knives. Though there are none, the show is still spectacular. **Isobune** (563-1030) is a sushi bar where the items are carried around the counter on little floating boats. Customers remove what looks interesting. **Kushitsuru** (922-9902) specializes in dushi age (skewered deep-fried foods), which are cooked and served at two special counters. Teriyaki dishes, tempura, sashimi, and an unusual oyster teppan yaki (oysters fried and served with a raw egg yolk for sauce and a side of sauteed bean sprouts) are also available. **Misono** (922-2728) is a tiny, country-rustic spot specializing in wappa-meshi (steamed fish or meat served over rice in a bamboo steaming box) in addition to more common items such as tempura, sukiyaki, sashimi (raw fish), and shabu shabu.

More interesting restaurants are located in other areas of the center. **Fuki-ya** (929-0127) has chefs who grill the meat, seafood, and vegetable items you pick from the robata-ya bar. **Kabuki Hibachi** (931-1122) allows diners to prepare their food on a grill located in the center of their table. **Sapporo-ya Ramen** (563-7400) has a noodle machine operating in its window.

For dessert visit the fast-food stand located across from **Mikado** (922-9450), a store which specializes in the popular Hello Kitty items. Order a taiyaki—a fish-shaped, waffle-like soft cookie filled with a sweet bean sauce. A few American pastry shops are also scattered throughout. Or stop in at **Benkyo-Do Co.** (922-1244), where Japanese pastries, candies, and rice crackers have been sold since 1906.

## MIKE'S CHINESE CUISINE
*5145 Geary Blvd./16th Ave., San Francisco, 752-0120; D W-M; $$; booster seats; no reservations; MC, V.*

Located far from the crush of Chinatown, this is one of the best Chinese restaurants in San Francisco. Tables are covered with white linens, making dining here feel special, and the tastefully decorated, well-insulated downstairs dining room keeps the noise level low. (Another room upstairs seats mainly larger parties.)

House specialties include crispy chicken, shredded barbecued chicken salad (cold smoked chicken with chopped almonds, lettuce, and a mustard dressing), and Peking duck (which must be ordered one day in advance).

Other winners on the menu include a spicy, fragrant hot and sour soup, an incredible smoky and tender Mongolian beef served on a bed of crispy rice noodles, and a large selection of both colorful sweet and sour dishes and pan-fried chow mein noodle dishes which are popular with my children.

If you have trouble deciding between so many tempting dishes, try one of the deluxe dinners. My favorite includes won ton soup, delicate fried won tons with sweet and sour sauce, tasty tenderloin with straw mushrooms, prawns with lobster sauce, sweet and sour pressed duck, fried rice, almond delight pudding (more like a delicately flavored almond gelatin), and, of course, fortune cookies and tea. We order just for the adults. If our teen is along, we order an additional dish of inexpensive, filling chow mein.

## MISSION ROCK RESORT
*817 China Basin Rd./3rd St., 621-5538; B & L daily, SunBr; $; booster seats; no reservations; AE, DC, MC, V.*

Known mainly to people who work in the area and boaters who dock in front while they stop to eat, this unpretentious spot is a relaxing find. The weathered deck is choice in fair weather, when you can view the huge ships docked nearby and gaze across the bay to Oakland. A small indoor dining area and bar is cozy in inclement weather.

The clientele dresses casually. Children are welcome and sometimes even given special treats by the servers.

The simple breakfast menu includes a variety of omelettes, plate-size hot cakes, and plain eggs served with nicely spiced homefries (heavy on the garlic) and toast or muffins. On Sundays eggs Benedict are available and served with a complimentary glass of champagne. For lunch it's soups, salads, sandwiches, and hamburgers, as well as fried scallops, oysters, and prawns.

## NEW ASIA
*772 Pacific Ave./Stockton St., 391-6666; dim sum daily 8:30-3; $; highchairs, booster seats; no reservations; MC, V.*

Chinese dim sum makes an interesting change of pace for breakfast or lunch. This cavernous restaurant specializes in the tasty delicacies. Deep-fried shrimp toast topped with a tiny quail egg, deep-fried taro balls filled with sweet poi, and cloud-like pork bows are especially good.

There is usually a wait to be seated on the popular ground level, but immediate seating is often available upstairs. A "stationary" waitress brings tea, water, plates, and check. If you hesitate when you are offered a choice of eight teas, you will probably be pushed to order green tea because it is the most popular. "Mobile" waitresses bring food items around on pushcarts. Flag one down when you see something which looks appealing. If you're not Chinese, the waitresses pushing carts bearing exotic delicacies, such as duck's beaks and feet, usually won't even stop.

After feasting, the bill is determined by how many serving plates have accumulated on the table. Tips are divided by the entire staff. Dim sum-to-go is available at a take-out counter by the waiting area. My family enjoys getting little yellow custard cups there to eat for dessert as we browse around Chinatown.

See also page 14.

## NEW WOEY LOY GOEY CAFE

*699 Jackson St./Grant Ave., 982-7816; L & D daily; $; highchairs, booster seats, booths; no reservations; no cards.*

Though common in other areas, not many Chinese restaurants in San Francisco serve American food. You must go elsewhere for sandwiches, steaks, and chops. However, this subterranean restaurant has both a Chinese menu (with many varieties of chow fun, chow mein, and rice plates as well as plenty of tempting stir-fried dishes and a family-style dinner) and a down-home American menu (with a club house sandwich and a hamburger as well as a t-bone steak and grilled pork chops, not to mention cakes, pies, and jello for dessert).

And you can take your choice of where to sit: in comfortable booths covered with pink vinyl, at tables with chairs, or at a long counter with swivel stools.

Personally, I was won over by just the name.

## NORTH BEACH PIZZA

*1499 Grant Ave./Union St., 433-2444; L & D daily; $; booster seats, booths; take-out delivery; no reservations; AE, DC, MC, V.*

Lacking pretension and finesse, this restaurant serves a working class kind of pizza. When we visited, customers included macho men dressed casually in white tank tops; some updated the look with an earring dangling from an ear. There were plenty of families, too.

Seated in a comfortable booth, my family felt relaxed in the easy atmosphere. We always order pepperoni and cheese pizza, and we found the spicy-hot sausage topping here particularly tasty. The thickish bread-like crust impressed us adults less, but the kids were too busy eating to critique. A delicious antipasto salad (Romaine lettuce, Feta cheese, marinated peppers, tomatoes, and salami) we enjoyed with our pizza is more than enough for a party of four.

The common varieties of pizza toppings and pastas (spaghetti, ravioli, lasagne) are all available. Next time I plan to try one of the more unusual items such as barbecued ribs or chicken, or maybe a submarine sandwich.

Note that the phone rings off the hook for take-out orders. If you live in the area, you may want to give it a try.

A branch is one block down the street at 1310 (433-2444).

## NORTH CHINA
*2315 Van Ness Ave./Green St., 673-8201; L & D M-Sat; $$; highchairs, booster seats; ask about validated parking; reservations suggested; AE, MC, V.*

Dress the kids up, give them a refresher course on restraint, and head out to this elegant Chinese restaurant. Tastefully decorated with crisp tablecloths and fresh flowers, the superior cuisine here draws me back again and again.

Excellent appetizers include dramatically-served sizzling rice soup, spicy hot and sour soup, exceptionally good potstickers, and a cold appetizer plate consisting of honey-glazed spareribs, chicken salad with sesame dressing, spiced slices of beef, fried and baked prawns, and smoked fish.

Some of my favorite dishes are dry-braised beef (dipped in egg batter and then flash-fried), mu shu pork (a mix of pork, onion, bamboo shoots, and hoisin sauce rolled in homemade crepes; chicken, shrimp, and mushroom versions also available), spicy kung pao shrimp, Szechwan beef (buttery-tender bits of beef mixed with crunchy shreds of celery and carrots and tossed with a slightly hot sauce), and smoked tea duck (marinated, smoked, steamed, and finally flash-fried just before serving).

My children are especially fond of the steamed rolls. One inexpensive order brings six sweet-dough rolls.

## OCEAN
*726 Clement St./9th Ave., 221-3351; L & D daily; $$; highchairs; no reservations; MC, V.*

Located on a street heavily laden with Chinese restaurants, this one stands out. The atmosphere is noisy and formica-casual. It's the food that brings people in and makes them willing to line up at the door. To most enjoy yourself at dinner, plan to arrive before 6, or get together a party of six or more people so that you can make a reservation.

The emphasis is on fresh seafood prepared Hong Kong-style with light sauces and very little seasoning, but other regional dishes are offered. Exotic seafood items include conche, lobster, abalone, eel, soft-shelled turtle, catfish, crayfish, jellyfish, river snails, and frog. The more common crab, squid, oyster, clam, and rock cod are also available fresh when possible. Many of these special seafood dishes are not on the menu, and information about them is not always easy to extract from the server.

My children choose to believe that the tanks of live fish which dot the restaurant arc there merely for decorative purposes. Fresh fish lovers will prefer to believe otherwise. (On one visit here a cook came to remove a lobster from the tank behind our table. The lobster didn't like the idea and gave a big splash with his bound claw, getting my husband wet. Now that's *fresh* lobster!)

My children particularly like the chicken with cashew nuts and almonds (big chunks of tender chicken mixed with bright chunks of vegetables, slices of ginger, and nuts) and Mongolian beef (tender beef mixed with a tasty sauce and large slices of green onion, then topped with color-ful shrimp chips). Szechwan-style shrimp is cooked lightly and served attractively on a bed of sliced green tomatoes topped with cilantro. The superb house spareribs, prepared with a mildly spicy sauce and served on a bed of red tomato slices topped with cilantro, are like mini-pork chops and make wonderful leftovers.

For dessert it's orange slices or another fruit. Sorry, no fortune cookies.

## OCEAN CITY
*644 Broadway/Columbus Ave., 982-2328; dim sum daily 9-3; $; highchairs, booster seats; reservations accepted; AE, MC, V.*

This giant, bustling dim sum house is related to a famous restaurant of the same name in Hong Kong which seats 8,000 diners! This branch has three floors. Dim sum is served on floors two and three. Though floor two alone seats 280 people, there still is usually a wait to get in. Avoid Labor Day. One year 3,000 people celebrated here over dim sum!

Once seated, if the carts don't get to you fast enough, flag down someone who looks in charge and order what you want directly from the kitchen. Taro balls and roast duck are particularly good here.

See also page 14.

## OLD UNCLE GAYLORD'S ICE CREAM PARLOR
*1900 Market St./Laguna St., 864-1971; daily 7am-8pm; $; no reservations; no cards.*

The decor here is striking art deco, and high ceilings provide an airy, spacious feeling.

Nothing artificial is used in the ice creams, which are all made by the old-fashioned bucket and rock salt method. If you are curious about just what does go into the exotic flavors (lotus cream, rum raisin, raspberry fudge—to name just a few) of delicious *icy* cream, ask for the free flier which lists all ingredients. Fancy coffees, pastries, and croissant sandwiches are also available.

A branch is at 721 Irving Street (759-1614). Branches are also in Oakland (see p. 152). The main ice cream and cookie factory is in Petaluma (707/778-6008). Visit it for a behind-the-scenes tour of ice cream making.

## O SOLE MIO
*2031 Chestnut St./Fillmore St., 931-9008; L M-F, D daily; $-$$; booster seats, booths; ask server about children's portions; no reservations; DC, MC, V.*

Once your eyes adjust to the dim lighting, you begin to notice that you've walked into what appears to be a heavily-laden grape arbor. The proverbial red-checked tablecloths adorn tables in this tiny pizzeria, and hand-painted murals and picture postcards decorate the walls. Old-fashioned miniature jukeboxes are conveniently located at the larger tables. They don't work, but requests for selections by the likes of Enrico Caruso, Mario Lanza, and Joan Sutherland can be arranged with your server.

The menu offers a large variety of pizzas prepared with an excellent homemade crust, as well as assorted pasta (including spaghetti and ravioli), chicken, and veal dishes.

Evenings are noisy and busy, and there is sometimes a short wait.

## PASAND
*1875 Union St., 922-4498.*
For description see page 152.

## POLLY ANN ICE CREAM
*3142 Noriega St./39th Ave., 664-2472; daily 11-10, F & Sat to 11; $; no cards.*

Claiming to be the only ice cream store in the world where you can take your dog for a free ice cream cone, Polly Ann is notable for yet other reasons. Where else can you get a constantly changing choice of over 425 flavors of ice cream? Where else does the owner make all of his own ice cream and smile happily as he declares, "Tonight I think I'll make watermelon?"

Fifty-two flavors are available every day. Some of the flavors are seasonal, and some are trendy—like Batman (black vanilla with lemon swirl) which is currently the #1 seller. Among the many unusual flavors are bumpy freeway (rocky road with colored marshmallows), sunflower seed, cantaloupe, chocolate peanut butter, and American beauty (made with *real* rose petals). Adults seem to favor the Irish coffee, piña colada, and Turkish coffee. Believe it or not, there are even some very traditional flavors available.

And mom, if the kids haven't eaten all of their vegetables for dinner but you still want to go out for an ice cream, treat them to a cone filled with *vegetable* ice cream! Carrot, corn, and zucchini are also sometimes available. According to the owner, "Anything is possible."

For a small additional charge any cone will be dipped into chocolate topping. And if this isn't enough of a choice to boggle your mind and satisfy your tummy, Polly Ann also dispenses a "suicide float" (two scoops of sherbet and a mix of all the soft drinks in their machine), frostees, and frozen candy bars.

And there's still more—but I'll let you discover the rest for yourself. So pile your kids and dogs into the car and head out for a tasty experience. Oh yes, babies get a free cone, too.

## THE POT STICKER
*150 Waverly Pl./Washington St., 397-9985; 335 Noe St./Market, 861-6868.*
For description see page 199.

## SALMAGUNDI

*442 Geary St./Mason St., 441-0894; L & D daily; $; highchairs, booster seats; no reservations; AE, MC, V.*

Because it is located right across the street from the Geary and Curran Theatres, I save this spot to visit when in the theater district for a performance. It is also only a few blocks from Union Square and makes a good luncheon stop when shopping there.

Service is cafeteria-style. Seating is tiered in a spacious, well-lit dining area. This is one of the few places I've observed people dining with so many kids in tow that one table was set up for the adults and another separate one for the children.

Each day there is a choice of three made-from-scratch soups. (Call 982-5603 for the current day's selections.) The repertoire includes thick, satisfying U.S. Senate ham hock and bean, icy dilled cucumber (in summer only), proper Bostonian clam chowder, and sopa de tortilla. I can personally vouch for the chunk Italian sausage, and the split pea with ham is *almost* as good as my mother used to make. A bowl includes free refills. Also available are green salad, bread rolls, a pasta torte, quiche, sandwiches, cheese, fruit, and homemade desserts and pastries. Service is cafeteria-style.

Branches are at Two Embarcadero Center (982-5603) and 39 Grove Street (431-7337).

## SAM WO

*813 Washington St./Grant Ave., 982-0596; L & D M-Sat; $; no reservations; no cards.*

People used to come here for the experience of being insulted (and to watch the reaction of others when they were insulted) by Edsel Ford Fong—the infamous waiter who once reigned over the second floor. When he was around even the wildest kid sat back glassy-eyed in an attempt to take it all in. Unfortunately, for those of us who actually became fond of him, Fong passed away in 1984. I doubt a replacement could ever be found.

So now the main reason to visit is for the fresh homemade noodles and the unusual layout of the tiny dining rooms.

To enter the restaurant you must pass through the cramped and busy kitchen and then climb the narrow stairs to the second or third floors.

This reminds me of entering a submarine, only you are going up instead of down.

Diners sit on stools at tables topped with real marble. After your order is taken it is shouted down the ancient dumbwaiter via which the finished dishes are later delivered to your waiter. The house specialty, noodle soup, is available in twelve varieties. Won ton soups and chow fun dishes (wonderful flat, chewy rice noodles stir-fried with a choice of meats and greens) are also on the menu. The cold roast pork rice noodle roll is especially good and is even better with a bit of hot mustard sauce. Children seem to like the fried donuts, also served cold and cut in bite-sized pieces.

Note that you will not find soft drinks, milk, or coffee on the menu, and no fortune cookies arrive with the amazingly inexpensive check.

## SANPPO
*1702 Post St./Buchanan St., 346-3486; L & D Tu-Sun; $$; highchairs, booster seats; child's plate; no reservations; no cards.*

The line at the door is a tip-off that there is something worth waiting for inside. A cozy, country-Japanese decor welcomes diners and soothes them when they are finally seated. Then service is fast. (We once spent less time seated inside than we did outside in line!)

Among the interesting appetizers are gomaae spinach (uncooked and sprinkled with sesame seeds) and harusame salad (sweet potato noodles mixed with lettuce, onion, and a creamy dressing). My favorite item is the light tempura; the prawns virtually melt in your mouth. My children make a meal of the gyoza, which are similar to Chinese potstickers and also available in soup form mixed with glass noodles, cabbage, and bean curd (gyoza nabe). Other interesting entrees on the extensive menu include fresh deep-fried oysters and nasu hasamiyaki (grilled slices of ginger-marinated beef and eggplant). A large selection of noodle dishes (udon, soba, ramen) are also available.

Dinners come with miso soup, pickled cabbage, rice, and green tea.

## SCOTT'S SEAFOOD GRILL & BAR
*2400 Lombard St., 563-8988; 3 Embarcadero, 981-0622.*

For description see page 154.

## SEARS
*439 Powell St./Sutter St., 986-1160; B & L W-Sun; $; booster seats; no reservations; no cards.*

This is a downtown institution known for its extensive menu, and it's always busy. Expect a wait in line before you sit at one of the tables covered with lacy crocheted cloths—which are covered again with protective see-through plastic. Try not to get irritated by the abruptness of the "hostess" and rushing waitresses by knowing that when you do sit down, you can look forward to fast service.

For breakfast, which is available all day, choose their famous eighteen silver dollar pancakes, crisp waffles, french toast made with sour dough bread dipped in eggs and cream and served with homemade strawberry preserves, banana nut bread, an imposing fresh fruit bowl (a must in summer), a huge baked apple with cream, or homemade yogurt. It is disappointing to discover that the hash browns and orange juice are the frozen variety.

The lunch menu offers hot entrees, salads, and sandwiches—including a hamburger and grilled cheese. I especially favor the homemade desserts: cakes, pies (including deep-dish varieties), and their specialty—a huge dome of an apple dumpling.

Though there are no children's items, there are plenty of things on the menu which children enjoy eating.

## ST. FRANCIS FOUNTAIN
*2801 24th St./York St., 826-4200; L & D daily; $; booster seats, booths; children's portions; no reservations; no cards.*

Run by the same family since 1918, this informal diner-style restaurant was last decorated in 1949. It claims to be "the oldest ice cream parlor in San Francisco." Visitors can try any of the twenty flavors of house-made fourteen per cent butterfat ice cream in such delights as giant double-dip sodas or triple-scoop milkshakes served in an old-time metal cannister. Sundae syrup toppings (banana, cherry, chocolate, lemon, marshmallow, and more) are homemade, too. There is even an authentic New York egg cream.

Most items on the menu are made from scratch: soups, salads, sandwiches (including grilled cheese). Sandwiches are prepared with homemade mayo and served with a side of potato salad.

At the front candy counter you can purchase made-on-the-premises peanut brittle, German-style fudge, and marshmallows as well as hand-dipped raspberry creams and rum truffles. Best sellers are rocky road, walnut fudge, and coconut clusters.

**La Victoria Bakery and Grocery** (2937 24th St./Alabama St., 550-9292), a Mexican pastry shop, is nearby. As you enter take a tray and tongs from the counter and then browse among the tantalizing pastry displays. Choose a jelly roll, a pastry horn filled with lemon custard, or some other such goodie. The shop also sells milk, canned Mexican fruit drinks, fresh tortillas, piñatas, and various Mexican condiments.

A small restaurant operates in the back. Casual, with its menu completely in Spanish, it reminds me of restaurants I've experienced in Mexico. The food is cheap and good (particularly the salsas), and there are highchairs and booster seats.

Another pastry shop, **Dominguez Mexican Bakery** (2953 24th St., 821-1717), is located across the street and offers similar treats. Olé! Also noteworthy is **La Palma Market** (2884 24th St./Florida St., 647-1500), where Mexican cooking supplies, homemade tortillas, and short-order items may be purchased. Colorful, inexpensive piñatas are also available.

## TAIWAN
*445 Clement St., 387-1789; 289 Columbus Ave., 989-6789.*
For description see page 157.

## T.G.I. FRIDAY'S
*685 Beach St./Hyde St., at Fisherman's Wharf, 775-8443.*
For description see page 201.

## TOMMASO'S
*1045 Kearny St./Broadway, 398-9696; D Tu-Sun; booster seats; no reservations; MC, V.*

In 1935, when this spot was known as Lupo's, it was the first restaurant to bring pizza to the West Coast. And for quite awhile it was the only restaurant in the United States to bake all its foods in a genuine oakwood-burning brick oven. In fact, world-renowned Chez Panisse in Berkeley used this oven as a model for their own, which then began producing a trend-setting mini-pizza.

The entry-way is usually crowded with hungry hordes willing to wait in line for the reasonably-priced, delicious Neapolitan fare. Even movie director Francis Ford Coppola has been known to dash in from his nearby office; sometimes he whips up his own creations in the kitchen.

Truly a family operation, the owner is a waiter, his sister is hostess, his mother and another sister are cooks, his father keeps the books, and his wife does a little bit of everything.

Seating in the dimly-lit cellar consists of both a large community dining table and smaller tables in semi-private compartments separated by wooden partitions. Murals depicting murky scenes of Naples decorate the walls.

We always begin with one of the delightful marinated salads—broccoli, string beans, or roasted peppers tossed with olive oil, lemon juice, and herbs.

Over a dozen types of pizza are made with whole-milk mozzarella, and the thin, crisp-yet-chewy crusts are superb. Several calzones—a sort of pizza turnover—are also available.

Pastas include homemade ravioli and spaghetti tossed with olive oil, garlic, and either fresh parsley or sauteed broccoli. Half-orders of ravioli and simple pastas (toppings include butter, marinara, and meat sauce) may be ordered for children.

All this and seafood, veal, and chicken entrees as well.

For dessert there's cannoli, a good spumoni ice cream, and a wonderful custard and whipped cream confection referred to as St. Honoré cake.

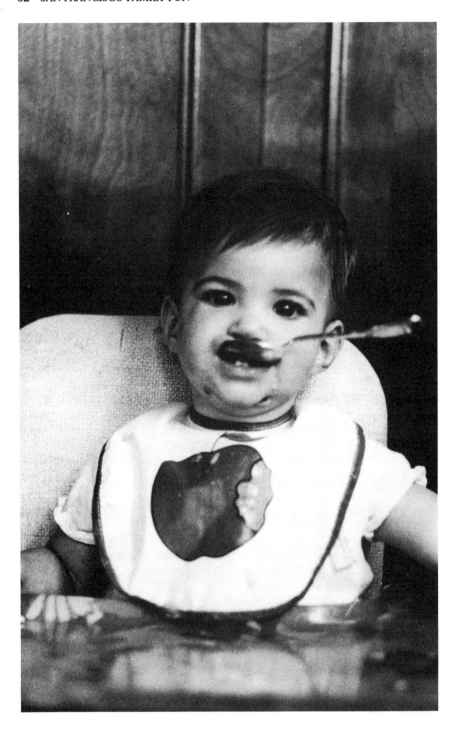

## TUNG FONG

*808 Pacific Ave./Stockton St., 362-7115; dim sum Thur-Tu 9-3; $; highchairs, booster seats; no reservations; no cards.*

Smaller and quieter than other dim sum houses, this restaurant has servers who describe each item on the cart and give service with a smile. You don't have to constantly crane your neck and be ready to signal the servers to stop; they come to you.

Especially delicious are the foil-wrapped chicken (a thigh baked to juicy perfection in a sticky, tasty barbecue sauce) and chow fun (a cold, soft stuffed noodle). Other items are similar to what are seen elsewhere.

See also page 14.

## UPSTAIRS AT THE CLIFF HOUSE

*1090 Point Lobos Ave., 387-5847; B, L, & D daily; $$; highchairs, booster seats, booths; free parking area adjoins; no reservations; AE, DC, MC, V.*

Perched at the edge of the sea, the Cliff House has been around for quite some time. Since 1850 to be exact, but in three different versions—having twice burned to the ground. Though it has gone through many changes, it has always been a restaurant. Since 1977 it has been part of the National Park Service's Golden Gate National Recreation Area.

Nowadays visitors may choose between two dining rooms and a bar—all featuring magnificent views of the ocean and adjacent **Seal Rocks**. Downstairs **The Phineas T. Barnacle** (386-7630) serves a casual menu of soups, salads, and sandwiches as well as snacks and mixed drinks. Next door **The Seafood & Beverage Co.** (386- 3330) serves a more formal menu of fresh seafood.

The informal atmosphere and cozy decor Upstairs makes it the best dining choice for families at breakfast or lunch. The menu offers 30 different omelettes. The tastiest just could be #17—a combination of spicy linguica sausage, mashed avocado, tangy tomato chunks, and melted Swiss cheese. Omelettes are served with a basket of toasted whole wheat English muffins and grilled potatoes.

Other items on the menu include hot and cold sandwiches, a Louis salad, chile, New England clam chowder, a hamburger, and a variety of desserts including cheesecake, German chocolate cake, and hot apple crisp with whipped cream.

No children's portions are available, but two children may share an order. The owner assures me the kitchen will be glad to prepare a hot dog, grilled cheese sandwich, or peanut butter & jelly sandwich upon request.

In the evening the menu becomes more pricey with pasta and seafood entrees.

## YANK SING
*427 Battery St./Clay St., 362-1640 & 781-1111; M-F 11-3, Sat & Sun 10-4; $; highchairs, boosters seats; reservations suggested; AE, DC, MC, V.*

If you are familiar with dim sum restaurants, you will know something is different here as soon as you spot the doorman spiffily attired in a short red jacket and white gloves. And though I personally favor the ambiance of Chinatown's dim sum palaces, there are some compelling reasons to forsake tradition and visit this upscale version in its Financial District location.

One big reason is that location. Parking in Chinatown is always a hassle. Parking on Battery is easier, especially on Sunday. And the Embarcadero Center garage, located just across the street, offers free parking from 9 a.m. to 3 p.m. on Sundays and holidays.

Another reason is the convenience of being able to make phone reservations. At other popular dim sum spots you must put you name on a list when you arrive and then wait—often as long as an hour. Not too much fun with kids in tow.

And yet another reason is the wide variety of excellent dim sum dishes (over 80 kinds). Selections include cloud-soft rice noodles stuffed with a choice of meats, succulent stuffed black mushroom caps, deep-fried crab claws (which my youngest enjoyed immensely until I absentmindedly told her what she was eating), and sweet taro balls. The more common potstickers, fried won tons, and steamed barbecued pork bows are also available.

The tasteful, brightly-lit interior is a labyrinth of dining rooms. Tablecloths, cloth napkins, and fresh flowers grace each table. Downstairs there is a peaceful bamboo fountain and beautiful etched-glass partitions.

Diners are given large glasses of ice water and may select from a drink menu which includes mixed drinks, soft drinks, and even Perrier, as well as the ever-popular tea.

Servers are friendly and answer questions about the items on their carts as best they can. And if something you want isn't on the cart, they will arrange for it to be brought directly from the kitchen.

My youngest is particularly fond of the dessert items. She ate the wedges of orange peel filled with beautifully shimmering orange jello all by herself. But all of us were crazy about the flaky-crusted custard tarts served warm from the oven—the best I've ever had.

Indeed, the only disappointment I experienced here was that the restaurant has also updated their method of tabulating the bill. Charges are added to the table tab as items are selected instead of tabulating the bill at the end of the meal by adding up the number of serving plates accumulated. But that is a very small quarrel with what is overall an outstanding dim sum restaurant.

It is a Cantonese custom to introduce a new baby to family and friends at a Red Egg and Ginger Party. Named for some of the food items included in the luncheon menu, these parties are catered by the restaurant and pre-set menus are available.

Yank Sing was the first dim sum parlor in San Francisco to serve the cuisine as it was known in Hong Kong. Orignally it was located on Broadway, where it opened in 1957.

See also page 14.

A branch is located at 49 Stevenson Street at 1st Street (495-4510).

## YET WAH
*2140 Clement St./23rd Ave., 387-8040; L & D daily; $$; highchairs, booster seats; reservations suggested; AE, DC, CB, MC, V.*

I remember when Yet Wah was just a little hole-in-the-wall on Clement Street. Now it has blossomed into something more.

The long menu lists over 200 dishes, and the quality is generally good. My favorites include hot and sour soup, fried won tons stuffed with Chinese sausage, mu shu pork, Szechwan spiced beef, ginger garlic lamb, and kuo teh (or potstickers), which are also especially liked by my children. Explore the menu yourself and enjoy the adventure of trying something new. How about dragon's eye fruit for dessert?

Branches are at 5238 Diamond Heights Boulevard (282-0404) and Pier 39 (434-4430). Branches are also in Concord (see p. 158), Foster City, (see p. 202), and Larkspur (see p. 220).

---

# — PICNIC PICK-UPS —

---

## CARAVANSARY
*2257 Chestnut St./Pierce St., 921-0534; M-Sat 9-8, Sun 9-5; pre-packed picnic boxes by reservation; beer, wine; B & L in sit-down area; AE, MC, V.*

Store specialties include aram sandwiches (made with softened Armenian cracker bread into which is rolled lettuce, tomato, herbed cream cheese, and roast beef, turkey, salami, or pesto), hummus (a pureed mixture of chickpeas, tahini, and garlic), and Greek salads with Feta cheese. Assorted cheeses, salads, fruits, vegetables, and pastries are also available.

## EL FARO
*2399 Folsom St./20th St., 647-3716; daily 6:30-8; pre-packed picnic by reservation; beer; B & L in sit-down area; no cards.*

Among the authentic Mexican deli fare offered here are soft tacos, guacamole with tortilla chips, and a large selection of Mexican beers and fruit sodas. The gigantic burritos are filled with guacamole, cheese, beans, rice, and a choice of beef, chicken, or pork. Regular deli sandwiches are also available.

Branches are located at 82 1st Street (495-4426) and 1200 Polk Street (771-9700). Branches are also located in Concord (see p. 161) and South San Francisco (see p. 202).

## LA FERME BEAUJOLAISE

*2000 Hyde St./Union St., 441-6913; M-Sat 8-7:30, Sun 9-6; pre-packed picnic boxes by reservation; beer, wine; B, L, D in sit-down area; MC, V.*

This classy shop is modeled after one of the same name located in Lyon, France. Choose from interesting French pastries and breads, croissants, pâtés, cheeses, wines, and a variety of prepared food items.

## LUCCA DELICATESSEN

*2120 Chestnut St./Steiner St., 921-7873; M 10-6:30, Tu-Sat 9-6:30, Sun 9-6; pre-packed picnic boxes by reservation; beer, wine; validated parking; no cards.*

This deli has been owned by the same family since 1931.

Made-to-order sandwiches are constructed from specialty meats and cheeses and priced by weight. A variety of homemade salads, including one with pig's feet, are available, as are handmade breadsticks and a large selection of imported Italian wines.

## SAY CHEESE

*856 Cole St./Carl, 665-5020; M-F 10-7, Sat 10-6, Sun 10-5; pre-packed picnic boxes by reservation; AE, MC, V.*

Hot soup and a variety of deli sandwiches, salads, and cheese spreads are available. Selections include over 200 kinds of cheese, a variety of pâtés and crackers, and homemade cookies.

## STOYANOF'S

*1240 9th Ave./Lincoln Ave., 664-3664; Tu-Sun 10-9:30; pre-packed picnic boxes by reservation; beer, wine; L & D in sit-down area; AE, MC, V.*

Located close to Golden Gate Park, this small, pleasant Greek restaurant offers cafeteria-style service. But if you ask, they will pack it to go. Try a borek (flaky pastry made of filo dough and stuffed with choice of meat mixture, cheese, or spinach). The Greek salad made with Feta cheese is good, and for dessert there is a light, flaky baklava. Everything is made in-house.

## VIVANDE PORTA VIA

*2125 Fillmore St./California St., 346-4430; M-F 10-7, Sat 10-6, Sun 10-5; pre-packed picnic boxes; beer, wine; L in sit-down area; AE, DC, MC, V.*

All items here are prepared in the heavenly-smelling open kitchen and are, in keeping with the literal meaning of the deli's name, "food to carry away."

The Italian fare varies, but main dishes might include succulent roasted chicken, mushroom or chicken turnovers in a wonderful flaky crust, or torta Milanese (a tall pie layered with ham, spinach, and cheese). Salads include cannellini beans and caviar, caponata (eggplant with raisins and pine nuts), several fresh pastas, and a house-smoked chicken tossed with fresh peas, cucumbers, and homemade mayonnaise.

Sandwiches are made to order with freshly-baked breads. An unusual version consists of two baked slices of eggplant stuffed with slices of provolone and mortadella. A variety of crackers, olives, and other supporting items are also available.

An assortment of tempting dolci (sweets) beckon from a filled display case. Chocolate lovers should note that truffle heaven, Cocolat (2119 Fillmore St., 567-1223), is located just a few doors away.

# What To Do

## — HISTORIC SITES —

### ALCATRAZ ISLAND
*800/445-8880 or 546-2896; daily 8:45-4:15; adults $7.50, 5-11 $4; reservations suggested.*

Before Alcatraz was opened to the public in 1973, it served as a fort in the 19th century and as a federal penitentiary from 1934 to 1963. From 1969 to 1971 it was occupied by Indians. During the time it was a maximum security prison, it was home to some of the country's most hardened criminals: Al Capone, George "Machine Gun" Kelly, Robert "Birdman of Alcatraz" Stroud.

And it's as good as it's cracked up to be: the boat ride, the tour, and the 360-degree bay view.

Boats are boarded at Pier 41. After the short, scenic ride to this infamous island, you are on your own to follow a self-guided tour. Ranger-led tours are sometime scheduled. A top-notch audio tour of the cell block—narrated by former inmates and guards—is also available for an additional fee (adults $2.50, 5-11 $1).

Wear comfortable shoes, dress warmly, and expect cool, windy weather—even in the summer.

An alternate **Round The Rock Tour** (adults $7.50, 4-11 $4) is also available. It operates during the summer and on holidays. Narrated by Frank Heaney, a former Alcatraz guard and now a Park Service Ranger, this tour doesn't land but goes around the island twice and points out areas not usually seen. Reservations are not necessary, but you should call for the current schedule.

It is interesting to note that the 214-foot-tall lighthouse here was built in 1854 and was the first on the West Coast.

### CHINATOWN
The most memorable way to enter Chinatown is on foot through the ornate archway located on Grant Avenue at Bush Street. However, most locals miss this experience in favor of driving to the heart of the action in their cars. Either way, a walk along pedestrian-crowded Grant Avenue, the city's oldest street, is quite an experience.

#### • Chinese Culture Center
*750 Kearney, 986-1822.*

A **Spring Festival** is scheduled each year during Chinese New Year. Call for the schedule of crafts demonstrations, exhibits, and performances

of Chinese dance and music.

Cultural and culinary tours of Chinatown are scheduled year-round:

• Participants on the **Culinary Walk** are introduced to Chinese cuisine with stops in markets, a fortune cookie factory, an herb shop, and a tea shop. The tour concludes with a dim sum lunch. (Wednesdays at 10:30 a.m.; adults $18, under 12 $9.)

• The **Heritage Walk** stresses the history and cultural achievements of the area. Stops may include a Chinese newspaper office, a Chinese temple, and a historical society. (Saturdays at 2; adults $9, under 18 $2.)

• **Chinese New Year Walks** are given only during that time of year. A history of the holiday is presented, and all participants sample special Chinese sweets from a "Tray of Togetherness." Reserve several months in advance. (Adults $10, under 18 $6.)

These walks are sponsored by the Chinese Culture Foundation. All require reservations.

### • Fortune Cookie Factories

Always fun after a meal in Chinatown is a walk through the narrow streets and alleys to find a fortune cookie factory. Though the workers aren't often anxious to see tourists, you can usually get at least a glimpse of the action by poking your head in the door or peeking in through a window. All will be glad to sell you cookies, and bags of broken "misfortune" cookies can usually be picked up at bargain prices.

• **Fortune Bakery** (570 Green St./Stockton St., 421-3713; M-Sat 8:30-4) is located in the heart of North Beach. This heavenly-smelling bakery makes a variety of Chinese baked goods. • **Golden Gate Fortune Cookies Company** (56 Ross Alley/Washington St., 781-3956; daily 9-8) is tucked away in a picturesque alley in the very heart of Chinatown. • **Lane Heung Bakery** (1507 Grant Ave./Union St., 982-9723; M-Sat 9-3) is located on the outskirts of North Beach. It sells cookies with x-rated messages. You may also arrange to insert messages of your own composition. Call for details. • **Mee Mee Bakery** (1328 Stockton St./Broadway, 362-3204; M-Sat 9-6) is located on the outskirts of Chinatown, where it meets North Beach. This factory sells x-rated cookies, chocolate and strawberry fortune cookies, and delicious mini-almond cookies.

• **Herb Shops**

In most of these interesting and somewhat mysterious shops, aromatic herbs are measured out on scales (some are the old-fashioned hand-held variety) and then tallied clickety-clack by the clerk on an abacus. Unless you actually want to purchase something, you'll probably feel like a fish out of water if you go inside. I advise just peeking in the doorway or window.

The following shops are all in the heart of Chinatown: **On Ning Tong Co.** (1045 Stockton St./Jackson St.); **Superior Trading Co.** (839 Washington St./Grant Ave.); **Great China Art Co.** (857 Washington/Stockton). Of special note is **Che Sun Tong Co.** (729 Washington St.). The herbalist there speaks English.

• **Temples**

Though there are many temples in Chinatown, only one seems to welcome visitors: **Tin How Temple** (125-129 Waverly Pl./Washington St.; daily 10-5, 7-9). Located in the heart of Chinatown in an alley known for its ornate painted balconies, this temple is easy to find. Just follow the scent of incense up the narrow wooden stairs to the fourth floor. Built in 1852, it is the oldest Chinese temple in the U.S. Though there is no charge to visit, donations are appreciated and an appropriate reverent behavior is expected. Bear in mind that the temple is actually used for worship.

**CLIFF HOUSE VISITORS CENTER**
*Point Lobos Ave./48th Ave., 556-8642; daily 10-4; free.*

Learn the history of the Cliff House area from the 1890s to the present.

Adjacent **Sutro Baths**, once the world's largest indoor swimming pool complex, was filled with ocean water via an ingenious system developed by Adolph Sutro. The pools could hold 10,000 swimmers and 7,500 observors! Free ranger-led tours of the ruins are scheduled each month.

Just outside, the **Musee Mecanique** is filled with old arcade games, some dating from the 17th century. For a quarter you can operate a miniature steam shovel and collect 90 seconds worth of gumballs, or see naughty Marietta sunbathing in 3-D realism. Beeping modern video games are in the back, where they belong.

Nearby a reproduction of Leonardo daVinci's 16th-century **Giant Camera Obscura** (752-9422; daily 11-sunset weather permitting; adults $1, 2-12 50¢, under 2 free, free on your birthday) may be perused. The educational and entertaining tour is personalized.

Historic **Seal Rocks** may be viewed with the naked eye or through an antique telescope. Barking sea lions and brown pelicans share the space.

## COIT TOWER

*From Filbert St. follow Lombard St. to top of hill, 667-7107; daily 10-6; $1.50, 6-12 50¢, under 6 free; free parking lot adjoins.*

Located atop fashionable Telegraph Hill, this 210-foot tower offers magnificent 360-degree views of San Francisco and the Bay Area. Colorful murals on the ground floor walls depict area activities during the depression. The fee is for the elevator ride to the top. Parking is limited.

If you walk or take the bus up, you can then walk down the **Filbert Street Steps**, past the **Grace Marchant Garden**, to Levi Plaza.

## CROOKEDEST STREET IN THE WORLD
*Lombard St. between Hyde St. & Leavenworth St.*
This famous curvy street is one-way downhill.

## FORT POINT NATIONAL HISTORIC SITE
*Located directly under the San Francisco entrance to the Golden Gate Bridge; take Lincoln Blvd. to Long Ave., turn left, at bottom follow road along water to fort; 556-1693; daily 10-5; free; free parking lot adjoins.*

Built in 1861, this is a classic example of the brick forts built by the U.S. Army Engineers. Its four tiers were once home to 149 cannon. Now guides dressed in Civil War uniforms give daily tours.

Each winter from November through February, **Candlelight Fort Tours** are scheduled. They allow participants to see the fort from the viewpoint of a Civil War soldier. What was it like in the 1860s to live in drafty quarters heated by fireplaces and lit by candles? What kind of food was eaten, and how was it prepared? These questions and more are answered on the inside tour, which is followed by a walk through the 1870 gun emplacements located south of the fort. Tours are given from 6:30 to 9 p.m. Dress warmly, and bring a flashlight; candle lanterns are provided. Reservations are necessary, and participants must be age 15 or older. Call for current dates.

## GOLDEN GATE BRIDGE
Once called "the bridge that couldn't be built," this magnificent example of man's ingenuity and perseverence is one of San Francisco's most famous sights. Measuring 6,450 feet, it is the longest suspension bridge in the world, and its 746-foot-high towers are the largest ever built.

Crossing it is a must. Views are breathtaking. In your car you will pay a toll southbound only. You may walk or bicycle across at no cost. It is about two miles round-trip, and there are picnic tables available below the parking area on the San Francisco side.

Many people are disappointed to discover that the bridge is not a golden color. In fact, it is painted with a protective dull red-orange coating. The color was chosen to make it visible in dense fog. Once you accept that fact, you're in for a major visual treat.

## GRACE CATHEDRAL
*1051 Taylor St./California St., 776-6611; daily 8-6, tours available.*

Located on Nob Hill, this majestic French Gothic cathedral stands 265-feet tall and is the largest in the western U.S. It is graced with more than sixty opulent stained-glass windows, and its gilded bronze entrance doors are exact replicas of Lorenzo Ghiberti's Doors of Paradise at the Baptistry in Florence, Italy.

Concerts using the cathedral's renowned 7,286-pipe organ are often scheduled, sometimes accompanied by the 44-bell carillon. The cathe-

dral's reveberant acoustics and architecturally magnificent interior make these memorable experiences. Carillon recitals are scheduled on Wednesdays and Fridays from 5 to 5:15 p.m. and on Sundays from 3 to 3:15 p.m.

Annual **Cathedral Choir Christmas Concerts** feature the Grace Cathedral Choir of Men and Boys singing both traditional and new carols. They are wondrous, inspirational events. A Festival of Lessons and a Midnight Mass are traditional on Christmas Eve, and a celebratory New Year's Eve event is also scheduled each year.

Just a few years ago, the **Michaelmas Faire** became an annual September event in the cathedral. A medieval celebration, it honors St. Michael—the Prince of Angels. It features musical entertainment, cathedral tours, handcraft and food booths, and children's activities. Participants are invited to come in appropriate costume.

And every few years the cathedral is the unusual, yet appropriate, setting for a screening of the original 1923 silent film classic *The Hunchback of Notre Dame*. This is appropriate for children age 7 and older and is not to be missed.

### HISTORIC HOUSES

San Francisco is known for its abundance of beautiful turn-of-the-century Victorian houses. One of the pleasures of living here is visiting people who actually live in them. Visitors to the city interested in capturing a taste of that pleasure will enjoy stopping by one of the three historic homes open to the public for tours.

### • Haas-Lilienthal House

*2007 Franklin St./Jackson St., 441-3004. House tours W 12-4 & Sun 11-4:30; adults $4, under 12 $2; strollers not permitted. Walking tours Sun at 12:30; adults $3, under 12 $1.*

In 1886 architect Peter R. Schmidt built this 24-room, $7^1/_2$-bath home of fir and redwood for Alice and William Haas. It cost $18,500. Average homes then went for about $2,000. Family members occupied the house until 1973, when it was donated to the Foundation for San Francisco's Architectural Heritage.

The house survived the infamous 1906 earthquake relatively unscathed. The only visible damage is a small bulge in the plaster. It also escaped the fire which followed, though Mr. Haas's downtown offices were destroyed.

The first-story floor plan is standard Victorian: a front parlour, second parlour, dining room, kitchen, and pantry. In keeping with Victorian building ideas, it is filled with leaded and stained-glass windows and such details as wallpaper stencilled to resemble leather. Most of the furnishings are original to the house. A lovely and extensive set of matching art nouveau furniture is on display in the main bedroom.

Docents are helpful in explaining the unusual features of this beauti-

HAAS-LILIENTHAL HOUSE

fully restored house. For instance, in the breakfast room a window which is actually a Gibb door opens to the back porch. The kitchen has been left unaltered and is still used during special events and private parties held in the house. It features 1920s appliances, the original marble sink, and a "cold room" where food is stored at outside temperature.

The Foundation-sponsored **Pacific Heights Walking Tour** of the neighborhood this house is located in allows participants to see the exteriors of some of San Francisco's finest Victorian and Edwardian homes.

### • Octagon House
*2645 Gough St./Union St., 441-7512; open 2nd & 4th Thur & 2nd Sun of month, 1-3:30, closed Jan; by donation.*

Built in 1861, when this architectural style was a fad throughout the country, this eight-sided house is now one of only two left in San Francisco.

The National Society of Colonial Dames of America has restored and furnished it and turned it into the only colonial museum on the West Coast. Items on display date from 1700 to 1830 and are labeled with background information. Of special interest is the display featuring the signatures of 54 of the original 56 signers of the Declaration of Independence.

A kit for making a paper model of the house is available and makes an appropriate souvenir.

The house's well-groomed garden and adjacent **Allyne Park** are both perfect for an after-tour stroll.

### • Whittier Mansion
*2090 Jackson St./Laguna St., 567-1848; tours Tu-F at 1:30, Sat & Sun at 1:30 & 3; adults $3, children $1, free 1st W of month.*

Built in 1896, this four-story transition-style Victorian mansion has thirty rooms and three Queen Anne towers. Its solid construction allowed the house to survive the '06 quake with the loss of only a few rooftiles. Unusual in its construction, it is made of brick with a woodframe interior and red Arizona sandstone facing.

The hand-carved solid oak front door weighs almost a ton. Other special features include Belgian cut-crystal sconces, silverplated hardware, and a non-functioning Otis hydraulic elevator.

The front room features a hand-carved mahogany fireplace, a variety of oriental rugs, and some of the original furniture. Vintage paintings of Yosemite National Park adorn the walls, and very old carbon filament lightbulbs are still emitting light.

### • Painted Ladies
To see some of the most beautiful "painted ladies," as the city's many colorfully painted Victorian homes are sometimes called, visit the area around **Alamo Square** at Hayes and Steiner Streets.

### MISSION DOLORES
*Dolores St./16th St., 621-8203; daily 9-4; adults $1, under 13 free.*

The mission chapel, completed in 1791, is the oldest intact building in the city. Its cool adobe interior makes for a pleasant respite from the occasional warm San Francisco day. A tiny museum and picturesque, rustic cemetery complete the complex of the sixth mission in California's chain of 21.

A visit here is de rigueur for every school child and is especially appropriate for fourth graders.

### OLD MINT
*5th St./Mission St., 974-0788; M-F 10-4; free.*

Built in 1874, this majestic building survived the 1906 earthquake and fire. Said to be the only Greek Revival-style building ever built on the West Coast, it has been restored to its original grandeur and is now a National Historic Landmark.

Once the most active mint in the nation, many of its old vaults are filled with money-related exhibits. One holds over $1,000,000 in gold nuggets and millions more in a pyramid of gold bars. For a small fee visitors may strike a souvenir bronze medallion on a noisy 1869 coin press.

An informative film is shown each hour; a guided tour follows.

## — PERFORMING ARTS —

### BEACH BLANKET BABYLON

*678 Green St./Powell St., Club Fugazi, 421-4222; Sun at 3; $14-$18.*

Begun back in 1974 as an underground production, this fast-moving and humorous musical revue is known for its creative costumes and huge headdresses. The show changes periodically but always brings pleasure.

Sunday matinees are aimed at families and are the only performances open to minors (under age 21). No alcohol is served then, but guests may order soft drinks and juice. I think BBB is appropriate for children 5 and older. There is no profanity or violence, but note that there is plenty of humorous reference to assorted types of sex.

For the past 15 years all performances have sold out, so reserve your tickets early and arrive when the doors open at 2 p.m. to choose your table.

## GREATER TUNA

*340 Mason St./Geary St., Mason Street Theatre, 668-TUNA; Tu-F at 8, Sat at 6 & 9, Sun at 3 & 7; tickets $18-$20.*

This two-man play about the third smallest town in Texas sure is unusual. In the sophisticated theater district of our stylish city, this comedy offers audiences the chance to dress casually, swig a beer while they watch (locally-brewed Anchor Steam is de rigueur, of course), and "get down." The two actors who portray the town's twenty outrageous inhabitants have changed over the seven-year-long run, but the wacky lines remain the same.

Though some of the content would be objectionable out of context, in general the performance is appropriate for children. My 11-year-old objected to stereotypes and racist statements (good for her!) until I had a chance to explain to her about satire.

Seating is general admission, so arrive when the doors open one-half hour before curtain.

## KIDSHOWS

*Noe Valley Ministry, 1021 Sanchez St., 282-2317.*

For description see page 168.

## MAKE-A-CIRCUS

*776-8477; July-Sept; free.*

This creative entourage presents a pre-performance Penny Carnival, a circus show, and children's workshops in circus skills. Children who par-

MAKE-A-CIRCUS

ticipate in the workshops may then perform their newly-learned skills in a second circus show. Performances are held in parks throughout the Bay Area.

Call for current schedule.

## PICKLE FAMILY CIRCUS
*826-0747; locations and prices vary; food service.*

This San Francisco-based troupe is an unusual European-style one-ring circus with a 30-foot trapeze, a five-piece jazz band, and assorted jugglers, tumblers, and clowns—but no animals! Performances are scheduled year-round at parks throughout the Bay Area. Team up a visit to one with a picnic.

During the Christmas holidays, performances are always scheduled at the Palace of Fine Arts.

## SAN FRANCISCO CHILDREN'S OPERA
*Van Ness Ave./McAllister St., in Herbst Theatre, 386-9622; Nov-Apr; season tickets $25-$50.*

At this Saturday afternoon performance series, five operas recommended for ages 5 and older are scheduled once per month. The simple plots are based on fairy tales; stage settings and costumes are elaborate;

and a 30-piece orchestra accompanies the singers. These well-directed productions have just the right mixture of singing, talking, dancing, and humor to hold children's attention.

### SAN FRANCISCO SYMPHONY FAMILY CONCERTS
*201 Van Ness Ave./Grove St., Davies Symphony Hall, 431-5400; $6-$24.*

Selections at these child-oriented concerts are designed to both interest and educate young children in classical music. Call for current schedule.

Each December a performance of **Peter and the Wolf** is presented. I once had the priviledge of seeing ex-Pickle Family Circus clown Geoff Hoyle act as narrator. He did a magnificent job of physically illustrating the piece. In 1989 the job was handled by Bobby "Don't Worry, Be Happy" McFerrin. The orchestra also performs some traditional carols and concludes with a carol sing-along. This program is appropriate for all ages.

### STBS
*Stockton St./Union Square, 433-STBS; Tu-Sat noon-7:30pm.*

Day-of-performance, half-price tickets are available here for many music, dance, and theater events. Cash only.

### YOUNG PERFORMERS THEATRE
*Fort Mason Center, Bldg. C, Laguna St./Marina Blvd., 346-5550; schedule varies; adults $6, children $4; free parking lot adjoins.*

This is a company of professional adults and young actors in training. Imaginative stage settings and simple, effective costumes make their usually short, fast-moving productions fun for parents and young children alike. Recent productions include *Charlie and the Chocolate Factory*, *Wind in the Willows*, and *The Secret Garden*.

---

# — MUSEUMS —

# Art Museums

### CALIFORNIA PALACE OF THE LEGION OF HONOR
*34th Ave./Clement St., in Lincoln Park, 750-3600; W-Sun 10-5; adults $4, 12-17 $2, under 12 free, free 1st W of month; free parking lot adjoins; food service.*

Situated on a scenic knoll overlooking the Golden Gate Bridge, this is the only museum in the country exhibiting primarily French art. Rodin's earliest casting of his sculpture, The Thinker, greets visitors as they approach the entrance to this impressive marble structure, a reproduction of an 18th century Parisian palace for which it was named. Special children's programs are sometimes scheduled.

The entrance to the **Holocaust Memorial** is on the north side of the parking area. A semicircular stairway leads down to the area where the cast bronze, white-painted pieces created by sculptor George Segal are displayed.

## CARTOON ART MUSEUM
*665 3rd St./Townsend St., 546-3922; W-F 11-5, Sat 10-5; adults $2.50, under 13 $1, under 1 free; free parking lot adjoins.*

Situated on the fifth floor of a modern building located right in the middle of factory outlet heaven (see p. 106), this relatively new museum presents both a permanent collection and occasional special exhibits. Its aim is "to preserve this unique art form and to enrich the public's knowledge of its cultural and aesthetic value."

## THE MEXICAN MUSEUM
*Fort Mason Center, Bldg. D, Laguna St./Marina Blvd., 441-0404; W-Sun 12-5, 1st W of month 12-8; adults $2, 10-16 $1, under 10 free, free 1st W of month; free parking lot adjoins.*

Founded in 1975, this is the first museum in the U.S. devoted to Mexican and Mexican-American art. Lots of open space and a tendency to exhibit colorful artworks makes this a choice spot to visit with children. Exhibits change regularly. When space allows, items from its permanent pre-Columbian collection are displayed.

Be careful in the well-stocked, but cramped, gift shop. Prices are good, and there are some attractive and inexpensive items for children to purchase. Don't miss (and don't touch) the $300 Ferris wheel usually displayed by the entry.

## M. H. DE YOUNG MEMORIAL MUSEUM
*In Golden Gate Park, 750-3600; W-Sun 10-5; adults $4, 12-17 $2, under 12 free, free 1st W of month; food service.*

A significant collection of American paintings are displayed on this museum's colorful walls. The collection includes sculpture and decorative arts, from colonial times into the mid-20th century, and a large collection of period furniture arrangements. Its collection of trompe l'oeil paintings is the best in the country.

Ask for a free children's gallery guide at the Information Desk to keep your child busy during your visit. Using a theme such as eyes, hats, or animals, it will lead your children through the museum looking for something specific and help them look at art on a level they can understand. A special children's class, Doing and Viewing Art, is held each Saturday from 10:30 to noon. Operating on a drop-in basis for children ages 7 through 12, it includes a tour of a gallery and a related studio art experience. The class is free, and no pre-registration is required. For more information, call 750-3658. Children are also welcome on the museum's guided tours.

Each March the museum galleries are stunningly decorated with fresh flowers. For **Bouquets to Art**, members of Bay Area flower clubs and professional florists design arrangements inspired by museum paintings. Some mimic the paintings, others pick up the colors or feeling. Overall they enliven the galleries. The event lasts for only three days. Call for the current year's schedule.

The cafeteria-style **Cafe de Young** (752-0116; L W-Sun; $; no reservations; no cards) serves simple foods prepared eloquently. The kitchen makes most items from scratch using fresh ingredients, and the menu offers a selection of salads and sandwiches along with a daily soup and pasta salad special. When available, both the minestrone soup, laden with chunks of vegetables and sprinkled with Parmesan, and the potato salad, seasoned with dill and tossed with bacon and black olives, are outstanding. Wonderful flaky cinnamon croissants are brought in from a bakery. Desserts are a weak spot. Selections consist of simple items such as carrot cake and brownies, when the setting seems to scream for fine pastries to go with tea. Diners can sit in a warm inside area, where tables are decorated with fresh flowers, or outside at umbrella-shaded tables surrounding a garden fountain.

Adjoining the de Young, the **Asian Art Museum** displays the best Asian collection in the U.S.

## MUSEO ITALO-AMERICANO
*Fort Mason Center, Bldg. C, Laguna St./Marina Blvd., 673-2200; W-Sun 12-5; by donation.*

Dedicated to displaying the works of Italian and Italian-American artists, this museum's exhibit space is stark and quiet. An annual children's art show occurs each April.

## SAN FRANCISCO CRAFT & FOLK ART MUSEUM
*Fort Mason Center, Bldg. A, Laguna St./Marina Blvd., 775-0990; Tu-Sun 11-5; adults $1, 12-17 50¢; under 12 free, free Sat 10-12; free parking lot adjoins.*

Serving as a showcase for high quality contemporary crafts and folk art, this museum's exhibits change every two months.

## SAN FRANCISCO MUSEUM OF MODERN ART
*401 Van Ness Ave./McAllister St., 863-8800; Tu,W,F 10-5, Thur 10-9, Sat & Sun 11-5; adults $4, 6-16 $1.50, under 6 free, free each Tu; food service.*

This is the only museum in the West devoted entirely to 20th century art. Its collection includes abstract art, photography, and the work of acclaimed contemporary artists.

In addition to interesting jewelry, the museum gift shop has a wonderful selection of children's books.

# Children's Museums

### JOSEPHINE D. RANDALL JUNIOR MUSEUM
*199 Museum Way/Roosevelt Way, near 15th St., 554-9600; Tu-Sat 10-5; free; free parking lot adjoins.*

Located high on Twin Peaks, this small museum has an indoor mini-zoo inhabited by uncaged but tethered hawks and owls and other small, accessible animals—most of which are recovering from injuries inflicted in the wild. A highlight is the Petting Corral where children may hold rabbits, chickens, and ducks. Exhibits are few but include an operating seismograph as well as dinosaur and fossil displays. Nature walks, movies, and children's science and art classes are scheduled regularly.

On the first and fourth Saturday afternoon of each month, the **Golden Gate Model Railroaders** show off their model railroad.

### SAN FRANCISCO INTERNATIONAL TOY MUSEUM
*2801 Leavenworth St./Beach St., in The Cannery, 441-TOYS; Tu-Sat 10-5, Sun 11-5; $2, under 2 free.*

This isn't your usual museum. The world's first hands-on toy museum, it is designed especially for kids. And because kids enjoy it, so do their parents.

One section is devoted to new toys which children may not only touch but actually play with! Among the goodies are a basket containing thousands of Lego pieces, a kid-operated wooden rocking rowboat, and a complete Brio wooden train set with an elaborate layout. This play area offers a great opportunity to try out new toys with your child.

Antique displays include vintage dolls and carriages and Dinky transportation toys from the '30s and '40s. All the toys in this collection are no longer being manufactured.

# Floating Museums

The collection of historic ships berthed along the San Francisco waterfront is the largest (by weight) in the world. Moving west, they begin with the *USS Pampanito*, berthed near Pier 45, and end with the *S.S. Jeremiah O'Brien*, berthed at Fort Mason. Five are open to the public.

Though it would be possible to visit all the ships in one day, and this certainly would be an interesting way to see them, I don't recommend attempting it with young children. Parents are advised to stretch out this adventure and visit the ships one or two at a time.

## USS PAMPANITO
*At Pier 45, foot of Taylor St., 929-0202; Sun-Thur 9-6, F & Sat 9-9, in summer daily 9-9; adults $4, 12-17 $2, 6-11 $1, under 6 free.*

This 312-foot-long World War II submarine was built in Portsmouth, New Hampshire in 1943. She is credited with the September 12, 1944 sinking of a 10,500-ton Japanese transport and 5,100-ton tanker as well as the destruction of a third ship in the South China Sea. She also rescued a group of British and Australian POWs.

A self-guided tour is provided via an electronic wand which is activated at stations throughout the submarine. While walking through the cramped belly of the sub, the narrative helps you imagine what it must have been like for men to be cooped up in this small space for days at a time.

## SAN FRANCISCO MARITIME NATIONAL HISTORICAL PARK

### • Maritime Museum
*On Beach St. at foot of Polk St., across from Ghirardelli Square, 556-2904; daily 10-6, guided tours daily at 1:15 and 3; free.*

The architecturally interesting building housing this museum was built by the Works Project Administration (WPA) in 1939. Appropriately, it resembles a ship, though it was originally meant to be used as a nightclub and aquatic activities center.

The main floor displays parts of old ships, elaborately carved and painted figureheads, and exquisitely detailed ship models. The second floor is home to more models as well as artifacts, paintings, photos, and maps.

The museum hosts an annual **Festival of the Sea** in October. It features sea music concerts, demonstrations of sailor arts, lectures, films, and the reading of sea poetry.

### • Hyde Street Pier
*2905 Hyde St./Jefferson St., 556-3002; daily 10-5; adults $2, under 17 free, free first Tu of month.*

The ships moored on this scenic pier represent the time period from the turn of the century through World War II—a period of rapid growth for San Francisco begun by the 1849 Gold Rush. During this time the city was an important shipping center.

*Balclutha.* A Cape Horn sailing ship built in Scotland in 1886, this 301-foot steel-hulled merchant ship carried whiskey, wool, and rice, but mainly coal, to San Francisco. On her return sailings to Europe she carried grain from California. Typical of Victorian British merchant ships, she is described colorfully by the men who sailed her as a "blue water, square-rigged, lime juice windbag." She is the last of the Cape Horn fleet and ended her sailing career as an Alaskan salmon ship.

Renovated by donated labor and goods, she was opened to the public

THE BALCLUTHA

in 1955. Colorful figureheads, anchors, and other maritime artifacts are displayed in the hold below her main deck. In addition, interpretive exhibits depict life on board.

*Eureka.* Originally named the *Ukiah*, this double-ended, wooden-hulled ferry was built in Tiburon in 1890 to carry railroad cars across the bay. In 1922 she was rebuilt to carry cars and passengers and renamed the *Eureka*. Later she served as a commuter ferry (the largest in the world) between San Francisco and Sausalito, and yet later as a ferry for train passengers arriving in San Francisco from Oakland. She held 2,300 people plus 120 automobiles.

Her four-story "walking beam" steam engine is the only such engine still afloat in the United States. A model demonstrates its operation, and a ranger-guided tour through the engine room is scheduled daily at 3 p.m.

All three decks are open to the public. The lower deck houses a display of antique cars; the main deck features original benches and historical photo displays; and the wheel house provides a wind-sheltered view of the bay and the opportunity to turn the heavy captain's wheel.

***C.A. Thayer.*** A fleet of 900 ships once carried lumber from the north coast forests to California ports. Only two of these ships still exist. One is the *C.A. Thayer*—a three-mast lumber schooner built in Fairhaven (near Eureka) in 1895. She made her last trip in 1950 as a fishing ship. She was the very last commercial sailing ship in use on the West Coast and is now a registered National Historic Landmark.

Visitors may descend into her dank wooden hold to see the crew's bunk room and then ascend to the captain's lushly furnished, oak-paneled cabin—complete with a gilded canary cage.

A 25-minute film of her last voyage is shown at 2 and 4 p.m. each day. For a guided tour, call ahead.

A fascinating way to get to know this ship is at one of the **chantey sings** sponsored by the National Park Service. These monthly events are held in her cozy hold. Participants should dress warmly and bring something to sit on as well as a chantey or two to share. A little something to

whet the whistle wouldn't hurt either. A children's program is scheduled from 3 to 5 p.m.; an adult program runs from 8 p.m. to midnight. For current schedule and free reservations call 556-1871.

More ships are moored at the pier which are not open for boarding. As funds allow, it is planned to restore them and open them to the public.

*Alma.* This scow schooner was built in 1891 at Hunters Point. She is a specialized cargo carrier and the last of her kind still afloat. Her bluff bows and flat bottom were designed to accommodate bulk cargoes of coal, hay, and sand. When she was retired in 1958, she was being used for dredging oyster shells. She occasionally sails as the ambassador ship of the museum.

*Eppleton Hall.* This sidewheel tug was built in 1914 in England, where she was used in the canals to tow coal ships. Her steam engines were converted from coal to oil in 1970. They were called "grasshopper engines" because the side levers looked like the hindlegs of a grasshopper. Her two paddlewheels can turn in opposite directions at the same time, allowing her to turn on a dime.

"Eppie" is the only ship in the collection which was not directly associated with West Coast maritime history.

*Hercules.* An ocean-going tugboat built in 1907, the *Hercules* has a triple expansion steam engine. She towed log rafts to lumber mills and hauled the great ships out to sea. She will be moving temporarily to Fort Mason for repairs. It is not yet determined whether she will be opened for boarding during this period.

*Monterey Clipper.* This latest addition to the collection is a classic bay fishing boat. Built in 1923 by the Labruzzi Brothers boat works at Fisherman's Wharf, she is 28 feet long and was donated to the museum by two Napa fishermen. Her one-cylinder Hicks gasoline engine weighs almost a ton and still works.

*Wapama.* This last surviving example of a steam schooner is currently located at the US Army Corps of Engineers Bay Model Visitor Center in Sausalito (see p. 230), where she is being restored. She is open for free guided tours. For reservations call 556-2904.

**Non-floating displays** at the pier include a turn-of-the-century ark, or houseboat, which was once moored in Tiburon and used as a summer cottage. The reconstructed sales office of the Tubbs Cordage Company, which once stood at 23rd and 3rd Streets, is now used as the ranger office. The *Sea Fox* wheelhouse is all that remains of a 117-foot wooden-hulled tugboat of the Miki Miki (Hawaiian for "on time") class. There is also a smaller tug wheelhouse, the *Geo. Shima*, which was built in 1912. A restored donkey engine, used to load and unload cargo, is also on display and is sometimes operated for visitors.

## S.S. JEREMIAH O'BRIEN
*Fort Mason Center, near Bldg. A, Pier 3 East, Laguna St./Marina Blvd.; 441-3101; M-F 9-3, Sat & Sun 9-4; adults $2-$3, under 13 $1, families $5.*

This massive 441-foot vessel is the last unaltered Liberty Ship from World War II still in operating condition. Between 1941 and 1945, in an all-out effort to replace the cargo ships which were being sunk in huge numbers by enemy submarines, 2,751 Liberty Ships were built to transport troops and supplies. At that time shipyards operated around the clock. Each ship, assembled from pre-fabricated sections, took only six to eight weeks to build.

The *O'Brien* was built in South Portland, Maine in 1943. She was in operation for 33 years and sailed from England to Normandy during the D-Day invasion.

In 1978 she was declared a National Monument. Since then dedicated volunteers, many of whom served on similar ships, have been working to restore her to her original glory. She has been open to the public since 1980 and floats as "a memorial to those who designed, built, loaded, and sailed Liberty Ships, to the Merchant Marine, and to the maritime industry."

She is shockingly large and quite a surprise to discover hidden around the side of a Fort Mason pier. Visitors have access to almost every part of the ship, including sleeping quarters, captain's quarters, wheel house, and guns as well as the catwalks in the eerie three-story engine room.

The triple expansion steam engine is operated on the third weekend of each month (except in May and December). They cook in the galley then, and the resulting hot dogs and cookies are available for purchase.

Each May the ship sails the bay for its annual **Seamen's Memorial Cruise** and **Bay Cruise**. A buffet lunch and live music are included in the tax-deductible $75 ticket.

## OPEN SHIPS
For information about visiting ships which are open for viewing, call the Port of San Francisco at 391-8000.

# Science Museums

## CALIFORNIA ACADEMY OF SCIENCES
*In Golden Gate Park, 750-7145; daily 10-5; adults $4, 12-17 $2, 6-11 $1, under 6 free, free 1st W of month; food service; free parking lot adjoins. Planetarium: 750-7141; $1.25-$2.50. Laserium: 750-7138; Thur-Sun; adults $4.50-$5.50, 6-12 $3.50, no children under 6. Discovery Room: 750-7155; reservations necessary.*

Founded in 1853, this is the oldest scientific institution in the West. And this impressive museum complex grows better all the time. You and your child can experience a simulated earthquake, watch time march on

FINISHING THE "WILD CALIFORNIA" EXHIBIT

via a Foucault pendulum (children love watching the little blocks getting knocked over), and handle a variety of natural artifacts in the hard-to-find Discovery Room located near The Far Side Gallery. Exhibits include bird and animal dioramas, most notably the new Wild California (featuring life-size elephant seals and a 14,000-gallon aquarium) and the African Waterhole (with authentic animal sounds synchronized to a dawn-to-dusk lighting cycle). An impressive Gem and Mineral Hall displays a thirteen-pound mass of gold from the Mother Lode.

The **Steinhart Aquarium** exhibits hundreds of fish tanks as well as a popular black-footed penguin environment and dolphin tank. There is also a newly renovated California Tidepool, where visitors may handle live sea animals, and a Roundabout—a circular 10,000-gallon tank where the viewers are on the inside and the fish are on the outside. With over 1,000 species in its exhibits, it is said to have the most diverse collection in the world.

**Morrison Planetarium**, the largest in Northern California, presents daily shows. Each year during the month of December, **The Christmas Star** is presented. Viewers are taken back in time to view the night sky as it is believed to have appeared to the Wise Men in Nazareth almost 2,000 years ago. Discussion includes the various possibilities of what the Christmas Star actually was, as well as information on what you can see in the current night sky.

In the evening **Laserium** shows display pulsating images on the planetarium ceiling. (The term "laserium" is a combination of the words "laser" and "planetarium.") A lightshow is coordinated to a music track by a live "laserist." The schedule offers three different types of music: hard rock, pop, and classical. The sound level is plenty loud, but if you really want to crank it up, bring along a portable FM radio and headset and tune in to the special Laserium channel. Because of limited seating, it is wise to purchase tickets in advance. These shows are particularly popular with teens.

Bring a picnic lunch to enjoy in the outdoor courtyard. Bufano statues are scattered about there for children to play upon, and hungry seagulls gather to gobble up dropped crumbs.

## EXPLORATORIUM

*3601 Lyon St., in the Marina District near the entrance to the Golden Gate Bridge, 561-0360; W-Sun 10-5, W eve to 9:30; adults $6, 6-17 $2, under 6 free, ticket good for 6 months, free first W of month & every W eve; free parking lot adjoins; food service.*

Located inside the **Palace of Fine Arts,** which was designed by architect Bernard Maybeck in 1915 as part of the Panama-Pacific Exposition (an early World's Fair) and is now the world's largest artificial ruin, this cavernous museum makes scientific and natural phenomena understandable through a collection of over 600 hands-on exhibits. It has been described by a former editor of *Scientific American* as the best science museum in the world.

Visitors may experience a dizzying ride on a Momentum Machine, measure sweat production during a kiss or a tickle, and light up an enchanted tree by clapping their hands. To the shrieking delight of youngsters, a walk-in Shadow Box allows reverse images to remain on a wall.

Reservations must be made several months in advance to experience the **Tactile Dome** (563-7272), a geodesic dome with thirteen chambers through which visitors may walk, crawl, slide, climb, and tumble in complete darkness with only their sense of touch to guide them. This experience is not recommended for children under age 7.

An effervescent, irregularly held **Bubble Festival** celebrates the won-

ANTI-GRAVITY MIRROR

der and beauty of bubbles. Past exhibits have allowed visitors to participate in blowing unusual bubbles. Performers have included Tom Noddy
(who can blow bubbles inside bubbles, inside-out bubbles, and bubble
cubes), Eiffel Plasterer (who has blown a bubble which encased a person
and one which lasted 340 days, and who saves his old bubbles in jars),
David Stein (a New York City architect who claims to be able to make the
largest bubbles ever recorded: 50-foot tubular bubbles and 8-foot spheres),
and Sterling Johnson (a San Francisco lawyer who can blow a giant bubble
with his hands and then, soaped up and in his bathing suit, walk through it).

Before or after your visit, enjoy a picturesque picnic outside by the
large reflecting pond populated with ducks and even a few swans.

The **Wave Organ**, a project sponsored by the Exploratorium, is located
across Marina Boulevard at the eastern tip of the breakwater forming the
Marina Yacht Harbor. This unusual musical instrument was designed by
artist Peter Richards in collaboration with stonemason George Gonzales.
Consisting of more than 20 pipes which extend down through the breakwater into the bay, the organ provides a constant symphony of natural
music. Listeners may relax in a small granite and marble amphitheatre
and enjoy views of the San Francisco skyline. The organ plays most effec-
tively at high tide.

# Miscellaneous Museums

### THE AMERICAN CAROUSEL MUSEUM
*633 Beach St./Hyde St., 928-0550; daily 10-5, to 6 Apr-Oct; adults $2, 12-17 $1,
under 12 free, free 1st W of month.*

It is said that the best carousel figures were American, not European.
Unlike their stiffer European counterparts, American carousel horses are
more dramatic and varied. Unfortunately, of the several thousand carousels originally built in the U.S. between the 1870s and 1930s, only about
200 are left.

This museum has dedicated itself to preserving this art. Carousel figures displayed here have been chosen for their beautiful carving. Among
the approximately 70 figures are some early European animals and
examples from all the major American carousel makers. An especially interesting exhibit uses six figures to show the various stages of restoring a
wooden carousel horse. Adding to the atmosphere is the intermittent
music from a Wurlitzer band organ. Craftsmen are often seen at work in
the restoration workshop located in the back of the museum.

### CABLE CAR MUSEUM
*1201 Mason St./Washington St., 474-1887; daily 10-5; free.*

Located two blocks from the heart of Chinatown, this interesting museum is situated inside the lovely brick cable car barn dating from the

1880s. Here visitors may view the huge, noisy wheels which control the underground cables that move the cable cars. An assortment of old cable cars and artifacts are on display, and an informative film explains how the cable cars actually work.

To complete the experience, take a ride downtown on the Powell-Mason line. You can catch it across the street at Mason and Jackson.

## GUINNESS MUSEUM OF WORLD RECORDS
*235 Jefferson St./Taylor St., 771-9890; daily 10-10; adults $5.95, 5-11 $2.75, under 5 free.*

They're all here: the smallest bicycle, the tiniest book, the biggest electric guitar, and much, much, more.

## RIPLEY'S BELIEVE IT OR NOT! MUSEUM
*175 Jefferson St./Taylor St., 771-6188; Sun-Thur 10-10, Fri & Sat to midnight; adults $6.50, 13-17 $5.25, 5-12 $3.75, under 5 free.*

Among the 500-plus exhibits from Ripley's personal collection of oddities are the world's smallest violin and the world's largest shoe. See the entire Lord's Prayer written on a grain of rice. See a real shrunken head. All this and more, more, more. It's unbelievable!

## SAN FRANCISCO FIRE DEPARTMENT MUSEUM
*655 Presidio Ave./Pine St., 861-8000; Thur-Sun 1-4; free.*

You'll see an interesting collection of antique fire engines at this small museum. Of special interest is an ornate hand-pulled engine which dates from 1849 and is said to be San Francisco's, and California's, first fire engine.

## TREASURE ISLAND MUSEUM
*Treasure Island, Bldg. One, 395-5067; daily 10-3:30; free; free parking lot adjoins.*

The permanent exhibits here chronicle the history of the Navy, Marine Corps, and Coast Guard in the Pacific. A Jewels in the Bay exhibit covers California's last World's Fair (the Golden Gate International Exposition of 1939-40), America's first trans-oceanic commercial airplanes (the China Clipper Flying Boats of 1935-46), the histories of both Treasure Island and Yerba Buena Island, and the building of both the Golden Gate and Bay bridges.

A Children's Activities Sheet is available to help you find the exhibits which will particularly interest children. Ask for one when you arrive.

Allow time to take in the magnificent view of San Francisco which is available from outside the museum.

## THE WAX MUSEUM
*145 Jefferson St./Taylor St., 885-4975; daily 9am-10:30pm; adults $7.95, 6-12 $3.95, under 6 free.*

Several hundred wax celebrities are situated among an assortment of backgrounds. The Chamber of Horrors should intrigue older children. Fairyland should do the same for the younger ones.

---

# — OUTDOORS/PARKS —

---

## ANGEL ISLAND STATE PARK
*San Francisco departures from Pier 43$^1/_2$ at Fisherman's Wharf, 546-2815; adults $7, 5-11 $4, under 5 free. Tiburon departures from Main St., 435-2131; $4. Schedules vary but usually operate daily in summer, weekends only rest of year. State Park information: 435-1910; Visitors Center open Sat & Sun 11-3:30; picnic tables, food service.*

Half the fun of a trip to Angel Island is the ferry ride over. After a scenic ride to the island, visitors are deposited at Ayala Cove. Picnic tables and barbecue facilities are nearby, as is a pleasant little beach for sunbathing. (Wading is inviting but not recommended. The water is polluted.) Perfect for a picnic, the island also has a snackbar. But it is highly recommended that you put your repast in a day pack and hike to some remote spot away from the crowds.

Approximately twelve miles of well-marked trails and paved roads allow hikers to completely circle the 740-acre island. Some lead to old military ruins—reminders of the island's past as a prison for American Indians, as a holding camp for quarantined immigrants (the island was once called the "Ellis Island of the West"), as a prisoner-of-war camp, and as a missile defense base. A two-mile nature trail leads from the cove to the top of 781-foot Mount Livermore. There you'll find a picnic area and a 360-degree view of the Bay Area. A trail map is available at the Visitors Center.

For those who prefer not to walk, bus service is usually available during the summer. It is also a great idea to bring bicycles. Except for Park Service vehicles, cars are not permitted on the island—making biking particularly pleasant. If interested, inquire about ferry regulations regarding bikes.

A variety of guided tours are available. Call for more information. Camping in primitive "environmental" campsites can be arranged. For information call 800/952-5580.

## BEACHES
San Francisco is not the place to come to go to the beach. Head for Los Angeles if you are after *that* California. Still, the city does have a few

good spots to soak up some rays. The water, however, is usually either too cold or too dangerous for swimming.

### • Aquatic Park
*Foot of Polk St., 556-2904; free.*

Located in the people-congested area across the street from Ghirardelli Square, this is a good spot for children to wade. A lifeguard is on duty in summer, and there are great views of the bay.

### • Baker Beach
*Off Lincoln Blvd./25th Ave., 556-8371; daily dawn to dusk; free.*

The surf here is unsafe and the temperature is often chilly. Still there are usually plenty of people sunning and strolling, and the views of the Golden Gate bridge are spectacular.

**Battery Chamberlin** is located adjacent. Demonstrations of the 95,000-pound "disappearing gun" are conducted by rangers on weekends, and environmental programs are sometimes offered.

### • China Beach
*End of Seacliff Ave./28th Ave., 556-7894; dawn to dusk daily; free; picnic tables.*

Located in an exclusive residential area, this secluded cove is surprising to come upon. Visitors park on a bluff and then walk down steep stairs to the sheltered, sandy beach. The surf is gentle, so swimming and wading are possible, and lifeguards are on duty April through October. Changing rooms and restrooms are available.

## FORT FUNSTON
*South end of Great Highway at Skyline Blvd., 556-8371; daily 6-9.*

A short, paved loop trail offers stunning coastal views. However, the reason most people come here is to watch the hang-gliders do their stuff. An observation platform on a bluff above the ocean provides a bird's-eye view.

## GOLDEN GATE PARK

One of the world's great metropolitan parks, Golden Gate Park is loaded with family activities. Encompassing 1,017 acres, it is nearly 200 acres larger than Manhattan's Central Park, after which it was originally patterned. Once just sand dunes, it is now the largest man-made park in the world.

Here are the things you simply must not miss.

### • Biking/Skating

On Sundays John F. Kennedy Drive is closed to automobiles. Car traffic is replaced with heavy bike, skate, and pedestrian traffic. Skate and bike rentals are available at shops along Stanyan Street. Skates are also usually available from trucks stopped along Fulton Street.

## • Buffalo Paddock

When is the last time you saw a *real* buffalo? Foreign visitors seem particularly impressed with viewing this herd.

## • California Academy of Sciences

For description see page 89.

## • Children's Playground

*On Bowling Green Dr., between King and Kennedy Dr., east of the California Academy of Sciences; free parking lot adjoins; picnic tables; food service.*

Constructed in 1887, this was the very first playground in a U.S. public park. Today it is filled with creative modern play structures.

Located adjacent, an antique **Carrousel** (W-Sun 10-4, to 5 in summer; adults $1, 6-12 25¢; children under 39 inches tall free with parent) makes its rounds within a protective hippodrome enclosure. Built in 1914 by Herschell-Spillman, it has 62 beautifully painted hand-carved animals and still operates its original Gebruder band organ.

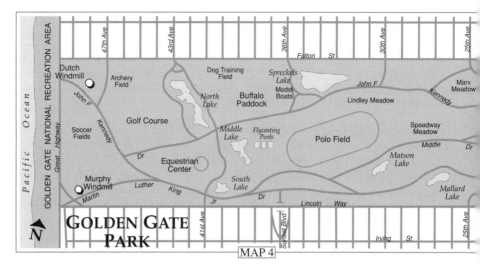

### • Conservatory of Flowers

*666-7107; daily 9-5, to 6 Apr-Oct; adults $1.50, 6-12 75¢, under 6 free, free 1st W of month; free parking lot adjoins.*

Built in Ireland in 1878 and modeled after the Palm House in London's Kew Gardens, this impressive example of Victorian architecture consists of a central dome flanked by two wings. It is the oldest remaining building in the park.

See if you can find the conservatory's oldest and largest plant—a Philodendron speciosum. Other noteworthy items to search out are the primitive cycads (from the dinosaur era) and the two ponds—one filled with tropical water lilies and the other planted in classic Victorian-style with ferns.

Seasonal displays change every two months. Of special note are the poinsettias which appear during the Christmas season.

### • Equestrian Center

*At west end of John F. Kennedy Dr., 668-7360; M-F 9-7, Sat & Sun 9-5.*

Riding lessons are available on a one-time or ongoing basis. Call for details. No hourly rentals are available, and children must be at least 8 years old.

### • Japanese Tea Garden and Teahouse

*Next to the de Young Museum, 666-7107; daily 9-5:30. Garden: adults $2, 6-12 $1, under 6 free; strollers not permitted. Tea: $1/person; no reservations; no cards.*

This garden is enjoyable to stroll through at any time of day, any time of year, and in almost any kind of weather. Be sure to take the kids to the "wishing bridge" (actually a drum bridge), where they can climb up the steep arch, make a wish, and throw a coin in the pond below. Adults

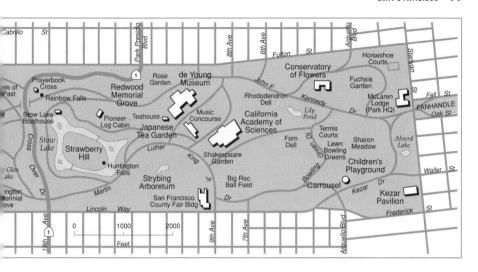

sometimes have a little more trouble maneuvering the sharp arc. You'll also want to climb up or down the steep steps leading to a miniature red pagoda. And keep your eyes peeled for the undulating dragon hedge.

Everyone seems to enjoy stopping for refreshment at the inviting outdoor teahouse, where tea and oriental cookies are served by waitresses clad in traditional Japanese kimonos. It is quite pleasant and relaxing to observe nature while leisurely sipping jasmine or green tea and munching on exotic cookies.

An interesting note: Makoto Hagiwara, who designed the garden in 1893 for the Mid-Winter Exposition, is credited with introducing the fortune cookie to America in 1914.

### • M. H. de Young Memorial Museum

For description see page 82.

### • Shakespeare Garden

*Behind the California Academy of Sciences.*

This garden is planted with the 150 varieties of flowers mentioned in William's plays.

### • Stow Lake Boathouse
*752-0347; Tu-Sun 10-3:45, daily in summer; paddle boats, row boats, & electric boats $8-$11/hour; free parking lot adjoins; picnic tables, food service.*

A boat on Stow Lake provides both an unusual and memorable picnic spot. After pushing off in a row boat, it's pleasant to find a cove where there isn't too much water movement and then get down to the business of eating a picnic meal.

When we tossed bread to the ducks and seagulls on one of our picnics here, they fairly sank our boat with enthusiasm. Be sure not to indulge in this bit of fancy until you are through eating—or the gulls may take off with your entire lunch.

Cushions, which double as life preservers, are provided in the boats. Though the water is shallow and it isn't possible to get very far from shore, you may want to bring along your own life vests for children or non-swimmers. Also, as the boats are often wet inside, consider bringing along a blanket to sit on.

### • Strybing Arboretum
*Entrance adjoins the San Francisco County Fair Bldg. (formerly the Hall of Flowers), 661-1316; M-F 8-4:30, Sat & Sun 10-5; free.*

Known for its magnolia and rhododendron collections, this lovely garden displays over 6,000 different plant species. Many are unique to this climate, and most are labeled. Of special note are the Japanese-style Moon-viewing Garden, the Arthur Menzies Garden of California Native Plants, the redwood forest, the small fragrance garden, and the Biblical Garden. It also is home to a duck pond with several swans in residence.

Free tours are scheduled at 1:30 on the second and fourth Monday and Saturday of each month. Plants currently in bloom are stressed.

### • Walking Tours
*221-1311; Sat & Sun May-Oct; free.*

All of these walks are led by volunteers and require no reservations. Except for the Japanese Tea Garden tour, which lasts 45 minutes, all tours run from $1^1/2$ to 2 hours.

Participants on the **Strawberry Hill Tour** enjoy a spectacular view of the Golden Gate Bridge and San Francisco from atop the hill. They see Huntington Falls, explore the Pioneer Log Cabin, and visit the Redwood Memorial Grove and the Rose Garden. (Saturdays at 11; meet at the park map between the Japanese Tea Garden and the de Young Museum.)

On the **East End Tour** walkers see some little-known spots such as the horseshoe courts and Fuchsia Garden. They stroll through the Rhododendron and Fern Dells and visit Children's Playground. (Sundays at 11; meet in front of McLaren Lodge at Fell and Stanyan Streets.)

The **Japanese Garden Tour** covers the history and design of the garden. (2nd, 4th, and 5th Sunday of the month at 2; pay admission and meet inside the main gate.)

The **West End Tour** takes in Spreckels Lake, the restored windmill, and the Buffalo Paddock. (1st Sunday of month at 2; meet at park map at Spreckels Lake/36th Ave.)

The **Lloyd Lake Tour** explores Portals of the Past, Rainbow Falls, Prayerbook Cross, and other park secrets. (3rd Sunday of month at 2; meet at park map in front of Lloyd Lake.)

## MOUNTAIN LAKE PARK
*Entrance at Lake St./Funston Ave.*

This park, well-hidden from the street, is an unexpected delight when you come upon it. Facilities include a path by the lake, a basketball court, tennis courts, a parcourse that begins at 9th Avenue, and a large, well-equipped playground off 12th Avenue. There are even ducks to feed.

Spring-fed Mountain Lake supplied all of the city's water between 1852 and 1870.

## SAN FRANCISCO ZOO
*Sloat Blvd./45th Ave., 753-7061; daily 10-5; adults $6, 12-15 $3, 5-12 $1, under 5 free, free 1st W of month; free parking lot adjoins; picnic tables; food service; stroller rentals ($2/day).*

A ride on the Zebra Zephyr tram gives a quick introduction to the layout of this scenic zoo. Of special note are Monkey Island (inhabited with spider monkeys), the half-acre Gorilla World (the world's largest gorilla habitat), and the Primate Discovery Center with its unusual, perhaps, unique, nocturnal primates exhibit. The lions are particularly interesting to visit when they are fed each afternoon from 2 to 3—except Monday, when they fast.

In the separate **Children's Zoo** (adults $1, under 2 free) you'll find a petting area inhabited by sheep and goats. California's only **Insect Zoo**, and one of only four in the U.S. (the others are in Cincinnati, Washington, D.C., and Tucson), is also located here. It is populated with three-inch walking sticks, giant Costa Rican wood cockroaches, and honeybees complete with a functioning hive. In an adjacent butterfly garden, native plants are labeled with the type of butterfly they attract.

Don't miss taking a ride on the antique **carousel** located just outside the Children's Zoo. Originally built in 1921 by the William Detzel Carving Company, it was beautifully restored in 1980. And do allow time for children to romp on the gargantuan playground across the way.

All ages are welcome to enter the popular three-mile family-oriented **Zoo Run** held each January. The course winds through the zoo, allowing participants to swing by the Primate Discovery Center, lope past the giraffes, and strut alongside Penguin Island. A more challenging seven-mile run is also scheduled. All participants receive a commemorative t-shirt, free admission to the zoo for the day, and end-of-the-line refreshments.

INSECT ZOO

Each year in May members of the Zoological Society are invited to a **Night Tour at the Zoo.** Entertainment, demonstrations, behind-the-scenes tours, and admission are all free, and a picnic dinner is available for a small charge. Support the zoo and find out just what happens at the zoo after dark.

NIGHT TOUR AT THE ZOO

## — SHOPPING —

### BASIC BROWN BEAR FACTORY & STORE

*444 DeHaro St./17th St., 626-0781; M-Sat 10-5, tours Sat at 11 & 2 or by appointment.*

Bears of all kinds—from your basic brown to your quite elaborate creamy-colored Beary Godmother dressed in pink satin wings and carrying a magic wand—are available in this tiny shop. The bears are not sold anywhere else, so they make a perfect souvenir. The close-to-wholesale prices range from $1.50 for a mouse to $129 for a four-foot tall, fully-jointed bear with leather paws. There are many more in between.

This is one of the few stuffed animal factories still manufacturing within the U.S. Some of its operations can be observed in the back of the sales shop. Sewing machines and cutting tables are upstairs. Call ahead if you'd like to make an appointment to stuff your own specialty bear using their World War II-era machine that once pumped up life preservers; a generic baby bear ($6.50) is always available for stuffing.

### THE CANNERY

*Beach St./Leavenworth St./Hyde St./Jefferson St.; 771-3112; most shops open M-F 10-6, Sun 11-6.*

Built in 1907, this charming red brick shopping complex was once the world's largest fruit and vegetable cannery. It now holds 50 shops, galleries, restaurants, and other diversions. Tenants described in this book include the San Francisco International Toy Museum (see p. 84) and the San Francisco School of Cooking (see p. 20).

Free entertainment by the city's finest street performers is often scheduled under the century-old olive trees in the pleasant courtyard.

### COST PLUS IMPORTS

*2552 Taylor St., near Fisherman's Wharf, 928-6200; M-Sat 10-9, Sun 11-7.*

This gigantic importer has long been a favorite shopping stop for many visitors to the area. Back in the '60s I used to bring out-of-towners here to get "hippie" supplies: batik bedspreads, incense, candles, etc.

Imports from around the world include jewelry, kitchenware, furniture, baskets, and toys. It is a favorite spot for my daughter to get rid of her allowance.

### ESPRIT FACTORY OUTLET

*499 Illinois St./16th St., 957-2550; M-F 10-8, Sat 10-7, Sun 11-5.*

This popular line of clothing for kids and teens (mainly girls) originates in San Francisco. Lines aren't too much of a problem if you avoid sales, but bargain hunters have been known to wait for over an hour just to get in.

If you find all the shopping makes you hungry, a stylish hi-tech cafe is located adjacent. There you can get an assortment of salads, trendy pizzas, sandwiches, and drinks. Or perhaps you might just want to settle in there while the kids shop.

## FACTORY OUTLET HEAVEN

This is my name for the area around Third and Brannan Streets. Just walk around and follow the herds into the various outlet stores offering all manner of bargains. Hours run roughly Monday through Saturday 10 to 4.

Of special note to those of you with girls is the **Gunne Sax** outlet at 35 Stanford Alley. This clothes manufacturer is known for its frilly party dresses.

## GHIRARDELLI SQUARE
*900 North Point St./Larkin St., 775-5500; daily 10-6, to 9 in summer.*

Built in 1900 as a chocolate factory and converted into a festival marketplace in 1964, this beautiful brick complex is said to have been the nation's first quaint, upscale shopping center. Now it is a National Historic Landmark and home to 63 shops and 13 restaurants.

If the weather is fair, stop in at **The Kite Shop** to select a kite from their interesting collection. (To fly it, just cross the street to Aquatic Park. When you've finished with this pleasant dalliance, you'll probably still have a colorful souvenir to take home.) Other interesting shops include **The Nature Company**, which specializes in quality items related to nature, **Goosebumps** for unusual gifts and souvenirs, **Bears to Go** for a honeypot of a selection of bearaphernalia, and **Sweet Zoo** for unique stuffed animals.

Restaurants which are particularly good for families include the Ghirardelli Chocolate Manufactory (see p. 34) and Compadres Mexican Bar & Grill (see p. 29). For sit-down snacks try **La Nouvelle Patisserie** and **Ghirardelli's**. For walk-away snacks try **The Corn Popper** (32 fun flavors) or **Findley's Fabulous Fudge** (said to be the country's best).

Street performers are scheduled on the courtyard stage each weekend.

## JAPAN CENTER
*Three square blocks bounded by Post, Geary, Laguna, and Fillmore Streets, 922-6776; open daily, hours vary; some businesses validate for the center's fee lot (entrance on Geary St. near Webster St.).*

This five-acre cultural center houses art galleries, traditional Japanese baths, a Japanese-style market, a movie theater complex, a hotel, 33 shops, and 18 restaurants. Designed like an indoor mall, there are a series of passageways permitting you to avoid crossing streets to get from one building to another. A five-tiered, 100-foot-high **Peace Pagoda** is illuminated at

GHIRARDELLI SQUARE, WITH THE HYDE STREET PIER AND
ALCATRAZ IN THE BACKGROUND

night, and an eternal flame, brought from the Sumiyoshi Shrine in Osaka, burns above a reflecting pool.

A **Cherry Blossom Festival** is scheduled each April. This elaborate Japanese-style celebration of spring usually includes traditional dancing

and martial arts demonstrations, taiko drum and koto performances, a bonsai exhibit, and tea ceremonies. A Japanese food bazaar operates continuously. The festival culminates with a colorful Japanese-style parade. For current information call 563-2313.

See also page 51.

### PIER 39
*Embarcadero/Beach St., 981-8030; most businesses open 10:30-8:30, in summer 8:30-10:30; free; fee ($1/20 min.) parking lot adjoins.*

Pier 39 has been steeped in controversy since its opening. I've heard locals decry its commercialism and then lapse into vagueries about what is wrong with it. My own opinion is that many of the shops tend to be expensive, and most of the restaurant lunch menus are pricey. (By comparison, dinner prices are reasonable). But all in all it is pleasant to visit and offers superb views of the bay.

Street performers entertain regularly. (In fact, the annual **International Street Performers Festival** is held here. See page 245 for more information.) Bumper cars and a vast video arcade are located inside the **Funtasia** entertainment center at the pier entrance, as is **The San Francisco Experience** (982-0327)—a multi-media film offering the chance to experience a simulated earthquake. You can also ride the **Mindscraper**—the country's first simulated roller coaster. A great souvenir is provided by **Music Tracks** (981-1777), the concession that lets you record yourself singing your favorite oldie with background accompaniment. (How about "I Left My Heart In San Francisco?") A modern double-decker Italian fiberglass **merry-go-round** is located at the other end of the pier.

There are over 130 shops. One specializes in music boxes, another in chocolate, another in Disney merchandise. More specialize in Christmas merchandise, in magic paraphernalia, in puppets, in puzzles, and in items for the left-handed person.

Most of the twelve full-service restaurants have seafood menus, but Italian, Chinese, and French cuisines are also represented. Menu boards are located in various spots, giving visitors a chance to analyze the offerings and prices.

Two fast-food centers allow visitors to choose an inexpensive meal from a variety of food booths featuring items such as fish & chips, bagels, hamburgers, and hot pretzels. A large **Swensen's Ice Cream Parlor** serves up sundaes, sodas, and cones. Yet more stands (there are a total of twenty) are scattered along the pier dispensing chocolate chip cookies, churros (long Mexican donuts), caramel apples, popcorn, and the like. You're not going to go hungry here.

### SUCH A BUSINESS
*1 Rhode Island St., 431-1703; M-Sat 10-6, Thur to 7, Sun 12-5.*

Everything you could possibly need for a new baby or young child can be found here: furniture, bedding, strollers, clothing, toys, books. The selection is extensive. And all the necessary equipment is available for rent: strollers, cribs, highchairs, etc. Each item rents for $3 per day or $15 per week.

The store also provides a children's play area and carries no war toys.

### UNION SQUARE/DOWNTOWN

#### • F.A.O. Schwarz
*48 Stockton St./O'Farrell St., 394-8700; daily 10-6.*

Sometimes I think adults like this store even better than children. The city's largest toy store, it is a lavishly decorated, three-story wonderland filled with elaborate toy displays and exclusive, unusual, and trend-setting merchandise.

Shoppers are greeted at the door by a live toy soldier. Steps from the entrance is a whimsical two-story mechanical clock tower that emits charming music.

Merchandise, of course, changes regularly. Currently the Don't Misses include a 40-inch-tall stuffed gorilla ($75), a plush rocking bluebird for toddlers ($225), a full-size velveteen horse ($7,500), and a gas-powered $2/3$-

scale red Ferrari ($14,500). The store also features the widest selection of Madame Alexander dolls in the Bay Area. And, believe it or not, a few items are available for around $1.

## • F. W. Woolworth Co.
*898 Market St./Powell St., 986-2164; M-F 8:30-8, Sat to 6:30, Sun 10-6.*

Located adjacent to the cable car turnaround, the world's largest dime store is fun to wander through. Fast food, travel supplies, souvenirs, and other good things await your perusal.

## • Kinderzimmer
*250 Sutter St./Grant Ave., 986-4594; M-Sat 10-6.*

Meaning literally "children's room" in German, this spacious store features colorful, high-quality European toys that are made to last. In addition to stuffed animals and plush rocking horses with real leather saddles, there are outdoor swings and a variety of interesting toy vehicles—tractors, cranes, bulldozers. Quality children's furniture is also available.

## • Macy's Electronics Department
*Macy's West, Union Square, Stockton St./O'Farrell St., 5th floor, 397-3333; M-F 9:30-9, Sat to 6:30, Sun 11-6.*

The very latest in electronic marvels are displayed in this futuristic department. The state-of-the-art merchandise includes some toys. Don't miss it.

## • Robison's Exclusively For Pets
*135 Maiden Lane, 421-0310; M-F 10-5:45, Sat to 5.*

This pet store is famous for its part in Alfred Hitchcock's thriller *The Birds*. It's the perfect spot to pick up a gift for your pet. Choose anything from inexpensive gourmet treats for dogs or cats to expensive Chanel collars and leads. They even stock Burberrys coats for dogs. An assortment of live dogs, cats, and birds is also available.

## • Sanrio
*216 Stockton St./Geary St., 981-5568; M-F 9-8, Sat 10-8, Sun 10-6.*

Children age 10 and under—especially girls—are sure to get excited about the extensive collection of Hello Kitty products found in this store. Fortunately, most are inexpensive.

## UNION STREET
This trendy area is filled with interesting upscale shops and restaurants. Many are located inside old Victorians, and flower stands add a seasonal burst of color. It is reminiscent of Madison Avenue in Manhattan.

The four blocks running between Fillmore and Octavia Streets have the heaviest concentration of shops, but boutiques continue on in both directions and down sidestreets.

With kids in tow, you'll want to check out **Familiar** (#1828), a store of charming children's clothing imported from Japan. A wooden maze is available in an outdoor yard area to occupy children while you shop.

## — TOURS —

# Guided Boat Tours

### BLUE AND GOLD FLEET BAY TOURS
*781-7877; daily from 10, from 11 in Jan & Feb; adults $12, 5-18 $6, under 5 free.*

A 1¼-hour narrated cruise of the bay takes you out under the world's most beautiful bridge—the Golden Gate—and the world's longest bridge— the 8¼-mile-long San Francisco/Oakland Bay Bridge. It also passes close to Alcatraz Island. Snack service is available. A three-hour dinner cruise with live music is also available in the summer. Tours leave from Pier 39.

### RUBY SAILING YACHT
*185 Berry St., at the China Basin Bldg., 861-2165; daily at 12:30 & 6; adults $25, under 10 $12.50; reservations necessary.*

Captain Joshua Pryor built the 64-foot sloop *Ruby* himself. He also sails it himself.

On the lunch cruise guests may dine on deli sandwiches either on deck or below deck in the salon. The 1½-hour trip circles Alcatraz. An evening trip, lasting 2½ hours and including hors d'oeuvres, sails to Sausalito. Beer and wine are available at additional charge.

### WHALE-WATCHING TOURS
*Oceanic Society: 474-3385; Sat & Sun, Jan-Apr; full day $34-$42/person, half-day $23-$28. Whale Center: 654-6621.*

If it's adventure you seek, consider a trip offshore to view the annual migration of the California grey whales. The non-profit Oceanic Society sponsors boat trips with two professional naturalists on board to explain all about the whales and interpret their behavior. Full day trips board in San Francisco; children must be at least age 10. Half-day trips board at Pillar Point Harbor in Princeton-by-the-Sea; children must be at least age 5.

**Farallon Islands Excursions** are offered July through November. Located just 25 miles across the Pacific Ocean from the Golden Gate Bridge, this National Wildlife Refuge supports the largest seabird rookery in the eastern Pacific south of Alaska. These islands are the summer home to a quarter-million sea birds—including tufted puffins, loons, and auklets. Children must be at least age 10 to take the $50 per person, eighthour trips.

The Whale Center operates similar excursions.

# Guided Bus Tours

### CABLE CAR CHARTERS
*922-2425; fares vary.*
The novelty here is riding in a motorized cable car for the various tours. Reservations are not necessary. Boarding occurs at Fisherman's Wharf near Pier 41 or at the front door of some downtown hotels. Call for details.

### GRAY LINE TOURS
*558-9400; fares vary, children under 5 free.*
Day tours by bus are available of San Francisco, Muir Woods/ Sausalito, and the Wine Country. Dinner tours of San Francisco and the Bay Area are also available. Some tours are aboard red double-decker, London-style buses. Call for a complete schedule. Reservations are required.

### NEAR ESCAPES
*386-8687 (FUN-TOURS); fee varies.*
Guided tours of unusual destinations are the specialty of this business. Past escapes have included Shop Till You Drop (a shopping spree of clothing outlets) and Graveyard Shift: The Colma Cemeteries (a visit to the graves of Wyatt Earp, Levi Strauss, and Benny Bufano as well as to a pet cemetery). Transportation, guide, and snack were included on both of these trips. Children are welcome; minimum ages are always stated. Call for a current schedule.

# Guided Walking Tours

It's no secret that San Francisco is a walker's paradise. The city's naturally intriguing streets become even more interesting when walked with a knowledgeable guide. Even natives have been known to learn something new on such a tour.

### ART DECO ARCHITECTURAL TOURS
*552-DECO; most Sundays in non-rainy season; $3.*
See the Bay Area's best examples of streamlined art deco architecture. Tours last approximately $1^1/_2$ hours and take place in both the East Bay and San Francisco. Call for current schedule.

### CHINATOWN WALKS
For description see page 70.

## CITY GUIDES
*558-3981.*

Sponsored by the Friends of the San Francisco Public Library, these informative tours cover most of the city: Alamo Square, Cathedral Hill Churches, City Hall, Coit Tower, Grace Cathedral, Haight-Ashbury, Historic Market Street, Jackson Square/Portsmouth Square, Japantown, Mission Murals, Montgomery Street, Nob Hill, North Beach, Pacific Heights Victorians, Presidio Museum, San Francisco Fire Department Museum, Union Square . . . and more!

All tours are free and last approximately 1½ hours.

For a free schedule send a stamped, self-addressed envelope to: City Guides, Main Library, Civic Center, San Francisco 94102.

## DASHIELL HAMMETT TOUR
*564-7021; Sat & Sun at noon, May-Aug; by appointment rest of year; adults $5, under 15 free; meet in front of Main Library, 200 Larkin St./McAllister St.*

While dashing off trivia and anecdotes, guide Don Herron leads walkers to landmarks from *The Maltese Falcon* and to all Hammett's known San Francisco residences. Herron, who is always appropriately attired in trench coat and fedora, has operated this tour since 1977. It is said to be the longest ongoing literary tour in the country. It lasts four hours and covers approximately three miles. No reservations are necessary. Rain or shine, do wear your trench coat, too.

## GOLDEN GATE PARK GUIDED WALKING TOURS
For description see page 101.

## PACIFIC HEIGHTS WALKING TOUR
For details see page 76.

## STRYBING ARBORETUM WALKING TOUR
For details see page 101.

# Do-It-Yourself Tours

## CABLE CAR RIDE
*673-6864; daily 6am-1am; adults $1.50, 5-17 75¢.*

One of the best do-it-yourself tours of the city is a nine-mile-per-hour cable car ride. Catch one at the turnaround located at the base of Powell Street and take it up and over the hills all the way to the bay. You won't get better views anywhere.

Ticket machines are provided at some stops, but you can also just jump on at stops along the routes and then pay the conductor.

Did you know that these beloved objects have operated since 1873

and were designated the country's first moving National Historic Landmark in 1964? Before they were developed in 1873 by Andrew Hallidie,
horses had to pull carts up the city's steep hills. Many died in the process.
Now 26 "single-enders" operate on the two Powell Street routes, and 11
"double-enders" operate on the California Street run.

### 49-MILE DRIVE

This planned driving route through San Francisco hits most of the
high points. For a free map of the route, contact the San Francisco Convention & Visitors Bureau (see p. 4).

# Where To Stay

San Francisco, everyone's favorite city, is also a very adult-oriented town. In order to have a good time here with children, a parent must know where to stay. To help you, I've prepared a collection of what I think are the city's best family lodgings.

I find that my own family is usually most content when we are booked into a hotel with family amenities. I don't enjoy being in a hotel that makes having children along a burden. I'm sure you don't either. So all the hotels I recommend here welcome children, and all will assist you in securing a babysitter. Unless otherwise noted, all have free cribs, roll-aways (which vary from free to $20/night), color TVS, and at least some combination bathtub/showers. When reserving, inquire about packages; some good deals are available on weekends. Note that because space in this gorgeous city is at a premium and the weather is generally quite cool, swimming pools—a popular family amenity—are rare indeed.

Families of four or more are usually more comfortable in a suite. Sometimes, but certainly not always, the additional cost over a standard room is quite reasonable for all the gained space.

## — UNION SQUARE —

This is a super area to stay in, especially if you don't have a car to deal with. (Hotels mentioned charge $8.50 to $18 per day for parking.) All these hotels are well-located—within a few blocks of downtown, the theater district, and the cable car line. Many are quaint, smaller establishments working hard to provide the European-style small hotel experience.

### THE CARTWRIGHT
*524 Sutter St./Powell St., 421-2865, 800/652-1858 in CA, 800/227-3844 rest of US, 800/654-1858 in Canada; 2 people/$85-$95, 5 suites/$135-$155, children under 3 stay free in parents' room; no rollaways; some refrigerators; highchairs in dining room.*

This European-style 8-story hotel was built in 1914 for the Panama-Pacific Exposition. Each of its 114 pleasant rooms is distinctively furnished with antiques. Fresh flowers and floral wallpaper add to the cozy, European feel. Regular rooms can accomodate guests with an infant, but larger families with older children will need a suite.

An inexpensive breakfast and lunch are available in the dining room, **Teddy's**, and a complimentary tea is served each afternoon in the pleasant lobby.

Reputed to be San Francisco's most popular small hotel, it is conveniently located on a fashionable shopping street just one block from Union Square.

### CHANCELLOR HOTEL

*433 Powell St./Post St., 362-2004, 800/428-4748, 2 people/$89, 6 suites/$130-$155;*
*children under 3 stay free in parents' room; room service with children's items; high-*
*chairs and children's portions in dining room.*

This solid 16-story hotel was built in 1914. It is just a half-block from
Union Square and the cable car stop and has 140 pleasantly decorated
rooms. Double-paned windows deaden street sound.

The dining room, **By the Square**, features Italian specialties.

### FOUR SEASONS CLIFT

*495 Geary St./Taylor St., 775-4700, 800/332-3442; 2/$180-$280, 71 suites/$265-*
*$1,000; refrigerators in all rooms; room service menu with children's items; highchairs,*
*booster seats, and children's menu in dining room.*

Over $5 million was spent recently to refurbish this historic 17-story
luxury hotel. The 329 large rooms have high ceilings and are beautifully
decorated. Thick terry robes are provided, and a hair dryer and scale is in
each room.

A special family plan includes two connecting rooms charged at the
single occupancy rate so that children can have a separate room. This
hotel is making a point of providing family services. Toys are available for
toddlers and magazines for teens. Children's books and board games may
be checked out from the desk. VCRs are in every suite, and Nintendo

games and children's movies are available on free loan from the desk. Bedtime snacks such as cookies and milk or popcorn and soda are available from room service. The concierge has loaner strollers and will help plan family sightseeing trips.

An exquisite **afternoon tea** (see also p. 251) is served in the lobby, and California cuisine prepared with the finest ingredients is available in the elegant, highly acclaimed French Room (see p. 33).

The hefty tab here puts this hotel on the list of the world's rich and famous. The likes of Mick Jagger, Madonna, and former President Jimmy Carter have stayed here. Service for guests is high-priority for the staff, and everyone enjoys royal treatment—celebrity or not. Even kids!

### THE HANDLERY UNION SQUARE HOTEL
*351 Geary St./Powell St., 781-7800, 800/223-0888; 2 people/$100-$150, 20 suites/ $110-$250; children under 15 stay free in parents' room; (no rollaways); some refrigerators; room service; highchairs, booster seats, children's portions in dining room.*

Located just a half-block from Union Square, this 8-story hotel was built in 1908. Remodeled in 1989, it has 377 rooms. Of special interest to families is the outdoor heated pool. This is the best deal in the area if you bring your car. The rate for parking is a bargain $8.50 per day.

**New Joe's,** the street-level restaurant, is under separate management. It has a mesquite grill, and the menu offers pastas and pizzas and other things that kids like.

### HOLIDAY INN UNION SQUARE
*480 Sutter St./Powell St., 398-8900, 800/HOLIDAY; 2 people/$110, 7 suites/$350- $700; children under 18 stay free in parents' room; some refrigerators; room service with children's items; highchairs, booster seats, children's portions in dining room.*

Not everyone wants quaint. Built in 1973, this is a modern 30-story high-rise hotel with 401 rooms.

Not to be missed is a visit to the **S. Holmes Esq. Public House and Drinking Salon** on the 30th floor. You can enjoy a magnificent view there along with a pretty good drink. The bar makes special children's cocktails. Additionally, there is an interesting museum of Sherlock Holmes paraphernalia to peruse. Carrying this theme further, the hotel's doorman is dressed in Sherlock Holmes regalia.

### HOTEL DIVA
*440 Geary St./Mason St., 885-0200, 800/553-1900; 2 people $119-$139, 25 suites/ $139; children under 12 stay free in parents' room; no rollaways; refrigerators in all rooms; room service with children's items; highchairs and booster seats in dining room.*

This 7-story hotel, built in 1913, features an unexpected hi-tech decor. Each of its 108 spacious rooms is decorated in neutral black, white, and grey—snazzed up with touches of chrome. Lacquered furnishings complement the contemporary design and lighting throughout.

The two-room suites are especially comfortable and well-priced for families. Each has a wallbed in the living area.

Teens might especially enjoy the somewhat punkish feel of the decor and may appreciate the four TVs mounted on the wall behind the artsy check-in desk in the stark lobby. Each room is equipped with a VCR, and over 300 tapes are available for rental.

Teens might also find it fun to browse in the hotel's **Satellite Gallery**, which is described as "an alternative exhibition space that encourages the promotion of emerging artists in San Francisco and the Bay Area."

All this, plus the hotel restaurant is the **California Pizza Kitchen**, and a complimentary continental breakfast is served on each floor, too!

## HOTEL UNION SQUARE
*114 Powell St./Ellis St., 776-1876, 800/553-1900; 2/$69-$129, 7 suites/$180-$280; children under 12 free in parents' room; room service; highchairs and booster seats in dining room.*

Located just steps from the cable car turnaround, this comfortably elegant 6-story hotel was completely renovated in 1982. Decorated in a tailored contemporary style, the 131 spacious rooms, some with two double beds, work well for families.

**Mermaids Seafood Bar** operates off the lobby, and a complimentary continental breakfast and local newspaper are provided each morning.

This is where Dashiell Hammett wrote *The Maltese Falcon*.

## KENSINGTON PARK HOTEL
*450 Post St./Powell St., 788-6400, 800/553-1900; 2 people/$110-$120, 2 suites/$160-$350; children under 12 stay free in parents' room; some refrigerators; room service.*

Built in Gothic-style architecture in 1923, this tastefully decorated 12-story hotel has 83 rooms—each with a telephone in the bathroom. The entire eighth floor is non-smoking. Terry robes are provided, and shoes are shined for free when left outside the door at night.

Complimentary afternoon sherry and tea is served in the attractive lobby, and a pianist entertains. A continental breakfast, complete with the morning paper, is provided on each floor.

**Theatre on the Square** (433-9500), which sometimes offers plays appropriate for the whole family, is on the hotel's second floor.

## THE KING GEORGE HOTEL
*334 Mason St./Geary St., 781-5050, 800/288-6005; 2 people/$93, 2 suites/$186; children under 12 stay free in parents' room; some refrigerators; room service with children's items.*

Located just one block from Union Square, this pleasant 9-story hotel was built in 1914. Thomas Edison was an original investor, and it was he who convinced management to switch from gaslight to electricity. Thick walls make the 138 spacious rooms very quiet. Suites are the best arrangement for families, and each has a small kitchen.

For a small additional charge, guests can enjoy a continental breakfast and/or afternoon tea in The Bread & Honey Tea Room (see p. 26). A large bowl of complimentary apples is always available at the desk for snacks. Room service is provided by **Lori's Diner**, located next door. Featuring a '50s decor, Lori's is open 24 hours and dispenses family-friendly foods such as burgers, fries, shakes, and even onion rings.

## VILLA FLORENCE
*225 Powell St./Geary, 397-7700, 800/243-5700 in CA, 800/553-4411 rest of US; 2 people/$109-$119, 36 suites/$139-$189; children stay free in parents' room; refrigerators; room service.*

Built in 1908, this 7-story hotel has 177 attractively decorated rooms. Its highly convenient location is about as close to the cable car turn-around as you can get.

**Kuleto's** restaurant operates off the lobby, serving the trendiest Italian cuisine in elegant surroundings. Reserve a booth and dine early, and maybe you can get away with taking kids. There are no highchairs or booster seats.

## THE WESTIN ST. FRANCIS
*335 Powell St./Geary St., 397-7000, 800/228-3000; 2/$180-305, suites/$300-$1,725!; children under 18 stay free in parents' room; refrigerators in all rooms; room service; highchairs, booster seats, children's portions in dining rooms.*

This classy landmark hotel, built in 1904, has a superb location opening right onto Union Square. It has an older section and a newer 32-story tower—combining for a total of 1,200 rooms.

The glass elevator operating outside the tower goes non-stop from the lobby to the 32nd floor in less than 30 seconds. And children love going 'round and 'round in the revolving entrance door off the main lobby.

This is the only hotel in the world that washes its money. Arnold Batliner, who is as old as the hotel, has been the coinwasher since 1960. During that time he has washed over $15 million in coins. The hotel began this custom in 1938, when silver dollars were used extensively. It was meant to keep women's white gloves from being soiled by dirty coins. Now all hotel change is washed.

A weekend package makes rooms available at half-price, and there are sometimes value packages available during holiday periods. This is an especially enjoyable hotel to stay in during the Christmas season, when its festively decorated lobby is the setting for holiday entertainment.

Restaurants include upscale **Victor's** dinner room, the medium-priced **Dutch Kitchen** coffee shop, and the elegant Compass Rose for snacks (see p. 30).

---

# — THE EMBARCADERO —

---

## HYATT REGENCY SAN FRANCISCO
*5 Embarcadero Center/California St., 788-1234, 800/233-1234; 2 people/$139-$268, 44 suites/$350-$945, children under 18 stay free in parents' room; refrigerators in all rooms; room service with children's items; highchairs, booster seats, and children's portions in dining rooms; parking $17/day.*

Built in 1973, this elegant hotel has 803 rooms. According to a hotel spokesperson, "Children love it. There is always a lot of activity in the lobby and no need to be quiet. **Embarcadero Center** and **Justin Herman Plaza** are great places to run around in." (Note that Justin Herman Plaza is where the **Vaillancourt Fountain** is located. This fountain, which looks like the aftermath of an earthquake, is popularly called "10 on the Richter.") This is all true, plus the hotel has nifty glass elevators running the height of its 17-story atrium interior. **Camp Hyatt**, a children's activity program, operates year-round. Call for current schedule and prices.

The hotel is especially nice to stay in during the Christmas holidays as they go all-out with Christmas activities. Especially fun for children is the Breakfast with Santa program (see p. 252).

## PARK HYATT SAN FRANCISCO
*333 Battery St./Clay St., 392-1234, 800/233-1234; 2/$260-$295, 37 suites/$295-$1,500, children under 18 free in parents' room; room service with children's items; highchairs, booster seats, and children's portions in dining room; parking $17/day.*

Built in 1989, this brand-new hotel is conveniently located across the street from the upscale **Embarcadero Center** shopping complex. It is 24 stories high, and each of the 360 rooms has a bay or city view.

Luxurious in every way, the hotel has fine art decorating its public areas. All guests are provided with terrycloth bathrobes, and overnight shoe polishing is available.

Fresh fruit is stocked in all rooms. A complimentary continental

breakfast is served each morning, and afternoon tea is available in the lobby. The hotel's elegant yet comfortable **Park Grill** restaurant sports a clubby atmosphere and serves beautifully prepared dishes for adults—things like Caesar salad and crab cakes and grilled fresh fish with creative sauces. Children are made happy with their own surprisingly inexpensive menu. It offers things like alphabet soup, chicken nuggets, and a grilled cheese sandwich.

Hyatt's wonderful **Camp Hyatt** program, for children ages 3 through 15, operates here, too. It is available on weekends year-round and daily during the summer and holiday periods. Children are kept entertained by an enthusiastic staff. Sometimes they even get cooking lessons in the hotel's kitchen. Charges run $5 per hour or $25 per day.

## — CHINATOWN/NORTH BEACH —

### ROYAL PACIFIC MOTOR INN
*661 Broadway/Columbus Ave., 781-6661, 800/545-5574; 2 people/$61-$72, 8 suites/ $75-$85; children under 16 free in parents' room; cribs/$6; free parking.*

This 5-story modern motel has 74 rooms. A sauna is available to guests, and a complimentary continental breakfast is served December through April. The rest of the year breakfast can be secured inexpensively by crossing the street to enjoy dim sum at Ocean City (see p. 56).

## — MOTEL ROW —

Approximately 25 motels are located in the 20-block corridor stretching along Lombard Street from Van Ness Avenue to the Presidio.

## — OUTER GEARY —

This quiet part of town is just ten blocks from Union Square. Both of these hotels are located in Japantown and have an oriental flavor.

### BEST WESTERN KYOTO INN
*1800 Sutter St./Buchanan St., 921-4000, 800/528-1234; 2 people/$81-$87, 2 suites/ $130-$200, children 18 and under stay free in parents' room; dining room; parking $5/ day.*

This modern 8-story motel has 125 rooms and is a member of the Best Western chain. The majority of the rooms have two double beds; 60 have a steam bath.

## MIYAKO HOTEL

*1625 Post St./Laguna St., 922-3200, 800/533-4567; 2 people/$125-$350, 14 suites/ $240-$350; children 18 and under free in parents' room; some refrigerators; room service; highchairs and booster seats in dining room; parking $7.50/day.*

Opened in 1968, this 13-story hotel has just undergone an extensive $10 million renovation. Its 218 rooms range from fully traditional Japanese-style, with futon feather beds on tatami mats, to western-style with oriental touches. Most rooms have deep furo bathing tubs, and some suites have a private redwood sauna. The tasteful lobby overlooks a Japanese garden where guests are welcome to stroll.

---

# — THE BEACH —

---

## OCEAN PARK MOTEL

*2690 46th Ave./Wawona St., 566-7020; 2 people/$41-$50, 13 suites/$50-$97; some kitchens; free parking.*

This 2-story art deco-style motel dates from the '30s, when it was the city's first motorcourt. Maintaining its original nautical decor, some windows are shaped as portholes. There are 24 attractive and homey rooms, two of which have bathtubs. A barbecue area and outdoor hot tub are also available. All this in a quiet area near the ocean and just a block from the zoo.

---

# — GOLDEN GATE PARK —

---

## STANYAN PARK HOTEL

*750 Stanyan St./ Waller St., 751-1000; 2 people/$73-$160, 6 suites/$110-$165; children under 3 free in parents' room; kitchens in suites; parking $5/day.*

Located in the Haight-Ashbury area near Golden Gate Park, this 1904 3-story Victorian survived the great quake of '06. It has been renovated and turned into a pleasant hotel with 36 attractively decorated rooms. A complimentary continental breakfast is served each morning.

---

# — FISHERMAN'S WHARF —

---

I (and many other local residents) simply can't understand why this area is so popular with tourists. It is terribly congested here, and all the motels look the same. But popular it is. So, since you insist, here are some of the better family lodgings.

A STREET CLOWN AT FISHERMAN'S WHARF

## BAYSIDE BOAT & BREAKFAST

*Pier 39, 291-8411, 800/BOAT-BED; 2 people/$115-$250, + $50/additional 2 people; 6 suites/$200-$300; all have kitchens; room service; parking $2/day.*

Spend the night on a yacht anchored near Fisherman's Wharf. Some have a private jacuzzi and/or sauna. A continental breakfast is included.

## HYDE PARK SUITES

*2655 Hyde St./Northpoint St., 771-0200, 800/227-3608; 24 suites, 2 people/$165-$220; children under 12 free in parents' room; all kitchens; room service; parking $12/day.*

This smallish, 3-story building lets you feel like you're living in the city instead of just visiting. In addition to offering most of the comforts of home, it is located right on the Hyde Street cable car line and is very close to the best aspects of the Fisherman's Wharf area. A newspaper is delivered to the door each morning, and a complimentary continental breakfast is served in the lobby.

## SHERATON AT FISHERMAN'S WHARF

*2500 Mason St./Beach St., 362-5500, 800/325-3535; 2 people/$120-$220, 7 suites/$325-$500; children under 17 stay free in parents' room; room service with children's items; highchairs and booster seats in dining room; parking $9/day.*

This huge 4-story, 525-room contemporary-style hotel features that rarest of San Francisco amenities—a heated (summer only) swimming pool.

## TRAVELODGE AT THE WHARF

*250 Beach St./Powell St., 392-6700, 800/255-3050; 2 people/$79-$170, 5 suites/$125-$250; children under 18 free in parents' room; some refrigerators; highchairs, booster seats, children's portions in dining room; free parking.*

Newly renovated, this conveniently located 4-story motel has 250 rooms. It also has an enclosed landscaped courtyard with a heated outdoor pool.

# — MISCELLANEOUS —

## THE AMERICAN PROPERTY EXCHANGE

*863-8484, 800/747-7784; $495-$1,100/wk; cribs $50/wk; .*

Live like a native. This service will help you find lodging in interesting residential areas. All units have kitchens and parking spaces; some have heated pools, tennis courts, and exercise rooms.

## BED & BREAKFAST INTERNATIONAL

*525-4569; 2 people/$44-$100; children under 2 stay free in parents' room; 2-night minimum.*

At least a dozen of the San Francisco host homes listed with this reservations service are appropriate for children. Most cannot accommodate more than two people in a room, but a 20% reduction is given for children staying in a second room. Amenities, of course, vary with the property. Call for details.

## THE MANSION HOTEL
*2220 Sacramento St./Laguna St., 929-9444; 2 people/$89-$250, 2 suites/$134-$154, children under 6 free in parent's room; color TVs available upon request; one refrigerator; room service; booster seats in dining room; parking $10/day.*

The owner of this beautifully restored 1887 twin-turreted Queen Anne Victorian doesn't believe in restrictions, so children, being people, are welcome. However he doesn't encourage bringing children to the Magic Concert—held on Thursday, Friday, and Saturday evenings—because it is meant to be a show for adults. Barbra Streisand has stayed here with her kids, and if it's good enough for Barbra . . . It's also been good enough for Paul Simon, Joan Baez, Diahann Carroll, and George McGovern.

Guests have use of a billiard table located in a real Billiard Room, among pig murals and a mini-museum of memorabilia. They are free to wander through the house and admire the large Turner oil painting, wall-size turn-of-the-century stained glass mural, and impressive collection of Beniamino Bufano sculptures. In fact, according to owner Robert Pritikin, cousin of the diet guy and author of *Christ Was an Ad Man*, there are approximately "100 tons" of Bufano art scattered throughout the house and surrounding garden. "It is the largest definitive collection ever displayed," he says.

Tennis courts are nearby, and a complimentary full breakfast is served each morning.

Children may especially enjoy meeting Senator Chambers, a blue and yellow macaw that lives in the parlor. There's also a merry-go-round pig to find. And the maids and butlers dress up in Victorian-style finery.

Even though this hotel is located out in the fashionable Pacific Heights residential neighborhood, it isn't that far away from the action. A cable car stop is just four blocks away.

## SAN FRANCISCO INTERNATIONAL HOSTEL
*Fort Mason, Bldg. 240, Bay St./Franklin St., 771-7277; $10/person, $5/child under 18 with parent; 3-night maximum; no cribs; limited free parking.*

Situated on a peaceful knoll with a magnificent view of the bay, this one-story building once was a Civil War barracks. Now it holds 160 dormitory beds spread among 20 rooms. Family rooms are available by reservation, and a fully-equipped kitchen is available for meal preparation.

As in all hostels, each guest helps with a ten-minute chore, and alcohol is prohibited. Guests do not have access to the premises from 2 to 4:30 p.m., and there is a midnight curfew on weeknights.

Opened in 1980, this is the largest and busiest hostel in the country and is particularly popular with foreign visitors.

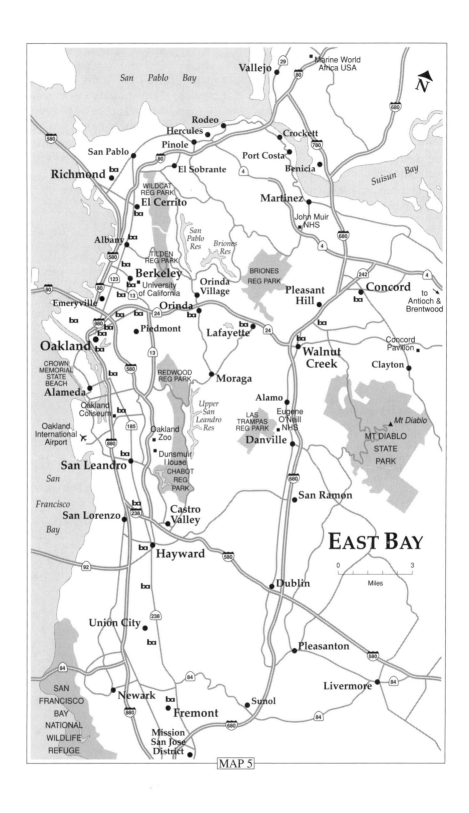

EAST BAY

MAP 5

# East Bay

## Where To Eat

### ARTURO'S

*2383 N. Main St./Ygnacio Valley Rd., Walnut Creek, 937-7891; L M-F, D daily, SunBr; $$; highchairs, booster seats, booths; separate children's menu; free parking lot adjoins; reservations suggested; AE, MC, V.*

The lovely wicker-furnished front room here is at its best at lunch time, when the sun streams in from the overhead skylight. The back room is darker, with some large, comfortable booths. Interesting photos decorate the wall.

For appetizers the nachos (cornchips topped with guacamole and melted cheese) are practically a meal in themselves. The cheese crisp (a giant flour tortilla topped with melted cheese) and guacamole are also tasty choices.

Entrees include combination plates, four kinds of hamburgers, and several salads. I particularly like the quesadilla (a flour tortilla filled with melted Jack cheese, green chilis, and shredded beef), enchiladas verdes (chicken enchiladas covered with a green tomatillo sauce and sour cream), and chimichanga (a deep-fried beef burrito topped with guacamole and sour cream). Steak and seafood entrees are also available.

The children's menu offers nachos, a bean taco and burrito, and a cheese enchilada. A hamburger, hot dog, grilled cheese sandwich, and peanut butter & jelly sandwich are also available. Each entree includes a beverage, ice cream, and trip to a treat-laden piñata. Children may also enjoy ordering a non-alcoholic Margarita, with the glass rim dipped in sugar instead of salt.

### BENIHANA OF TOKYO

*1989 Diamond Blvd., in Willows Shopping Center, Concord, 827-4220.*

For description see page 52.

## BERKELEY THAI HOUSE

*2511 Channing Way/Telegraph Ave., Berkeley, 843-7352; L & D daily; $; highchairs, booster seats; reservations suggested at dinner; MC, V.*

In good weather, it is quite pleasant to sit out on the wooden deck here. On colder days, or in the evening, the cozy inside dining room, which is pleasantly decorated with Indonesian artifacts, is preferable.

Specials are chalked on a board by the entrance and are usually a good bet. I once enjoyed an interesting stir-fried chicken and shrimp dish made with shitake mushrooms, baby corn, water chestnuts, and a few fiery-hot peppers.

Most dishes are simply-seasoned and frugal with the hot peppers. My favorite item is basil chicken sauteed with mint leaves, sliced onion, and hot chilis. I am also fond of moo prik-khing—a stir-fry dish consisting of pork and fresh green beans in a spicy sauce. Cashew nut chicken is also a winner, as is panang neur—beef and sweet basil in a spicy red curry sauce with a coconut milk base. My husband usually orders pad thai—a sweet and very orange noodle dish flavored with ground peanuts, bean sprouts, bean cake, and a few tiny shrimp.

My daughter favors both the Thai iced tea, swirled with half-and-half, and the fried banana. However, she dislikes the "Thai dessert"—a pudding flavored with rose water and texturized with kernels of corn.

See also page 16.

## BERTOLA'S

*4659 Telegraph Ave./Shattuck Ave., Oakland, 547-9301; L M-F, D daily; $; highchairs, booster seats; children's portions; free parking lot adjoins; no reservations; no cards.*

Renowned for low prices, this restaurant continues to offer large portions of Italian family-style fare at bargain rates. If there is a wait, inflation-defying $1.50 well drinks are available at a large bar just off the entrance.

The largest, noisiest family will fit in comfortably with the Italian atmosphere of red-checked tablecloths, mock brick walls, and hearty background laughter. Seating is a combination of long communal tables and individual tables.

Entree choices are roasted chicken, ground round, pot roast, veal, steak, and prime rib. Dinners include an ample bowl of delicious homemade minestrone soup, green salad, warm french bread, spaghetti topped with a tasty meat sauce, and fresh vegetables. Arrive hungry.

## BETTE'S OCEAN VIEW DINER

*1807 4th St./Hearst Ave., Berkeley, 644-3230; B & L daily; $; booster seats, booths; no reservations; no cards.*

This is a choice spot for a weekend breakfast when the kids wake you up *real early* and you don't have the energy to cook. And it sure beats starving until the brunch places open up.

It's fun to sit on a counter stool here and watch the cooks hustle. But with a family in tow, it's better to miss a little of the action and choose one of the comfortable red vinyl booths or a table. That is, once you get *in*. Because this casual, noisy diner, with its 1950s truckstop decor and menu of traditional American food, is so popular the wait can run to thirty minutes. Names are taken and, in the morning, coffee is made available to ease the wait. And all the while the funky jukebox is busy mixing '50s tunes with reggae.

Among the interesting and extensive breakfast choices are spicy scrambled eggs, steak and eggs, four kinds of omelettes, griddle cakes with *real* maple syrup, and french toast. Blintzes are available on Sundays and Mondays. Combination plates include The New York (smoked salmon, bagel, cream cheese, red onion, and tomato) and The Philadelphia (scrapple, poached eggs, toast, and grilled tomato). Plain eggs are served with a choice of homefries, toast, muffin, or scone. Even my fussy young daughter was satisfied by a bowl of cold cereal with fruit. And if plain coffee doesn't do it for you, espresso and cappuccino are also available.

Lunch is a satisfying assortment of well-prepared classic sandwiches, homemade soups, and homey items like meatloaf, grilled bockwurst, and potato pancakes. Thick old-fashioned milkshakes are available, too, but oddly no hamburgers or fries.

By the way. About that ocean view. There is none. Ocean View is the name of the neighborhood in which the restaurant is located.

Before you leave, don't forget to stop in next door at **Bette's To Go** (548-9494; M-Sat 6:30-5, Sun 8-4). Breakfast pastries, sandwiches, and salads are available along with an array of other goodies—including brownies and chocolate cookies. Consider picking up picnic supplies and heading out for further family adventure.

## BRENNAN'S
*720 University Ave./4th St., Berkeley, 841-0960; L & D daily; $; booster seats; free parking lot adjoins; no reservations; no cards.*

Always crowded and boisterous, this Berkeley institution has a huge rectangular bar dominating the center of its hall-like dining room.

A drawback for families is that children can be hard to keep track of in the cafeteria line. It is best to find a table first, and leave one adult at the table with the children while another goes to get the food. Also, there are no booths, and some people find the formica tables and mix-matched chairs not quite comfortable enough. I say at these prices you can't have everything.

The hofbrau-style food is basically meat and potatoes. The bargain hot sandwiches, served with made-from-scratch mashed potatoes smothered in gravy, are my favorite. Side dishes include a tasty stuffing and a choice of macaroni, potato salad, or coleslaw. Corned beef served with a wedge of cabbage is very good, as are the roast beef and fresh, juicy turkey. Hot dogs are also available, and on Mondays and Tuesdays you can get a very good corned beef hash. Homemade desserts include pies, custard, and a creamy cheesecake.

So head here on a night when you want to chow down but don't want to cook, splurge, or get dressed up.

## CACTUS TAQUERIA

*5940 College Ave./Harwood Ave., Oakland, 547-1305; L & D daily; $; highchairs, booster seats, booths; no reservations; no cards.*

Mexican fast-food at its best is served here in attractive surroundings. Tables and chairs are painted in Santa Fe-style pastels, with cactus cut-outs separating tables.

You pick your drink while waiting in line, place your order at the counter, and then wait a short time for your number to be called.

Tacos, burritos, tostadas, and tortas (a baguette sandwich) are prepared with a choice of interesting fillings—all prepared on the premises from scratch. I am absolutely addicted to the spicy chilorio (shredded roast pork seasoned with dried chilies, garlic, cumin, and oregano). It is incredible. Other fillings include pollo verde (shredded chicken seasoned with roasted tomatillos, green chilies, garlic, and onions), birria (not the traditional goat but instead roast lamb and veal marinated with oregano, cumin, garlic, cloves, and black pepper), and a mild carne mochomos (shredded beef braised with onions and spices and then fried).

Good choices for kids are a soft taco or a quesadilla (crisp flour tortilla filled with melted cheese).

Crisp chips come with each order, and superb salsas are on the tables: a tangy green tomatillo, a fresh tomato-cilantro-onion, and a smoky mole.

## CAFFE GIOVANNI

*2420 Shattuck Ave./Channing Way, Berkeley, 843-6678; L & D daily; $$; highchairs, booster seats; children's portions; reservations suggested; AE, DC, MC, V.*

Giovanni's was among the first restaurants I dined at en famille following the birth of my first child. Through the years we've been back many times and have always enjoyed the noisy, pleasant atmosphere.

The menu pleases families because there are so many choices: a variety of calzones, fresh fish specials, sandwiches, salads, and even a hamburger. On our most recent visit, I ordered my favorite veal scaloppini Marsala. As always, it was smothered with plenty of mushrooms. My husband, who always orders something different, tried a delicate fettuccine al pesto prepared with broccoli flowerettes, toasted whole pinenuts, and fresh pasta. That noisy baby has turned into a teenage food machine. His ravioli Mama Savaria, filled with ricotta cheese and topped with marinara sauce, was gone in a flash. Our complete dinners were served with warm triangles of focaccia bread, homemade minestrone soup, and a tossed green salad.

The burning question on this visit was what would our 15-year-old Italian exchange student order in an American Italian restaurant? The answer: pizza. She declared the crust less crisp than her favorite at home but ate it without further complaint.

Dolci are prepared in-house by a pastry chef and are continuously changing. There is always a tray of goodies to choose from. Usually it includes a mousse, sometimes a cannoli. Zabaglione is always available by request.

Should you have to wait, you can either watch the cooks at work (they provide quite a show) or have a well-made, unusual drink like a banana cow, piña colada, or fresh strawberry daiquiri in the comfortable lounge area. Children might enjoy a piña fria or Italian soda.

## CASA DE EVA
*2826 Telegraph Ave./Oregon St., Berkeley, 540-9092; L Tu-F, D Tu-Sat; $; highchairs, booster seats; children's portions; no reservations; no cards.*

Consistently delicious and unusual Mexican food, good service, and reasonable prices make this an extremely popular restaurant with a loyal clientele. The atmosphere is warm and noisy, and the decor festive—with heavy wooden furniture, tile floors, and a striking kitchen archway covered with handpainted Mexican tiles.

All menu items are prepared from fresh ingredients of the highest quality. Especially wonderful are the enchilada verde (filled with shredded chicken and topped with a tangy tomatillo sauce and sour cream), the flauta (two tortillas rolled together and filled with shredded beef, fried, and topped with sour cream), the chalupa (a fat handmade corn tortilla base topped with spicy chorizo sausage, refried beans, shredded lettuce, and guacamole), and the avocado taco (shredded chicken inside a deep-fried rolled tortilla topped with guacamole). My children favor the cheese enchilada, quesadilla (a corn or flour tortilla stuffed with superb melted Jack cheese, smoky ham, and guacamole), and thick house-made fruit punch. Flour tortillas are made from scratch in the kitchen, and traditional tamales are available Thursday through Saturday. More common items are also on the interesting menu.

This remains one of my family's all-time favorite restaurants.

## CELIA'S
*2040 4th St., Berkeley, 549-1460.*
For description see page 29.

## CHEVYS

*2400 Mariner Square Dr., Alameda, 521-3768; L & D daily; $$; highchairs, booster seats, booths; separate children's menu; free parking lot adjoins; reservations suggested; AE, MC V.*

Located on the Alameda side of the Oakland Estuary, this Tex-Mex restaurant is decorated to resemble a border cantina. Its ambiance is noisy and happy, with Mexican music playing in the background. When the manager told me, "I've never heard a kid cry in my restaurant," I thought he meant because it was so noisy. He actually meant because kids have so much fun. Isn't that nice?

Popular with singles, the restaurant has a large upstairs bar. Children are welcome there, but the law says they may not actually sit at the bar. However, there are plenty of tables, and non-alcoholic kid's drinks are available. Should there be a wait to get in, you can also spend it checking out El Machino— the intriguing tortilla-making machine operating inside the main dining room.

Though there is ample seating indoors and you can get good views of the water from the back of the restaurant, my first choice on a warm day is outdoors on the deck. Tables there are sheltered by umbrellas and most have water views, plus there is plenty of space for kids to romp. In fact, they can actually go out on an adjacent lawn area and play.

We like to start off with one of the Margaritas served in a large beer mug. Thin, crisp freshly-fried tortilla chips and a tasty tomato salsa are served gratis.

The fajitas plate for two is usually enough for my entire family. It consists of freshly-made flour tortillas and a pound of sizzling, delicious Texas skirt steak that is marinated and then grilled over mesquite. Chicken and combination versions are also available. Superb flavored rice, simmered whole beans, guacamole, and pico de gallo are included as fillings. You pile onto your tortilla whatever you want and then chow down.

Other interesting items on the menu include broiled jumbo shrimp, broiled quail, and great tamales with a chewy, tasty filling. There are also plenty of the usual tacos and enchiladas. A la carte portions are good choices for children.

Desserts include sopapillas dripping with honey, empañadas (tortilla dough with an apple-raisin filling, deep-fried and topped with powdered sugar), and flan. If dessert makes you feel guilty, you might want to walk it off along the path fronting the estuary.

Branches are in El Cerrito at 6 El Cerrito Plaza (526-2551) and in Pleasant Hill at 650 Ellinwood Way (685-6651). Branches are also in San Francisco (see p. 29), Redwood City (see p. 191), and Greenbrae (see p. 212).

## CHINA STATION
*700 University Ave./3rd St., Berkeley, 548-7880; L & D daily; $ $; highchairs, booster seats; free parking lot adjoins; reservations suggested; AE, DC, MC, V.*

Located inside what was formerly the Berkeley Southern Pacific railroad depot, this popular Chinese restaurant features a cozy interior. Natural wood trim and green-shaded wall lamps give it an elegant, yet casual, feeling.

Since Cantonese and Szechwan seafoods are its specialty, you're wise to try the wonderfully seasoned, and very messy, crab in black bean sauce, the spicy-hot Szechwan prawns, and the deep-fried rock cod filets in a sweet and sour sauce dappled with pineapple, peaches, onion, and green pepper. My children like the lemon chicken—crispy-skinned chicken breasts topped with lemon rounds and surrounded with bright red maraschino cherries—and the fat and juicy potstickers. Also particularly good are the ginger beef, beef with fresh asparagus, and the filling noodle dishes (especially the chow fun). The extensive menu also offers live Maine lobster and minced squab in lettuce cups.

A large drink menu offers children and non-drinkers a punchless piña colada and strawberry daiquiri, a Pac-man (ginger ale with lemon juice, grenadine, and bitters), and an Unfuzzy Navel (peach nectar with lemon and orange juice and grenadine). Exotic mixed drinks are available from a large bar adjoining the waiting area. They include a Hurricana (rum punch) and a lichee iced tea. A variety of beers and wines are also available.

For dessert you really must try the fried milk puffs—deep-fried milk-flour balls, creamy and light, served hot and sprinkled with powdered sugar. Delicious and unusual.

Service is attentive. There is attention to detail, and the personnel seem actually to care whether or not they have pleased you. Portions tend to be small, but the presentation is refined and the quality of ingredients high.

To the special delight of young and old alike, trains still rumble by periodically.

## CLAREMONT RESORT PAVILION ROOM
*Ashby Ave./Domingo Ave., Oakland, 843-3000; SunBr; $ $ $; highchairs, booster seats; children's prices; 2-hr. free validation in adjoining parking lot; reservations suggested; AE, DC, MC, V.*

Located right on the border between Berkeley and Oakland, the Claremont Resort and Tennis Club is a surprising find: a full-service resort in the middle of a tightly-packed residential area.

The elegant dining room, decorated in soothing shades of pale pink and seafoam green, features tall ceilings and views of the bay that don't stop. From the windows you can also see some of the modern art sculptures which are scattered about the grounds. Definitely request a window table when you reserve.

The elegant Sunday brunch is the best time to dine here with children. When dressed up in their best clothes and properly warned ahead of time about what to expect ("Be good or no . . . for the entire week."), kids often come through with excellent, or at least passable, behavior.

Several buffet tables are set up for brunch: salads and fresh fruit; seafood (prawns, crab, salmon); meats, cheeses, and breads. (Don't miss the absolutely wonderful sticky buns.) There is also a design-your-own-omelette station where you can watch your invention being prepared.

Guests may return to the buffet as often as they wish to sample the attractive and tasty items. But do leave room for the dessert buffet, which is laden with a selection of fine cakes, chocolate eclairs, chocolate fondue, and several flavors of mousse.

If all this isn't much too much, entrees are available for just a few dollars more: grilled salmon oriental (with ginger-soy glaze and cilantro butter), whole grain pancakes, a waffle, beef kabobs, eggs Benedict.

Exotic libations are also available at additional cost. Among the selections are a gorgeous mimosa (a mixture of fresh-squeezed orange juice and champagne served over a maraschino cherry in a tall glass), the inevitable Ramos fizz, and a non-alcoholic apple-berry smoothie.

## CROGAN'S BAR AND GRILL
*1387 Locust St./Cypress St., Walnut Creek, 933-7800; L & D daily; $$; highchairs, booster seats, booths; reservations suggested; AE, MC, V.*

The bar here prepares drinks from scratch using fresh, natural ingredients. Patrons crowd in dressed in everything from shorts to three-piece suits, and it is usually more crowded there than in the restaurant.

We always head right for the large and noisy dining room, resplendent with natural wood and beveled glass fixtures. My family of four has plenty of elbow room and privacy sitting in what rank among the largest booths I've even seen.

The menu changes daily. Though most items (fresh seafood, steak, corned beef and cabbage, assorted sandwiches, salads) are tempting, my hands-down favorite is the hamburger. It arrives cooked to specification and topped with a choice of cheddar, Swiss, or Monterey Jack cheese and with tomatoes, lettuce, onion, pickle, and large homemade fries on the side. That makes for one big meal. Even though it's plenty to satisfy my appetite, I usually can't resist ordering a side of what might be the world's largest and best onion rings (now available only by special request).

Children seem to appreciate that sodas are served in bottles, allowing them to pour just the right amount into their glasses by themselves. Desserts include a sinfully dense Chocolate Decadence, a smooth caramel custard topped with raspberry sauce, and a light, creamy chocolate mousse. They are made fresh each day by the restaurant's own pastry chef.

In warmer weather, a patio dining area is opened at lunch.

## DANVILLE HOTEL RESTAURANT & SALOON

*155 S. Hartz Ave./Prospect, Danville, 837-6627; L M-Sat, D daily, SunBr; $$; high-chairs, booster seats, booths; separate children's menu; take-out delivery; free parking lot adjoins; reservations suggested; AE, DC, MC, V.*

Each of the three dining rooms here is elegantly decorated in turn-of-the-century cozy. A favorite is the front room. That's because it has an operating fireplace and large, comfortable booths—worth asking for when you reserve.

Champagne is included in the brunch price and is poured throughout the meal, keeping diners content. Kids get bottomless glasses of sparkling cider.

After ordering, a small bowl of fresh fruit is served. Then a tin full of warm, puffy sopaipillas appears, with instructions from the server to tear off an end and squeeze in some honey. Remarkable self-restraint is required so as not to eat too many of these triangular Mexican pastries before the entree arrives.

Among the entrees are a classic eggs Benedict and a delicious, delicate eggs Alaska, made like the classic dish but with the twist of flaky smoked salmon instead of Canadian bacon and with a sprinkling of dill in the hollandaise. Mexican Scramble consists of chorizo sauteed with onions and bell peppers and served on a flour tortilla topped with cheese. For those watching calories and cholesterol, the Healthy Miner's Breakfast offers scrambled eggs made with a bearable egg substitute and several of Bruce Aidell's tasty chicken apple sausages. It's only 342 calories.

A separate children's menu is served with crayons and designed to be colored and taken home. Brunch choices are cinnamon-raisin french toast, scrambled eggs and bacon, or a hamburger and french fries. All come with a Shirley Temple cocktail.

## EDY'S

*2201 Shattuck Ave./Allston Way, Berkeley, 843-3096; B, L, & D daily; $; highchairs, booster seats, booths; reservations accepted; MC, V.*

Opened in 1932, this ice cream parlor has been remodeled several times. But it still has its original wooden booths, which were carved in Germany in the '30s, and it retains an old-fashioned feeling.

Classic hot fudge and caramel sundaes are topped with sauces made fresh from Old World recipes. The English toffee sundae is made with toasted almond and vanilla ice creams topped with caramel sauce, pieces of English toffee candy, whipped cream, and a cherry. Dreyer's ice cream is used exclusively. Sodas, freezes, and fancy cakes are also available.

The same menu, featuring a large selection of breakfast and lunch items, is available throughout the day.

## EMIL VILLA'S HICK'RY PIT

*1982 Pleasant Valley Rd./Broadway, in Rockridge Shopping Center, Oakland, 654-0915; B, L, & D daily; $; highchairs, booster seats, booths; separate children's menu; free parking lot adjoins; no reservations; no cards.*

This spacious restaurant was opened in 1981 to replace its predecessor at Telegraph and 44th, which had operated there since 1928.

The restaurant touts itself as "where the elite meet to eat meat" and claims that the pork used comes "from pigs that made hogs of themselves." The fare is barbecued meats—pork, beef, ham, turkey, chicken, and especially ribs—basted with a mild brown sauce or a slightly spicy red sauce and served in hot or cold sandwich form or as dinner plates. A hamburger and grilled cheese sandwich are also on the menu.

Dessert is a hunk of fresh-baked pie chosen from an always tempting array.

Best of all, service is fast.

Branches are in Concord at 1631 Willow Pass Road (827-9902), in Fremont at 39410 Fremont Boulevard (790-1992), in Hayward at 24047 Mission Boulevard (537-0734), in San Leandro at 1800 East 14th Street (357-2780), in Walnut Creek at 1495 South Main Street (935-7450), and in Vallejo at 3288 Sonoma Boulevard (707/643-9030). Branches are also in Campbell and Los Altos (see p. 194) and in Mill Valley (see p. 213).

## FATAPPLE'S

*7525 Fairmount Ave./Colusa Ave., El Cerrito, 528-3433; B, L, & D daily; $-$$; highchairs, booster seats; 100% non-smoking; free parking lot adjoins; no reservations; no cards.*

It's a fortunate thing the food here is so good, because after the typically long wait to get in no one is in the mood to accept anything less.

Seated on comfortable chairs at spacious, sturdy tables under a high open-beamed ceiling, diners select from a simple menu. The restaurant's forte is food made from scratch using *real* ingredients. Lean ground chuck used for hamburgers is ground on the premises; soup is made fresh; blue cheese salad dressing is made with the real stuff; robust coffee (from Peet's) is freshly ground and served with heavy whipping cream.

The tender rib-eye steak on the dinner menu can sometimes be gristly, making sticking to the one-third-pound charcoal-broiled hamburger the restaurant is famous for both a good idea and a bargain. Served on a toasted house-made bun (white or wheat), it is available with a variety of toppings. A good pasta salad made with fresh corkscrew pasta (from The Pasta Shop) is also recommended. It is tossed with a vinaigrette and topped with bits of turkey, colorful bursts of carrot sticks, and grated purple cabbage.

There are no children's items. Children may be happy sharing something or ordering a supplementary baked potato.

Varietal wines are available by the glass. Kids can share a not-too-thick, just-right shake served in a metal container.

For dessert you can't go wrong with a slice of the puffy, warm apple pie the restaurant is named for. Other pies (including a chocolate velvet and lemon meringue), cheesecake, and German chocolate cake are also available. Sugar shape cookies and other baked goods are available for take-out.

Breakfast features fresh-squeezed orange juice, wonderful crisp waffles served with 100% pure Vermont maple syrup, and freshly baked croissants, danish, and muffins.

The original Fatapple's is in Berkeley at 1346 Martin Luther King Jr. Way (526-2260).

## FENTONS CREAMERY
*4226 Piedmont Ave./Entrada Ave., Oakland, 658-7000; M-Sat 11am-11pm, Sun from noon; $; highchairs, booster seats; children's portions; free parking lot adjoins; no reservations; MC,V.*

What this well-established ice cream parlor lacks in atmosphere (one big room filled haphazardly with lemon-colored tables) it makes up for in the size of its portions. Some of the sundaes are appropriate for sharing among several people. The banana split easily serves four "normal" appetites. If all those people eating out of one bowl doesn't appeal to you, just ask for extra bowls. Drinks include milk shakes served in old-fashioned metal containers, sodas, floats, sherbet freezes, and fizzes (juice, sherbet, carbonated water, and an egg mixed into a froth). Taking into account varying appetites, sundaes come in small (1/3 pound ice cream), medium (3/4 pound), and large (over one pound).

For some reason the whipped cream here is always overwhipped and unpleasantly grainy. Consider asking to have it on the side, and certainly don't order extra until you have tasted it. Ice cream is fourteen per cent butterfat and is made on the premises, as is the hot fudge sauce.

The menu also includes several soups and salads, a hamburger, and an assortment of sandwiches, including grilled cheese and peanut butter & jelly. An excellent crab on sourdough is as popular here as the ice cream.

## FONDUE FRED

*2556 Telegraph Ave./Blake St., in Village Mall, Berkeley, 549-0850; L W-Sun, D daily; $$; highchairs, booster seats; reservations accepted; AE, MC, V.*

It was less than a week until his 16th birthday, so I didn't expect it to be easy to get our son to tag along for a family fondue feast. But fondue is one of his favorites, and I'd overlooked that to him dinner out meant he didn't have to do the dishes. It also meant he would get more practice driving the car in preparation for his up-coming license test.

So, seated on spacious park benches tucked under indestructible thickly-resined hatchcovers, my kids speared bread cubes and dipped them in a shared pot of smooth, bland classical Swiss cheese fondue. My husband and I were free to indulge in garlic and spicy chili pepper fondues.

Fondues are served with a generous salad composed of iceberg lettuce, sprouts, and shredded carrots. A tart vinaigrette dressing gets the old taste-buds in gear.

Our particularly pleasant waitress encouraged my son to order the "huge" coke which the menu claimed "is probably the largest glass you have ever seen." I think it was. We were sure he'd finally met his match, but he managed to down it all! When his younger sister accidentally toppled her "medium," the waitress appeared with sympathy and another coke. We adults sat back and let the piped-in jazz and our French Columbard work their magic.

For dessert a thin dark chocolate fondue for two was more than enough for all of us. At the sight of the generous platter of fruit, my excited daughter practically dove in and immediately confiscated most of the marshmallows. The adolescent tried a few chocolate-coated tidbits and then just stared at it all nervously, deep in thought about the complexion horrors that might develop if he ate any more.

## FUDDRUCKERS

*150 Longbrook Way/Contra Costa Blvd., in Ellinwood Square, Pleasant Hill, 825-1443; L & D daily; $; highchairs, booster seats, booths; children's portions; free parking lot adjoins; reservations accepted; AE, MC, V.*

Located near Highway 680, this spot is not easy to find if you are unfamiliar with the area. But it is worth the search if you have a hungry family of hamburger-lovers.

Diners get in the line, marked by boundaries of stacked boxes, and place their orders. Among the choices are 1/4-pound hot dogs, 1/3- and 1/2-pound hamburgers, and a 6-ounce rib-eye steak sandwich. Chicken and fish sandwiches and tacos are also available, as are side orders of sauteed onions, fries, and chile. Drinks include an assortment of really cold beers and bottomless soft drinks as well as colorful frozen "daiquiritas" in an assortment of unusual flavors—jungle juice, blue Hawaii, peach colada—and in both alcoholic and non-alcoholic versions.

After ordering, diners proceed to one of several seating areas in the attractive, spacious interior to select a table. Sitting at one, waiting for my food, I couldn't help but be reminded of a noisy, busy airport terminal. Names were even called out over loudspeakers, mimicking arrival and departure announcements.

After picking up their order, diners add the trimmings at a salad bar. Dessert choices are limited to ice cream (Dreyer's) and oven-fresh cookies and brownies. All bakery items are made on the premises.

Oh, yes. You can also order a bag of bones to take home to bowser.

If you have a sensitive child in tow, avoid letting them see the butcher shop near the door. Workers cut steaks and grind hamburger amid hanging sides of beef and are completely visible through a large window.

## FUDGE ALLEY
*376 Park St./Center St., in Rheem Valley Shopping Center, Moraga, 376-1003; open daily; $; booster seats, booths; children's portions; free parking lot adjoins; reservations accepted; no cards.*

This cozy ice cream parlour feels like it has been around forever. Menu items are what you would expect: sundaes, shakes, sodas, floats. All are made with either Dreyer's or Mary B. Best ice cream.

Chile, a hot dog, and a variety of sandwiches (including grilled cheese and peanut butter & jelly) are also available. All in all, this a a great spot for a quick treat.

## THE GOOD EARTH
*2175 Allston Way, Berkeley, 841-2555.*

For description see page 194.

## GRAMMA'S
*2740 Telegraph Ave./Ward St., Berkeley, 549-2145; SunBr, seatings at 10, 11:30, & 1; $$; highchairs, booster seats; children's portions; 100% non-smoking; reservations suggested; AE, DC, MC, V.*

With our own Gramma in tow, my entire family set out hungrily for an early brunch at Gramma's Victorian mansion. Having warned the kids to eat nothing before we left, we all arrived eager to experience a bounteous buffet.

My son, who is in the habit of putting on his plate and then eating one thing at a time, appreciated the themed buffet tables. First he filled his plate with spinach salad topped with a light raspberry vinaigrette. This was followed by baked ham glazed with champagne and ginger, crisply roasted chunks of baby red potatoes delicately flavored with fresh rosemary, and a portion of multi-colored bell pepper omelette. Then came an oversize orange-walnut muffin and, finally, portions of devilishly rich and fudgy chocolate-brandy-chestnut torte and pumpkin pie with hazelnut crust and fresh whipped cream topping.

My daughter, who is not fond of fussy food, did not change her feelings here. Upon her plate she allowed only a slice of orange decorated with cranberry sauce, a poached egg, and an irresistible heart-shaped waffle topped with rose butter and raspberry sauce. She also relished some of that dense chocolate cake and drank all of her milk.

We grown-ups enjoyed the above plus some more complex fare rejected soundly by the kids: the house pâté, tangy stoneground creole mustard, beets scented with orange, fig and cognac polenta, and a particularly light and wonderful pear roulade. All this plus champagne, vibrantly colored fresh-squeezed orange juice, and plenty of coffee.

Note that the seasonal menu changes approximately every six weeks.

Children 6 to 12 are charged half price; those under 6 are free. The brunch price includes tax, and tipping is discouraged.

## HOBEE'S
*5765 Christie Ave., in Powell Street Plaza, Emeryville, 652-5944; B & L daily, D F-Sat; $; highchairs, booster seats; separate children's menu; 100% non-smoking; free parking lot adjoins; no reservations; MC, V.*

Good wholesome food (lots of vegetables and tofu) served in a cheerful atmosphere in comfortable surroundings is the secret to success here. It is the perfect spot for a casual, inexpensive meal with the kids in tow.

Children get a placemat-size coloring sheet and a bucket of crayons to keep them busy. Their very own menu offers goodies such as pancakes, french toast, a grilled cheese sandwich, three kinds of burger (beef, tofu, chicken), and a cheese quesadilla. And they are given an appetizer plate of fruit—made to look like a face—to munch on while they wait to be served.

The regular breakfast menu, which is available all day, offers a selection of omelettes and scrambles as well as items such as whole wheat pancakes, cinnamon-orange swirl french toast, and granola. The orange and grapefruit juices are fresh-squeezed. Lunch brings on the salad bar, homemade soups, and a variety of sandwiches and hamburgers. A personal favorite is the quesadilla stuffed with a sauteed mixture of turkey, mushrooms, spinach, and onions.

Service is attentive, and iced tea comes with a free refill.

A branch is in Fremont at 39222 Fremont Boulevard (796-4779). Branches are also in San Bruno, Palo Alto, Mountain View, Cupertino, and San Jose (see p. 195).

## HUNAN RESTAURANT
*366 8th St., Oakland, 444-9255; L M-F, D daily, B Sat & Sun; $-$$; highchairs, booster seats; reservations suggested; MC, V.*

An attractive tile entryway leads into this pleasant restaurant. Servers wear short red jackets, accenting the decor much as the hot red chilies provide color and accent in the food.

Most stir-fried items are lightly sauced and spiced, and hot items are mild by my standards. Potstickers consist of a mild pork filling in tender wrappers. Crispy fried won tons have just the tiniest pocket of savory filling and are served with sweet and sour dipping sauce. Noisy sizzling rice soup is on the menu along with a flavorful, mild version of hot and sour soup filled with such good things as bean curd, bamboo shoots, egg, seaweed, green onions, and chunks of pork.

There are a wide variety of beef dishes, including a wonderful Szechwan beef mixed with yellow and green onions and sprinkled with hot red peppers. Tasty mu shu pork consists of egg, shredded pork, cabbage, black mushrooms, and chilies and is served with a plum sauce, green onions, cilantro, and pancakes to tuck it all into—sort of like a Chinese burrito. Crisp dry-braised green beans are mixed with minced pork and a garlicky sauce. Dramatic sizzling iron platters (chili sauce shrimp, ginger oyster, or beef and scallops) and several unusual casseroles (lion's head and fish head stews) are also available.

Weekend brunch consists of an unusual Northern-style Chinese breakfast. There are Chinese donuts (long, puffy, and fried—my kids love these), green onion pancakes (yes—*green onion*), potstickers, and plenty more. Even if you get carried away and order many items, the bill will remain low.

## THE ICE CREAMERY
*3276 Lakeshore Ave./Lake Park Ave., Oakland, 839-6161; daily 11am-midnight; $; highchairs; children's portions; free parking lot adjoins; reservations accepted; no cards.*

The sign in front reads "Purveyor of old-fashioned ice cream delicacies, scrumptious sandwiches, and pretty good pie." It's the truth. Diners here enjoy gigantic sundaes (child-sized versions are available), huge milkshakes served in old-fashioned metal mixer containers (enough for two or three people), fresh fruit freezes (mixtures of fruit juice, carbonated water, and sherbet), and delicatessen sandwiches (including grilled cheese, grilled peanut butter & jelly, and a hot dog). Some even enjoy the Kitchen Sink—a concoction made with scoops and scoops of ice cream, three bananas, assorted sauces, a topping of whipped cream and nuts and served in a replica of a sink!

Upon request, expectant mothers are served a free dill pickle along with their ice cream.

A branch is in Castro Valley at 3323 Castro Valley Boulevard (886-6158).

## JADE VILLA
*800 Broadway/8th St., Oakland, 839-1688; dim sum daily 9-2:30; $; booster seats; reservations suggested M-Sat, not taken on Sun; MC, V.*

There are many good dim sum restaurants in San Francisco's Chinatown. However, the difficulty with parking and long waits to be seated can be a deterrant. This spot in Oakland's smaller Chinatown allows enjoying an excellent meal of these tasty appetizers with less of a wait and easier parking.

Especially good items include the sweet deep-fried taro balls, nicely spiced pork-filled bows, delicate steamed shrimp dumplings, and exquisite deep-fried shrimp toasts topped with a pea. Unlike most San Francisco dim sum houses, where the bill is tallied at the end by counting the stack of plates accumulated, dishes here are added to the bill as selections are made.

The Cantonese-style dinner menu features fresh fish dishes and several reasonably priced family-style dinners.

See also page 14.

## JOY LUCK
*327 8th St./Webster St., Oakland, 832-4270; L & D W-M; $; highchairs, booster seats; reservations suggested; MC, V.*

Located in Oakland's tiny Chinatown, this Cantonese restaurant is a standout. Its exterior is bright tangerine-colored tile, making it easy to find. Inside lighting is low, the noise level high, and children abound.

Several family-style dinners are available. The least expensive includes won ton soup, crisp fried won tons with a generous amount of stuffing, egg roll, paper-wrapped chicken, chow mein, sweet and sour pork, shrimp fried rice, fortune cookies, and tea.

A la carte items include a tasty oyster sauce beef, delicious sweet and sour pineapple dishes (prawns, chicken, pork, spareribs, duck), a variety of seafood dishes, and egg foo young. Specialty dishes include exotic bird's nest soup, a seasonal crab with black bean sauce, and squab dishes. I am particularly fond of the chow fun noodle dishes (wide, chewy noodles made with rice flour), as is my particularly particular young daughter.

## KING TSIN
*1699-1701 Solano Ave./Tulare Ave., Berkeley, 525-9890; L & D daily; $$; highchairs, booster seats; reservations suggested; MC, V.*

Specializing in Mandarin Chinese cuisine, this popular restaurant is always crowded. Fortunately there is a comfortable bar area to wait in.

The cooks have the style down pat, so dishes are consistent. The extensive menu has a large choice of seafood items and includes most popular Chinese dishes. Portions are large.

Especially good are the delicately-crisp fried won tons, the hot and sour soup, the spiced prawns (coated in batter, deep-fried, and served with a thin, spicy sauce), the twice-cooked beef (in a sweet plum sauce accented with bamboo shoots and green onions), the spicy Mongolian beef (smothered in green onions and topping a bed of crisp rice noodles), and the asparagus, broccoli, snow pea, or string bean beef—depending on what is in season. The sizzling plates of beef, chicken, prawns, or scallops and the sizzling rice soup are all quite dramatic. If you're after the unusual, note the stewed shark's fin (must be ordered in advance), chicken livers with green onions, and sea cucumber in shrimp seeds.

When the owner is on the premises, pay your tab as you leave. Then you can watch him tally your bill with his abacus.

A branch is in Walnut Creek at 2280 Oak Grove Road (935-1238).

## KING YEN
*2984 College Ave./Alcatraz Ave., Berkeley, 845-1286; L & D daily; $$; highchairs, booster seats; no reservations; MC, V.*

Hunan and Szechwan styles of cooking are the specialty here. In my opinion the hot dishes are only medium hot, but the preparation is excellent. Three brothers are the exclusive cooks. This translates into no bad nights when the main cook is off.

Wall-to-wall carpet tempers the noise, colorful fresh flowers decorate the tables, and service is leisurely yet attentive. Portions tend to be large, and the shrimp is firm and sweet.

Crispy fried won tons are delicious and served with traditional sweet and sour dipping sauce spiraled with hot mustard. Thick, peppery hot and sour soup is filled with seaweed, egg, bamboo shoots, bean curd, and mushrooms. In the tasty Szechwan beef the meat is battered, deep-fried, and then stir-fried with a spicy sweet sauce. Delicately seasoned mu shu pork is a combination of shredded pork, bamboo shoots, mushrooms, and vegetables—meant to be stuffed into the flat pancakes it is served with and then spread with hoisin sauce and shredded green onions. (My young son once wanted nothing to do with the shredded "scallions" offered by the waiter until we told him they were only green onions.) Sauteed three ingredients is a spicy, saucy combination of shrimp, scallops, and chicken with bright green snow peas and bamboo shoots. Exotic beggar's chicken (stuffed with mushrooms and bamboo shoots and baked in clay) and Peking duck are available by advance order.

Fortune cookies and bright wedges of orange or cantaloupe end the feast.

Note that this restaurant is scheduled to move across the street.

## LARRY BLAKE'S
*2367 Telegraph Ave./Durant Ave., Berkeley, 848-0886; L & D daily, Sat & SunBr; $-$$; highchairs, booster seats, booths; reservations accepted; AE, DC, MC, V.*

A U.C. campus hangout since 1940, this restaurant is well-known for its hamburgers and steaks. But the menu also offers a grilled cheddar cheese sandwich, an excellent barbecued beef sandwich, and great barbecued pork ribs with a mild, tasty sweet sauce.

Weekdays lunch is served both downstairs, in the funky rathskellar, and upstairs, where there are excellent views of the sidewalk parade outside. Downstairs the floor is covered with sawdust, and seating is in old wooden booths. There is also a video game area, and most nights there is live music (children not admitted; cover charge).

Children tend to be looked upon adoringly by the mainly student clientele, allowing families to feel right at home.

## LA VAL'S
*1834 Euclid Ave./Hearst Ave., Berkeley, 843-5617; L & D daily; $; highchairs, booster seats, booths; no reservations; MC, V.*

Located on the quieter north side of the U.C. campus, this has long been a popular student hangout. Generally very noisy and full of boisterous students taking a break from studying, its atmosphere is very casual.

On a warm afternoon or evening the courtyard beer garden makes a great spot to enjoy a pizza and brew. Menu items also include a very good garlic bread and pastas such as ravioli, lasagne, and spaghetti as well as a hamburger, hot dog, and grilled cheese sandwich. But my family *always* gets pizza.

Inside there is more seating, most of it in a room decorated with forest murals and furnished with a mix-matched collection of chairs and formica tables. Live music and plays are often scheduled downstairs in the **Subterranean.** Food may be ordered there, and children are welcome; there is a cover charge.

If you're eating upstairs, you get in one line to place your food order and in another to purchase your drinks. Then you pick a table and wait for your number to be called. My family usually gets a salad when we place our order, and then munch on it while we wait. Older children like to use this waiting time to play a few video games; younger ones enjoy rides in the miniature car or a visit to the five-minute cartoon booth.

Branches are in Berkeley at 2516B Durant Avenue (845-5353), in Alameda at 891 Island Drive (521-7711), and in San Ramon at 2030 Twin Creeks Drive (838-2030).

For dessert, stroll a few doors down to **Schuyler's Ice Cream Cafe** (#1854) for a cone, or to **Pane e Cioccolata** (#1878) on the corner for a cookie or pastry.

## L. J. QUINN'S LIGHTHOUSE

*51 Embarcadero Cove, 16th Ave. exit off I880, Oakland, 536-2050; L & D daily, Sat & Sun Br; $$; highchairs, booster seats, children's portions; free parking lot adjoins; reservations suggested in restaurant, no reservations taken in pub; MC, V.*

Quinn's operates out of the attractively remodeled Oakland Harbor Lighthouse. Built in 1903 and replaced by an automatic beacon in 1966, it was purchased from the Coast Guard for just $1.

I wasn't expecting great food when I set out with my family for brunch in a lighthouse. I figured the novelty of the setting would outweigh the expertise of the kitchen. As mothers sometimes are, I was wrong.

Seated outside on an upstairs deck overlooking the quiet estuary, I relaxed over a tangy daiquiri made with fresh raspberries while my husband sipped a traditional Margarita. The kids were pleased with virgin versions. Because this was a late brunch, we kept the growls at bay with delicious hot sourdough garlic bread. And because you are allowed to throw the shells on the floor here, we also indulged in a basket of roasted peanuts. My youngest had a great time crunching the shells under foot.

Sometimes a traditional brunch menu is served in the downstairs dining room. At other times a lunch menu with just a few brunch items is available in the upstairs bar/pub. This was one of the latter times. My family tried both the tasty three-egg Jambalaya omelette—stuffed with a spicy creole mixture of shrimp, sausage, and chicken—and the classicly-prepared eggs Benedict. They arrived hot with sides of wonderful fried potatoes accented with bits of bacon and sweet peppers. Even the English muffins were hot and delicious.

Additional lunch items include pastas, seafood, a hamburger, and some Cajun items. Among the desserts are an apple pie and a rich, creamy chocolate swirl cheesecake served in a pool of raspberry sauce.

Lunch and dinner in the dining room are a bit more formal but still pleasant with children.

## MAIKO
*1629 San Pablo Ave./Cedar St., Berkeley, 525-1575; D Thur-M; $$; highchairs, booster seats; reservations suggested; AE, MC, V.*

Once past the windowless cement façade of this former bowling alley, diners enter a gigantic room decorated with a lovely central rock garden and fountain. Ceiling light fixtures mimic the moon.

Choice tables are arranged around the fountain, where the gentle sound of the running water has a soothing effect (though some children have been known to see it only as a hard-to-resist opportunity for tossing loose stones into water). Another area holds a sushi bar serviced by a toy train. Yet another area provides traditional tatami floor seating. (Children especially enjoy the unusual request to take off their shoes before entering this area. Be sure to check all socks for holes before you leave home!) If your kids move around a lot or need a highchair, opt for a regular table.

Kids and parents both like the custom of offering hot washcloths for use before dining.

The menu has a large selection of fish items but also includes sukiyaki and shabu shabu as well as tasty teriyakis—popular with children because they are in easy-to-eat pieces. Donburi are literally "meals in a bowl" consisting of assorted meats and vegetables served on top of rice; they are filling and delicious as well as a good buy. My own favorite is the wonderful, light tempura. Complete dinners include a marinated cucumber salad and dessert of vanilla or green tea ice cream.

Hot sake in tiny cups is a nice, soothing touch for weary moms and dads.

## MARIE CALLENDER'S
*6180 Stoneridge Mall Rd., Pleasanton, 734-0200; 250 Market Pl., San Ramon, 830-9000.*

For description see page 197.

## MAX'S DINER
*Crow Canyon/Hwy 680, San Ramon, 277-9300.*

For description see page 49.

## MAX'S OPERA CAFE
*1676 N. California Blvd., in Growers Square, Walnut Creek, 932-3434.*

For description see page 49.

## NANTUCKET FISH COMPANY
*Foot of Port St., Crockett, 787-2233; L M-Sat, D daily; $$; highchairs, booster seats; children's portions; free parking lot adjoins; no reservations; AE, DC, MC, V.*

Situated at the end of a twisting road under the Carquinez Bridge, on the other side of the tracks, this popular restaurant specializes in serving New England-style fresh fish items. Some are actually flown in from the East Coast. A board lists the fresh fish items and daily specials.

Most fish selections are available either charcoal-broiled or pan-fried. Shell fish is lightly breaded and deep-fried Cape Cod-style; it is also available in casseroles with Newburg or Mornay sauce. Shellfish cioppino is either old-fashioned style (in the shell) or lazy man's style (out of the shell). Lobster and steak comprise the higher-priced end of the menu. All dinners are served with a choice of either creamy white clam chowder or a salad topped with shrimp. They also include warm Parmesan cheese-topped french bread, a fresh vegetable prepared with flair, and a choice of either french fries or seasoned rice. Children's plates are a choice of a hamburger, fried clam strips, or fish & chips. Several unusual flavors of cheesecake (macademia nut, Kahlua and almond) are usually available for dessert.

The restaurant itself is unpretentious, and all tables have a view of the water. Best of all, though, for parents are the fantastic waitresses that really like children.

If there is a wait to be seated, you can stroll along the pier outside. It's also pleasant to just stand outside and look at the water. Drinks and seafood appetizers are available from the bar and may be enjoyed indoors or out.

A branch is in Benicia at 123 First Street (707/745-2233).

Crockett is the major center for sugar production on the West Coast. As you drive back to the freeway, the large red brick building you see to the east is the circa 1906 C & H Sugar refinery.

## NEW SUNSHINE RISTORANTE
*3891 Piedmont Ave./40th Ave., Oakland, 428-2500; D W-Sun; $$; highchairs, booster seats; reservations suggested; MC, V.*

Everything here, with the exception of the lasagne, is made to order. Lasagne is the exception because the chef is of the opinion that it tastes better when made the day before.

The thin-crusted sourdough pizza doesn't get soggy, and a large one is probably enough to feed a family of four. A large selection of popular toppings is available, as well as some trendy ones such as sundried tomatoes or prawns with pesto.

The menu also offers minestrone soup, a meatball sandwich, eggplant parmigiana, spaghetti, three kinds of ravioli (cheese, chicken, and seafood), and a good selection of pastas.

Wine varietals are available by the glass. Children may especially enjoy the Italian sodas, grenadine being a clear favorite.

For dessert there is a choice of either cheesecake or Italian "tiles"—pastry raviolis filled with chocolate and vanilla creams and served in a raspberry sauce. Magnifico!

This restaurant is located inside a converted Victorian. The best spot for families is at a comfortable table in the carpeted main dining room. The glass-roofed patio area, called the Sunshine Room, has tile floors and other hard surfaces off which family noises bounce quite loudly.

## OLD UNCLE GAYLORD'S ICE CREAM PARLOR
*3300 Grand Ave., Oakland, 763-7695; 4150 Piedmont Ave., Oakland, 547-5184.*

For description see page 56.

## ORTMAN'S ICE CREAM PARLOR
*1799 Solano Ave./Colusa Ave., Berkeley, 526-9830; M-F 7am-10pm, Sat & Sun to 11pm; $; booster seats; no reservtions; no cards.*

Decked out with a cheerful pink and white striped awning, this popular ice cream parlor has been dishing up ice cream goodies since 1945. There are sundaes in small and large versions, milkshakes served in metal mixing containers, and fruit phosphates served in sturdy, decorative glasses. The large sandwich selection includes a peanut butter & jelly, a grilled cheese, a double weiner and cheese, and a delightful crab served on buttered, toasted french bread. Each is served with a small cup of sherbet.

The limited seating consists of a counter with stools, one large communal table, and several small tables. If it's crowded, consider a walk-away cone.

## PASAND
*2286 Shattuck Ave./Bancroft Way, Berkeley, 549-2559; L & D daily; $-$$; highchairs, booster seats, booths; reservations taken but usually not necessary; AE, MC, V.*

Authentic South-Indian Madras cuisine is served here in casual, comfortable surroundings. Among the choices are Biriani entrees (a choice of chicken, lamb, or vegetables) mixed in a tasty, spicy Basmati rice and served with yogurt raita.

Other goodies on the extensive menu include items cooked over mesquite in a Tandoori oven (chicken tikka kabab is especially wonderful) and an assortment of vegetable and meat curries. Entrees are served a la carte or with all the trimmings: dahl (lentil curry), sambar (thick lentil soup), rasam (spicy tamarind soup), raita, poori (puffy deep-fried bread), papadum (a crisp lentil wafer), rice pilaf, mango chutney, and a honey-soaked gulab jambun for dessert.

For a smaller appetite try a masala dosa—a lentil flour crepe stuffed with a delicious vegetable curry. It is served with sambar and two sauces.

Spicing is mild unless you specifically request spicy-hot.

Indian music is performed live every night from 6:30 to 9:30. The musicians are seated on a raised stage in the main dining room.

Branches are in San Francisco (see p. 57), Santa Clara (see p. 198), and San Rafael (see p. 216).

## PICANTE TAQUERIA & CANTINA
*1328 Sixth St./Gilman St., Berkeley, 525-3121; L & D daily; $; highchairs, booster seats, booths; no reservations; no cards.*

Claiming to be the largest taqueria in the bay area, this spot is located in Berkeley's low-rent district. Noisy and casual, it has the feel of a south-of-the-border cantina. Unusual half-moon wooden booths line the side of an oblong room, with tables running down the center and a long bar lining the other side. Ceiling fans and tile floors add to the cantina ambiance.

Meals are ordered in the back. Choices include tacos, two sizes of burrito, tamales, corn or flour quesadillas (popular with children), and tostada salads. Fillings include carne asada, chili verde, chorizo (from a house recipe), pollo colorado, a bland version of carnitas, and a vegeterian mixture. The salsa, unspicy enough to be eaten by young children, is made with fresh tomatoes, onions, and cilantro.

A large selection of Mexican beer is available. Margaritas made with agave wine are available on Friday and Saturday evenings. Live music is also scheduled then from 8:30 to midnight, and there is no cover charge.

## PLEARN
*2050 University Ave./Shattuck Ave., Berkeley, 841-2148; L & D M-Sat; $$; booster seats; no reservations.*

This very popular restaurant offers a pleasant "Thai-tech" decor. Seating is at comfortable tables, and children attend in great numbers. There is often a wait, but my kids don't mind because shrimp chips are usually offered to help keep hunger pangs at bay.

Among the creative appetizers are yum-nua (a simply yummy mixture of beef slices seasoned with onion and ground chilies and tossed with fragrant mint leaves and lime juice) and tender beef satay. I find the curries disappointing, and always order stir-frys. Among my favorite are him-ma-pan (chicken with cashew nuts and chilies) and pat-prik-king (pork with chilies and string beans). For a pittance more, an entree can include both rice and an iceberg lettuce salad topped with a bright-yellow, tangy-sweet dressing. For dessert, a crispy batter-dipped, deep-fried banana topped with a light coconut sauce can be pleasant.

See also page 16.

## RUSTY PELICAN
*2455 Marine Square Dr., Alameda, 865-2166; SunBr, L M-F, D daily; $$; highchairs, booster seats, booths; children's portions; free parking lot adjoins; reservations suggested; AE, DC, MC, V.*

My whole family enjoys sitting here at brunch and watching the boats drift by. Occasionally one filled with hungry weekend sailors docks right at the restaurant.

Even with reservations, there is usually a wait. It can be pleasantly passed imbibing one of the usual Sunday morning drinks in the nicely appointed bar upstairs. Children may enjoy The Surfer, a combination of 7-Up or ginger ale and grenadine.

Brunch begins with a complimentary fresh fruit ambrosia, served as soon as you are seated by attentive waitresses attired in very short skirts. Presented in a tall glass and topped with a light sauce, the delightful fruit tides you over while perusing the menu. A basket of carrot, date-nut, and banana breads arrives soon after. (Cereal-deprived kids have been known to polish this off in nothing flat.) Complimentary champagne follows.

Among the entrees are an ample "pelican omelette" (filled with crab, shrimp, avocado, artichoke hearts, and Jack cheese) and a croissant Benedict. Children's portions consist of half an entree at half the price.

A branch is in San Ramon at 2323 San Ramon Valley Boulevard (820-6160). Another branch is in Cupertino (see p. 199).

## SCOTT'S SEAFOOD GRILL & BAR

*73 Jack London Square, Oakland, 444-3456; L & D daily; $$$; booster seats, booths; reservations essential; validated parking lot adjoins, valet parking available; AE, DC, MC, V.*

Best saved for a special occasion, Scott's offers few family amenities. But with that known in advance, it can provide a satisfying dining experience. Especially if you get a window table overlooking the Oakland Estuary.

Well-known for its extensive menu of fresh seafood, which changes every day, Scott's also offers a hamburger, several pastas, a New York and filet mignon steak, and a chicken item.

For my birthday celebration dinner I started with a cup of thick, creamy New England-style clam chowder—filled deliciously with sand-free clams and small pieces of properly cooked potato. My husband and teen shared a house salad consisting of crisp whole leaves of romaine lettuce and rounds of tomato and cucumber. Meanwhile, my young daughter, who eats very little, designed me a Happy Birthday card on her paper placemat.

My grilled Idaho rainbow trout was served boned and flat and topped with a light sauce and sprinkling of toasted almonds. I really wanted Maine lobster but the kids would have mutinied. The trout came with a side of french fries, prepared from fresh potatoes, and colorful, delicious steamed vegetables.

My husband enjoyed grilled Atlantic sea bass which had been marinated and topped with lemon butter. It came with a side of saffron-colored rice.

Our teen ordered what turned out to be one of the biggest cheeseburgers we've seen. Made with six to eight ounces of meat and topped with lettuce and three thick slices of tomato, it was too much for him to finish. Our daughter ate a few carrot sticks, a tomato slice, and a tad of rice culled from our various plates. The waitress was accommodating in providing her with an extra plate service at no charge.

Several varietal wines are available by the glass. Bar drinks may be ordered, and there are virgin drinks for kids. Among the dessert items is a semi-dense, semi-sweet chocolate mousse torte topped attractively with a whipped cream rose. We ordered one with four forks and two cappuccinos.

As we left, my daughter deposited a tip in the pianist's jar. Even though he was playing in the bar area, we had enjoyed the pleasant background music.

A branch is in Walnut Creek at 1333 North California Street (934-1300). Branches are also in San Francisco (see p. 59), Palo Alto, and San Jose (see p. 200).

## SIAM CUISINE
*1181 University Ave./San Pablo Ave., Berkeley, 548-3278; L M-Sat, D daily; $$; highchairs, booster seats; reservations suggested; AE, DC, MC, V.*

The very first Thai restaurant in the East Bay, this has long been a personal favorite. In fact, we took our children here years ago when it first opened and made our original discovery of how little there was on a Thai menu for kids to eat. We didn't take them again for a long, long time.

Recently I've discovered lard-nar on the menu (a rice noodle dish made with broccoli, beef, and a soy sauce gravy). My kids always like rice noodles, and they like this dish because it isn't exotic, spicy, or hot.

My daughter finds the iced tea here particularly interesting because the milk is served in a pitcher, permitting her to add it as she pleases to her tea. This allows for experiments in swirling which keep her occupied for a few minutes. Sometimes she likes the tender beef satay with its delicious peanut curry sauce, and sometimes she doesn't. My son, however, always does. Unfortunately for children, there are a no fried bananas on the menu.

And for we adults who are nuts about HOT, this is definitely the place. On the menu, each dish is categorized as to hotness—and (hot) means HOT!

We like to begin with deep-fried shrimp and pork toast (mild) served with a hot and sour cucumber salad. A lettuce and vegetable salad with spicy peanut dressing is made memorable with tamarind juice.

Delicious green curry pork (very hot) is indeed. Beef with hot pepper (hot), chicken with sweet basil (hot), and mus-u-man curry with beef, potatoes, peanuts, and coconut milk (medium) are also quite tasty. And the fresh fish filet of the day topped with a hot and spicy sauce (hot) is not to be missed.

I've rarely experienced a disappointing dish here.

See also page 16.

## SKATES

*100 Seawall Dr., foot of University Ave., Berkeley, 549-1900; L & D daily, SunBr; $$; highchairs, booster seats, booths; children's portions; free parking lot adjoins; reservations suggested; AE, MC, V.*

The dining room here is pleasantly decorated, with thick carpeting and ceiling fans, and there is a choice of sitting in large booths or at tables with chairs. Window tables feature three-bridge views.

Brunch items include a broccoli and cheddar cheese quiche, scrambled eggs, several omelettes (Mexican, seafood), and fresh fish grilled over Hawaiian kiawe wood. Eggs Benedict is prepared in the classic manner and served with unseasoned boiled red potatoes. All entrees include buttery croissants made fresh in the kitchen.

Fresh-squeezed orange and grapefruit juices and glasses of champagne are available along with a large assortment of wines, beers, and mixed drinks.

Items from the extensive lunch menu are also available during brunch. One intriguing possibility is deep-fried Cajun shrimp in coconut beer batter served with a spicy sauce. There is also a homemade focaccia (Italian pan bread), a hamburger with focaccia bun, and a variety of soups, salads, and pastas.

The dinner menu brings on more fresh fish items.

If you have room, desserts include a hot fudge sundae, a burnt cream (smooth, rich vanilla custard topped with a crisp burnt sugar crust), and, in season, a giant traditional strawberry shortcake.

## SPENGER'S FISH GROTTO

*1919 4th St./University Ave., Berkeley, 845-7771; B, L, & D daily; $$; highchairs, booster seats; separate children's menu; free parking lot adjoins; no reservations; DC, MC, V.*

Spenger's began life in 1890 as a country store. Then it became a fish market. After prohibition it finally evolved into a bar and restaurant.

Now this expansive restaurant easily qualifies as Berkeley's most popular. With a seating capacity of 400 people and a staff of 240, it is the largest restaurant in the Bay Area. Over 3,000 dinners are served every day (that's approximately a ton of seafood), making it number seven among independent restaurants in overall volume of business in the entire country!

It is always packed to overflowing, and there are always herds of children in attendance. And the wait is often at least one hour! I can't sit with my children that long and still retain enough energy to enjoy my meal.

To avoid the long wait, we arrive for dinner before 6 or after 9 or gather up a party of six or more people and make a reservation.

Excellent, reasonably-priced drinks are served in the bustling, cozy nautical bar. A second bar, larger but equally busy, offers an oyster bar and a four- by five-foot TV screen. That ought to help out with the kids, except that the TV isn't usually tuned to *Sesame Street* or cartoons.

When your name is finally called, you can look forward to a roaring-loud atmosphere and a menu offering a large selection of seafood items (fresh whenever the catch permits) as well as steak, froglegs, a hamburger, and a grilled cheese sandwich. A good seafood sampling is provided by the captain's plate: deep-fried prawns, oysters, scallops, and fish filet. The children's menu is a choice of grilled filet of sole, shrimp scatter, a hamburger patty, or deep-fried scallops.

Once your order is taken, the food arrives quickly. No desserts are on the menu, and I doubt you will want them because portions here are big.

A well-stocked fish market adjoins; the delicious house sourdough bread is available there for take-out.

## TAIWAN
*2071 University Ave./Shattuck Ave., Berkeley, 845-1456; B Sat & Sun, L & D daily; $; highchairs, booster seats; no reservations; AE, MC, V.*

Newly remodeled, this popular restaurant offers an extensive menu. Native Taiwanese specialties are among the representative dishes from most of the Chinese provinces. There is a good selection of vegetarian dishes.

My favorites are wok-fried spinach with garlic (steamed fresh spinach tossed with oil and generous amounts of chopped garlic), dry braised green beans (fresh green beans in a salty mixture of oyster sauce, garlic, and ground pork), General Tsao's chicken (bite-size pieces of chicken in a spicy red sauce), spicy fish-flavored chicken, beef a la Shangtung (deep-fried pieces of battered beef with a tasty sauce), the showy sizzling beef and chicken platters, Mongolian beef (tossed with black bean sauce and green onions and served over crisp rice noodles), and spicy prawns (in a tasty red sauce). Portions are generous. It is my opinion that the dishes marked "spicy hot" are not. This may be good news for those of you with timid taste buds.

More unusual items include Taiwan pickle cabbage with pork tripe soup, boneless duck web, and numerous squid dishes. Beggar's chicken and Peking duck are available when ordered one day in advance.

Not all items are appreciated by children. Pork a la Hunan, a salty blend of cabbage and cured pork, prompted our preteen to ask, "What's that bad smell on the table?" Order with care. Children do, however, enjoy watching cooks prepare noodles and dumplings in the kitchen visible from the sidewalk.

A weekend Chinese breakfast is very similar to that served at the Hunan Restaurant (see p. 144).

The fortune cookies here are unusually prophetic. The strip inside mine once read, "You would make an excellent critic."

Two branches are in San Francisco (see p. 61).

## TAQUERIA MEXICAN GRILL

*1359 Locust St./California Blvd., Walnut Creek, 932-8987; 150 Hartz Ave./Mt. Diablo Rd., Danville, 838-7292; 1847 Willow Pass Rd., in the Park-N-Shop Shopping Center, Concord, 676-3367.*

For description see page 219.

## TJ'S GINGERBREAD HOUSE

*741 5th St./Brush St., Oakland, 444-7373; L & D Tu-Sat, tea 2:30-4; $$-$$$; children's portions; reservations required; AE, DC, MC, V.*

To enjoy a Cajun-Creole meal at this unique restaurant, diners must first send in a stamped, self-addressed envelope requesting a menu. Then a call is made to reserve a date and place the meal order. This unusual procedure leaves one anticipating the experience.

Arrival at the colorful little empire that is TJ's meets expectations. The three dining rooms include two marvelous rooms in the original Victorian house, each boasting an extensive doll collection, and a newer gazebo annex built a few years ago.

Among the tempting appetizers are barbecued ribs, shrimp remoulade, and escargots. Or you can start with a colorful fresh fruit salad. (Meals here include salad and dessert.) Among the twenty-plus main courses is the house specialty—a tasty, mildly-spicy "spoon" jambalaya. It is heavy with ham, Louisiana hot sausage, and Cajun rice and topped with shrimp and four perfect fresh, firm prawns. Other entrees include Bayou catfish Etouffee (sauteed and blanketed in a piquante sauce), whiskey stuffed lobster, and sauteed quail. You really must get the menu to get the picture.

Entrees are served with sides of delicious "sassy" corn bread sitting in melted butter, wonderful lightly-steamed vegetables in a vinegar-butter dressing, and Cajun "come back" dirty rice. Dessert is a bowl of vanilla ice cream with a tiny frosted gingerbread man standing in the center. On the side sits a half of a very large ginger cake cookie studded with walnuts, raisins, and chocolate chips.

A child's setting includes everything but an entree—even fruit punch.

## YET WAH

*4635 Clayton Rd., Concord, 671-7044.*

For description see page 65.

## YOSHI'S
*6030 Claremont Ave./College Ave., Oakland, 652-9200; L M-F, D daily; $$; high-chairs, booster seats, booths; free parking lot adjoins; reservations suggested; AE, DC, MC, V.*

Portions at this tastefully decorated, casual Japanese restaurant are generous. Beautifully prepared tempura entrees include the classic prawn as well as calamari and all-vegetable versions. Sukiyaki, yakitori, and several teriyaki items are on the menu along with gyoza (Japanese potsickers), tonkatsu (a deep-fried breaded pork cutlet), and sashimi (raw tuna).

Entrees come with tasty soup broth, green salad, steamed rice, and fragrant genmai tea (green tea with roasted rice).

There is a tatami room with seating on a raised floor (open only at dinner) and a separate sushi bar. Live music is scheduled most nights in the upstairs bar.

## YUJEAN'S MODERN CUISINE OF CHINA
*843 San Pablo Ave./Solano Ave., Albany, 525-8557; L & D Tu-Sun; $$-$$$; high-chairs, booster seats; 100% non-smoking; reservations suggested; AE, MC, V.*

Featuring a sophisticated decor with high ceilings, white tablecloths, and fan-folded pale pink cloth napkins, this relatively upscale Chinese restaurant has been open just since 1987.

Unusual cuisine and a celebrated, well-priced wine list are the restaurant's claims to fame. (Some of the wines are in the $200 to $400 range!) Foodies mingle with families to sample the promised exquisite pairings. Though I've dined here many times, I cannot comment on the wine because I simply haven't accepted the idea of drinking wine with Chinese food. Beer, cola, or tea are my choices of drink. Fortunately, all of these are also available.

Another unusual feature (for a Chinese restaurant) is sophisticated service. Items are brought to the side of the table one at a time, placed on trays, and then served onto each diner's plate. Careful attention is given to arrangement, making for an attractive presentation. For my family, this extra attention to detail puts Yujean's into the category of a "special occasion" restaurant. Perhaps because of this, prices tend to be steeper and dishes smaller than we are accustomed to in other Chinese restaurants.

Though the menu changes frequently, offering new dishes and seasonal items, the quality and execution are consistent. Seafood is fresh. This is one of the few restaurants where I will order shrimp or prawns; I know they will have a firm texture and delicate taste.

Soups are served in individual portions. One person can have spicy hot and sour, another bland sizzling rice. My family appreciates this.

My kids always like potstickers. Here they are served six to a plate with bowls of hot sauce, hot mustard, and sweet and sour sauce for dipping. My daughter, who usually doesn't like anything crunchy, is fond of the light spring rolls. Though "ants climbing tree" is a wonderful dish (a base of minced pork, mushrooms, and water chestnuts topped with chopped peanuts and served on a lettuce leaf cup), its name usually prohibits our ordering it when the kids are along.

I haven't yet had a disappointing dish here. Favorites include beef a la Szechwan (made with matchstick beef and shreds of carrot and celery tossed with a spicy soy sauce mixture), chicken with honey-glazed cashews and shitake mushroom pieces, pork with garlic sauce (mixed with green onions and crunchy water chestnuts), and delicious crisp-skinned tea-smoked duck served with plum sauce and green onions and rolled in thin crepes. Other great choices include filet of fresh Alaskan salmon, prepared in varying inventive ways, and kung pao spicy prawns.

Fortune cookies end the meal. For a more exciting ending, order glazed fresh fruit consisting of a hard caramelized sugar glaze over an assortment of fresh seasonal fruits.

## ZACHARY'S CHICAGO PIZZA

*1853 Solano Ave./The Alameda, Berkeley, 525-5950; L & D daily; $; highchairs, booster seats; 100% non-smoking; no reservations; no cards.*

About that Chicago pizza. It isn't anything like the deep-dish Chicago pizza I have memory of downing at Chicago's famous Uno and Due's. But then, according to the menu, the restaurant doesn't claim that it is. It is a "stuffed pizza in the pan." Served de-panned, it looks a lot like a cheesecake. (The famous Chicago pizza of my memory was served in an iron frying pan.) One tasty version my family particularly likes is made with fresh Italian sausage, a tangy and chunky homemade tomato sauce, and a very rich, chewy mozzarella cheese. As promised on the menu, the made-from-scratch crust isn't soggy. A ten-inch pizza serves two adults and one kid, maybe with enough left over for a lunch the next day.

The pizza takes thirty minutes to cook. We pass the wait munching on a spinach salad made with well-washed spinach (no grit) and sprinkled with fresh mushrooms, crumbled bacon, and a mustard dressing. (Note that if there is a wait to be seated, you can pre-order your pizza so it is ready when you sit down.)

A "thin pizza," for which you can select your choice of toppings, is also available. Beverages and a house salad complete the menu.

Pizzas-to-go are available half-cooked—to be popped in the oven and finished at home.

A branch is in Oakland at 5801 College Avenue (655-6385).

---

## — PICNIC PICK-UPS —

---

## BETTE'S TO GO

*1807 4th St./Hearst Ave., Berkeley, 548-9494.*

For description see page 133.

## BROTHERS' BAGEL FACTORY

*1281 Gilman St./Santa Fe Ave., Berkeley, 524-3104; M-F 7-6, Sat 8-6, Sun 8-3; free parking lot adjoins; no cards.*

Twelve varieties of bagels are usually available, often warm from the oven. Pick up lox (choose from four kinds), cream cheese, and jams for assemblage at your picnic site, or have bagel sandwiches made to-go. Among the other sandwiches which can be prepared for take-out are tuna or chicken salad, smoked turkey and cheese, and roast beef. Halvah is avail-able for dessert, and drinks include milk, mineral waters, fresh-squeezed orange juice, and a variety of apple juices.

## EL FARO

*2280 Monument Blvd., Concord, 827-0976.*

For description see page 65.

## G.B. RATTO & CO. INTERNATIONAL GROCERS

*821 Washington St./9th St., Oakland, 832-6503; M-Sat 8-5; pre-packed picnic boxes by reservation; beer, wine; L in sit-down area; free parking lot adjoins; MC, V.*

Don't expect to just run in and run out at this wonderland of international foods. Family-operated since 1897, it is literally stuffed to the rafters with goodies. There are bins of grains and pastas, bulk spices, hanging sausages, garlic braids, and fresh breads. There is sauerkraut from Germany, pepper from India, and morel mushrooms from France. A long deli counter provides countless sandwich choices.

Personally, I prefer to have lunch in the adjoining informal cafeteria, then browse the grocery and select deli items to take home for dinner.

Friday night pasta dinners followed by live opera are scheduled from 6:30 to 9:30.

## LAKESIDE DELICATESSEN

*3257 Lakeshore Ave./MacArthur Blvd., Oakland, 832-4374; M-Sat 7:30-6, Sun 9:30-5; pre-packed picnic boxes by reservation; sit-down area, no table service; MC, V.*

In business since 1937, this old-time deli offers made-to-order sandwiches, bagels and cream cheese, house-made salads and hot entrees (enchiladas, ribs, lasagne, ravioli made with turkey and Swiss chard), fresh pastries, imported cheeses, hot and cold drinks, and the usual deli accompaniments.

## MADE TO ORDER

*1576 Hopkins St./Monterey, Berkeley, 524-7552; M-Sat 9:30-6; pre-packed picnic boxes by reservation; beer, wine; MC, V.*

Just as the name indicates, sandwiches here are made to order. A variety of interesting house-made salads, pâtés, cheeses, crackers, drinks, and sweets round out the offerings. Personal favorites include the sausage turnovers and Grandma's seasoned potato rounds.

And do stop in across the street at the legendary **Monterey Market** to pick up some fresh fruit for your picnic basket.

## PLEASANTON CHEESE FACTORY
*830 Main St., Pleasanton, 846-2577; daily 9-6; pre-packed picnic boxes by reservation; beer, wine; free parking lot adjoins; L in sit-down area, no table service; MC, V.*

Though they no longer make their own, this shop still provides a large variety of cheeses to choose from. Fresh breads (including an unusual Greek bread ring), crackers, wines, and accompaniments are also available.

An adjacent shop prepares gigantic sandwiches. The ham and cheese, salami and cheese, and just plain cheese on sheepherder's bread are all highly recommended.

It is quite pleasant to have your picnic right here. Select one of the cablespool tables outside and watching the world go by on Pleasanton's busy Main Street.

# What To Do

---

## — HISTORIC SITES —

---

### ARDENWOOD HISTORIC FARM
*34600 Ardenwood Blvd./Hwy 84, Fremont, 796-0663; Thur-Sun 10-4, Nov-Mar; adults $5, 4-18 $2.50, under 4 free; free parking lot adjoins; picnic tables, food service.*

Situated in a fragrant eucalyptus grove, this farm was built in the 1850s by a wealthy farmer. The old farm buildings, crop fields, and antique farm equipment have been restored. It is said to be the only historic farm park in the West and allows visitors to step back in time to view farm life in the 1880s.

Tours of the elegant **Patterson Home** are scheduled each hour. Demonstrations of typical farm chores vary with the season but may include shoeing a horse, sheepshearing, constructing a barrel, wheat threshing, milking a goat, or cheese making. Hands-on participation is encouraged.

Children can pet young farm animals, jump in a haystack, and roll around on grassy expanses. Sometimes rugs are hung out on the line for them to beat clean.

The admission fee includes rides on an unusual horse-drawn narrow-gauge railroad as well as on several haywagons and surreys. Special events are scheduled regularly.

### BLACK DIAMOND MINES REGIONAL PRESERVE
*In Antioch, take Hwy 4 east to Somersville Rd. exit, then go 3 miles south on Somersville Rd. to park entrance, 757-2620; daily 8-dusk; free; mining museum: adults $3, 7-11 $1.50, under 7 not admitted; free parking lot adjoins; picnic tables.*

From 1860 to 1906 this area was the largest coal mining district in California; over half the coal used in the state came from these mines. Visitors can hike over 30 miles of trails and visit historic Rose Hill Cemetery. Picnic facilities are available.

Self-guided tours of the **Underground Mining Museum** are available by advance reservation only. Hard-hats and flashlights are provided.

### EUGENE O'NEILL NATIONAL HISTORIC SITE
*In Danville, 838-0249; tours W-Sun at 10 & 1:30, reservations required; free.*

While living in Danville at **Tao House**, O'Neill wrote his last plays, among them *The Iceman Cometh, Long Day's Journey Into Night,* and *A Moon for the Misbegotten.* In 1976 the house was established as a national historic site to commemorate his contributions to American theater and to be used as a park for the performing arts. Finally in 1985, after years of negotiating between the National Park Service and nearby homeowners, Tao House was opened for public tours.

Because the tour is slow-moving and sprinkled generously with lectures, it is not recommended for children under 5.

### JOHN MUIR NATIONAL HISTORIC SITE
*4202 Alhambra Ave./Hwy. 4, Martinez, 228-8860; daily 10-4:30; adults $1, under 17 free, everyone free each Aug 25; free parking lot adjoins; picnic tables.*

After seeing a background film, visitors tour Muir's 19th century farmhouse. Then they are free to wander in the large garden filled with fruit trees and to visit the circa 1844 **Martinez Adobe** located there.

A **Victorian Tea** is scheduled each December. The house is decorated for the occasion in Christmas cheer, and participants are greeted by personalities from Muir's time. They are also entertained by a string trio and led in song by Victorian carolers. Refreshments include hot tea, coffee, and apple cider served with Victorian-style cookies. Tickets go on sale at the beginning of November and sell fast.

### MISSION SAN JOSE DE GUADALUPE
*43000 Mission Blvd./Washington Blvd., Fremont, 657-1797; daily 10-4:30; by donation.*

Marking the center of the oldest community in the East Bay, this mission was founded in 1797. It was the only mission built in the East Bay.

Part of the original adobe monastery wing remains and now holds exhibits.

Of particular note are the quiet graveyard and the beautifully decorated interior of the circa 1809 New England gothic-style **St. Joseph's Church.**

## UNIVERSITY OF CALIFORNIA, BERKELEY CAMPUS
*Telegraph Avenue/Bancroft Way, Berkeley, 642-6000.*

Pack up the kids and head out for the big U. The foremost attraction on the campus is, of course, higher learning. The university is known for academic excellence and boasts a faculty distinguished by ten Nobel Prize winners. Many noteworthy facilities on the 1200-acre campus are open to the public.

Wander around the beautiful campus, or take a guided tour. Free tours are available at the Visitor Center (University Hall, Room 101, Oxford/ University Ave., 642-5215, M-F at 1 & M, W, F at 10). Reservations are not necessary. A self-guiding tour brochure is always available.

### • Botanical Garden
*On Centennial Dr., 642-3343; daily 9-4:45; tours Sat & Sun at 1:30; free; free parking lot adjoins; picnic tables.*

Located behind the main campus in lush Strawberry Canyon, this "library of living plants" covers over 30 acres and contains over 8,000 different types of plants. The plants are organized into sixteen collections according to geographic origin, taxonomic affinity, and economic value. Of special interest are the herb garden, rhododendron dell, redwood grove, California native plants area, and Chinese medicinal herb garden stocked with over 90 rare plants. Children particularly enjoy the greenhouse filled with carniverous plants and the lily pond stocked with colorful koi. Grassy areas perfect for picnicking are scattered throughout this peaceful spot.

### • Campanile
*In center of campus, 642-3666.*

Modeled after the slightly taller campanile in St. Marks Square in Venice, this campus landmark stands 307 feet tall (30 stories). When classes are in session, concerts are hand-played on its 61-bell carillon three times each day (at 7:50 a.m., noon, and 6 p.m.). Each Sunday at 2 there is a 45-minute recital—a perfect time to enjoy a picnic in the surrounding area.

An elevator (daily 10-4:15; 50¢) takes visitors up 200 feet to an observation platform, where a 360-degree view of the area may be enjoyed.

### • Food Stalls
*Telegraph Ave./Bancroft Way, M-F 11-3, more or less; $; no reservations; no cards.*

Located at the entrance to the campus, these stands usually offer a

choice of donuts, soft pretzels, fresh juices and smoothies, falafel (a Middle Eastern vegetarian sandwich made with pocket bread), sandwiches, fresh fruit, Chinese, Mexican, and Japanese items . . . and much more.

Once you've gathered up your meal, find a nice spot on the nearby benches, steps, or grassy areas and then sit back and watch the amazing free floor show surrounding you.

This famous intersection attracts all types of entertainers—jugglers, musicians, revivalists—you name it. Keep your ears open for the free musical entertainment that often occurs on the lower **Sproul Plaza.**

### • Lawrence Hall of Science
For description see page 171.

### • Lowie Museum of Anthropology
*103 Kroeber Hall, Bancroft Way/College Ave., 643-7648; Tu-F 10-4:30, Sat & Sun 12-4:30; adults $1.50, 3-16 25¢, under 3 free.*

Part of the U.C. campus since 1901, this interesting museum stores the largest anthropological research collection (over 4 million artifacts) in the western United States. Exhibits change regularly.

## • Museum of Paleontology
*Earth Sciences Bldg., 1st, 2nd, & 3rd floors, 642-1821; M-F 8-5, Sat 8-12.*

This informal museum houses a variety of fossils, including a sabre tooth tiger—the California state fossil.

The Geology Department sponsors displays of photographs, rock specimens, and maps.

Also of interest in this building is the operating seismograph (earthquake recorder) located on the first floor.

---

## — PERFORMING ARTS —

---

### BERKELEY SHAKESPEARE FESTIVAL
*John Hinkel Park, Berkeley, 548-3422; June-Oct, W-Sat at 8, Sun at 2, some W & Sat matinees at 2; adults $10-$21, under 12 $10-$12.*

Dedicated to bringing Shakespeare to everyone—even children—this festival has been operating under the trees and the stars in **John Hinkel Park** since 1974. (It is scheduled to move to Orinda in 1991.)

The troupe expresses an interest in exposing young children to Shakespeare in a positive way. Children of all ages attend in great, happy numbers, and even the youngest are attentive to the action on stage. They seem to enjoy all the plays—even *Macbeth*. Because most people attending matinees are families, the audience then tends to be more tolerant of the sounds and movements of children.

Whatever you see, it helps to read the synopsis printed in the program to children ahead of time so that they can more easily follow the story.

Seating in the outdoor amphitheater is limited to 250 people per performance, allowing the audience a certain intimacy with the actors not possible in larger theaters. Seating is on the ground, so bring a padding of some sort to sit on as well as some pillows to buffer your back from the earthen wall.

It is customary to arrive about an hour early for a pre-performance picnic. Children may also enjoy the park's playground before and after the performance.

### CONCORD PAVILION
*2000 Kirker Pass Rd./Concord Blvd., Concord, 67-MUSIC; Apr-Oct; admission varies with show; fee ($3) parking lot adjoins; food service; strollers not permitted.*

Operated as a non-profit agency of the City of Concord, this stage presents top-name performers. Many programs are appropriate for children, while others are of interest mostly to teenagers or adults. The least expensive (and in my opinion the best) tickets are for lawn seating where you can enjoy a comfortable pre-performance picnic. Occasional free events are scheduled.

Bring protection from the sun during matinees and from the cold during evening performances. And don't forget a blanket. Bear in mind that the following are not allowed inside: bottles and cans (use a thermos or plastic container), animals, barbecues, lawn furniture, recording equipment, cameras.

If interested, inquire about the BART shuttle service.

### FANTASY FORUM
*350 Moraga Rd./Rheem Blvd., in the Rheem Theatre, Moraga, 943-5862; performances in Sept & Dec, troupe tours Bay Area Mar-June (call for schedule); tickets $4; free parking lot adjoins.*

Excitement runs high as children file into a theatrical performance by this troupe. Actors dressed in full storybook costume greet the audience and mingle with them once they are seated.

Children sit on a carpeted floor around the low stage. Cushioned seats are available for harder-to-please adults, but parents are welcome to join their children on the floor.

Fantasy Forum Actors Ensemble began presenting original musical adaptations of favorite fairy tales and stories in 1971. The troup consists of adults who work regular jobs during the week and devote their free time to acting. They are not paid for their efforts. They perform out of love. And so in a production of *Wizard of Oz* you see a corporate lawyer playing the Scarecrow without any brain, and a school principal who loves kids playing the Tin Man without any heart.

In keeping with a trim budget, the production is basically family-run: the founder is also the producer and director; his wife is one of the main actresses; his brother handles advance ticket sales; his father runs the ticket office during performances; his mother helps him write the scripts, music, and lyrics.

Zany humor, colorful staging and costumes, and exciting special effects make the performances appealing to all ages. Scripts play on several levels, with some jokes aimed over the kids' heads, especially at their parents. Children are encouraged by the script to speak out, and everyone loves it when they get excited or squeal with delight. And the company almost makes a trademark of always offering a moral lesson and of teaching the power of love and good acts.

When each performance is over and it is time to leave, children are bid farewell at the door by their new friends.

### KIDSHOWS
*2640 College Ave./Derby, Berkeley, 527-4977; Oct-Mar; tickets $5, under 1 free.*

This children's performance series for ages 3 through 8 presents programs in the beautiful redwood interior of the **Julia Morgan Theatre**. The intimate live theater programs are designed to inspire and move children, and parents usually enjoy them too. An informal atmosphere allows for interaction between the audience and the stage, so adults feel none of the usual pressure to hush their children.

Call for the current schedule.

Performances are also held in Walnut Creek at Civic Arts Theatre at 1963 Tice Valley Rd. (943-5862), in San Rafael (see p. 223), and in San Francisco (see p. 79).

## PACIFIC FILM ARCHIVE
*2625 Durant Ave./College Ave., Berkeley, 642-1412; adults $4.25, children $2.25; food service.*

Located in the basement of the University Art Museum and adjacent to The Swallow cafeteria, this film archive is known internationally for its film exhibition and scholarship.

Children's films are scheduled twice a month on Saturday afternoons at 3:30. Age recommendations are provided.

A charming **Teddy Bear Film Festival and Parade** is held annually in November on the weekend after Thanksgiving. Children are invited to bring their teddies and join in the informal parade which precedes. Favors

and balloons are awarded to all participants. Past films have included classics such as *A Pocket for Corduroy* (based on the book by Gary Templeton) and *Happy Birthday Moon* (an animated film about a bear who decides to give his friend, the moon, a birthday present). To avoid unbearable disappointment, purchase tickets in advance.

## PARAMOUNT THEATRE
*2025 Broadway/21st St., Oakland, 465-6400; tours 1st & 3rd Sat, $1/person; performances intermittent, $5-$11/person.*

This beautifully renovated art deco theater offers public tours. Note they are not appropriate for children under 10.

The theater also has an ongoing schedule of performances. Among the best for families are the **Organ Pops Series**, in which silent films are accompanied by live music, and the **Hollywood Movie Classics**, which features the best of the old movies. Based on personal experience, I recommend not taking children under age 5. Call for current schedule.

## U.C. THEATRE
*2036 University Ave./Shattuck Ave., Berkeley, 843-6267; adults $4.50-$5.50, under 12 $3.50.*

The big reason to come here is the ever-changing schedule of films. Something new (really something old) is shown every day on the huge screen (measuring 40 feet wide by 27 feet high) of the gargantuan 1917-vintage theater. Children's movies are also often revived. Call for current schedule.

Also of note are the snackbar items: good popcorn topped with real butter, made-from-scratch herbal ice tea, a variety of Calistoga waters, It's It and Haagen-Dazs ice creams, and Bette's Bake Shop goodies.

## WOODMINSTER AMPHITHEATER
*3300 Joaquin Miller Rd., off Hwy 13, Oakland, 531-9597; June-Sept; Thur-Sun, 8pm curtain; $8-$15, under 16 $1 discount; fee ($1.25) parking lot adjoins; picnic tables, food service.*

A pleasant way to spend a balmy summer evening is at a live performance here under the stars. The musical plays begin at dusk. Witnessing the deepening of evening and the slow appearance of the stars adds to the overall enjoyment of the production on stage.

The amphitheater seats approximately 1,500 people on tiers of wooden benches, and all seats offer good views of the stage.

Picnic tables are set up in redwood groves outside the theater and in an area behind the stage. Reservations are necessary. Refreshments at the concession are limited to peanuts, popcorn, soft drinks, and coffee.

Note that it sometimes gets chilly. Bring wraps. Also bring pillows or blankets to soften the strain of the wooden benches.

# — MUSEUMS —

## ALEXANDER LINDSAY JUNIOR MUSEUM
*1901 First Ave./Buena Vista, in Larkey Park, Walnut Creek, 935-1978; W-Sun 1-5; free.*

This small, hands-on museum houses a mini-zoo of animals which children can touch. For a small fee, children age 6 and older can **rent-a-pet** (rat, hamster, guinea pig, or rabbit) for a week at a time, cage included.

## JUDAH L. MAGNES MUSEUM
*2911 Russell St./College Ave., Berkeley, 849-2710; Sun-Thur 10-4; by donation; picnic tables.*

The first Jewish museum established in the western U.S., this institution exhibits Jewish ceremonial and fine arts from communities around the world. It is housed in a converted 1908 mansion, the gardens for which were landscaped by John McLaren, designer of Golden Gate Park.

Docent tours are available on Wednesdays and Sundays. Special children's programs are sometimes scheduled.

## LAWRENCE HALL OF SCIENCE
*Centennial Dr./Grizzly Peak Blvd., Berkeley, 642-5132; M-Sat 10-4:30, Sun 12-5; adults $3.50-$4, 7-18 $2.50-$3, 3-6 50¢-$1.50, under 3 free; free parking lot adjoins; food service.*

Located high in the hills behind the University of California campus, this participatory museum was established by the university in 1958 as a memorial to Ernest Orlando Lawrence. Lawrence developed the cyclotron and was the university's first Nobel laureate.

A button-pusher's paradise, it is filled with learning machines and computer games. There's also an Earthquake Information Center, a seismograph, and a mini-planetarium. A Wizard's Lab encourages do-it-yourself experiments—like standing your hair on end with static electricity—and a Biology Lab allows visitors to experiment with mazes and learn about a variety of small animals. Children's science classes and workshops are scheduled regularly, and children's films are shown on weekends and holidays. All this and a great gift shop, too!

**Dinosaur Days** begin each February and usually run through September. Life-like animated dinosaur models are displayed throughout the hall. Some are full size, and all make some sort of sound. Past supporting exhibits have included an assortment of real dinosaur fossils and a climb-in fiberglass dinosaur nest.

And yes, Virginia, there is junk food in Berkeley. It is alive and well at the **Galaxy Sandwich Shop** (642-3883), a short-order kitchen staffed mostly by U.C. students. Sandwiches are made in the kitchen, but you can also get soups, green salads, hot dogs, hamburgers, yogurt, and hard-

boiled eggs as well as muffins and fresh-baked cookies. Machines offer bags of chips, candy, and soft drinks. Thoughtfully, a computer, which is keyed to the menu and helps you score the nutritional value of your menu choices, is located in the hall outside the lunchroom.

This snackbar has an absolutely magnificent panoramic view of the bay and San Francisco. With a view like this, the facility could easily support an expensive gourmet restaurant. Fortunately for us, and in true

Berkeley fashion, this view has been reserved for "the people." I once saw a clever mom sipping coffee and mending clothes in this breathtaking setting—relaxing while her children were down the hall enjoying a film. Keep that in mind the next time you need a break and can't get a babysitter.

## LOWIE MUSEUM OF ANTHROPOLOGY

For description see page 166.

## MURIEL'S DOLL HOUSE MUSEUM

*33 Canyon Lake Dr., Port Costa, 787-2820; Tu-Sun 10-7; adults $1, 12 & under 25¢.*

Located in a wood-frame cottage a short walk down the road from the center of town, Muriel's collection includes between three and four thousand dolls. One of the latest additions is a Goodyear rubber doll made in 1851. Muriel personally tells visitors background stories.

The collection also includes some miniature scenes and a 1900 Bliss doll house. Don't miss seeing The Last Supper painted on a pinhead!

## MUSEUM OF PALEONTOLOGY

For description see page 167.

## OAKLAND MUSEUM

*1000 Oak St./10th St., Oakland, 273-3401; W-Sat 10-5, Sun 12-7; free; fee (40¢/hr) parking lot adjoins; food service.*

This beautifully designed tri-level museum is the only one in the state focusing on the art, natural sciences, and history of California. The state's history is presented as a panorama of man's experience in California dating from prehistoric times, and the Ecology Hall provides a miniature walk across the state—complete with appropriate plant and animal life.

Special children's programs are often scheduled.

Each spring, usually in April or May, there is a wonderful **Wildflower Show** in which hundreds of freshly-collected specimens are displayed. A different area of the state is represented each year.

## UNIVERSITY ART MUSEUM

*2626 Bancroft Way/College Ave., Berkeley, 642-1207; W-Sun 11-5; adults $3, 6-17 $2, under 6 free, admission free Thur 11-12; food service.*

Built in a cubist style of architecture, this U.C. museum is reminiscent of the Guggenheim in New York—except that it is angular instead of circular. Many people feel that the building itself is as interesting and unusual as its contents.

The museum's permanent collection stresses modern and Asian art and includes a large collection of paintings by Modernist Hans Hofmann.

In the basement, a casual cafeteria-style restaurant known as **The Swallow** (841-2409; L & D Tu-Sun; $; highchairs; children's portions; no reservations; no cards) is operated by a collective. Homemade soups and sandwiches are the menu mainstays, but daily specials usually include several creative salads (perhaps a potato and ham mixed with vinaigrette, or maybe a two-color corkscrew pasta with black olives, red and green peppers, and artichoke hearts tossed with an unusual cashew dressing), a quiche of the day, and something more substantial like baked chicken. A good choice for children are the half-sandwiches, served open-face on either whole wheat bread or a baguette.

Drinks include beer and wine and an assortment of Dr. Brown sodas, but no ice is provided. Desserts tend to be common but good—items like brownies and carrot cake.

Seating is in an attractive modern dining area with large windows looking out into the museum's sculpture garden, where diners may opt to enjoy their food al fresco.

---

# — OUTDOORS/PARKS —

---

### ADVENTURE PLAYGROUND
*Across from the Berkeley Marine Sports Center, 225 University Ave., Berkeley, 644-6530; Sat & Sun 11-4, open daily & for longer hours in summer; free; free parking lot adjoins; picnic tables.*

This unusual play area is styled after popular post-war European playgrounds. The story goes that after World War II an European playground designer built a series of modern playgrounds for children. But the kids continued, indeed preferred, to play in the bombed-out buildings and to construct their own play equipment from the plentiful rubble and debris. So at Adventure Playground there is a storage shed full of tools and scrap wood. Children can build forts and clubhouses and other things and leave them up, or tear them down, when they are done.

The playground also has a tire swing, a climbing net, and a fast-moving hanging trolley. Outside the fence there is a par course and a large grassy area with a more traditional tiny-tot play area.

Nearby, at the end of University Avenue near Skates restaurant, make note of the bow-and-arrow-weilding sculpture situated by the wayside. Apparently artist Fred Fierstein plopped it there himself in 1985 when he got tired of waiting for Berkeley politicians to decide to do it for him. He had offered **The Guardian** to the city at no cost, but it was rejected, after long deliberation, as too aggressive. Also, the animal appears to urinate when it rains. Recently Berkeley residents voted to keep it there. But things change. See it while you can.

## BERKELEY ROSE GARDEN
*On Euclid Ave. near Buena Vista Way, Berkeley, 644-6530; daily, sunrise to sunset; free.*

Planted at the turn of the century, this garden was originally conceived as a classical Greek arboretum. It is a particularly nice place to visit when the roses are in bloom in late spring and summer. Benches sheltered by arbors covered with climbing roses make for pleasant picnicking and provide gorgeous views of the bay and San Francisco. Tennis courts adjoin.

The garden is a popular spot for weddings, and most evenings find a knot of people at the top watching the sun set.

Across the street, **Codornices Park** features a playground with a long, exciting, and somewhat dangerous concrete slide.

## CHILDREN'S FAIRYLAND U.S.A.
*Grand Ave./Bellevue Ave., Oakland, 832-3609; in summer daily 10-4:30, in spring & fall W-Sun, in winter Sat & Sun; adults $2, 1-12 $1.50, under 1 free; fee parking lot adjoins; picnic tables, food service.*

This Fairyland was the first in the United States. In addition to seeing Mother Goose rhymes and fairy tales come to life, children are entertained with puppet shows, a mini-zoo of domestic animals, a maze, slides, and rides on a mini-carousel and -Ferris wheel. A "magic key" may be purchased for unlocking stories located throughout the enchanted land.

An orange pumpkin snackbar dispenses good, inexpensive foods: hot dogs, bagels with cream cheese, ice slushes made with fresh fruit, animal cookies, peanut butter & jelly sandwiches. You can even buy ice cream cones filled with feed pellets for the park's animals.

Very special programs are scheduled around the various holidays. For the annual **Jack-O-Lantern Jamboree** everyone is encouraged to come in costume and bring a bag for trick-or-treating at the fairytale theme sets. Children must be accompanied by an adult, and tickets must be purchased in advance. After Christmas, children are given the rare opportunity to spontaneously **Thank Santa** in person. The jolly one strolls the grounds, usually on the 26th and 27th. Call for current details on both events.

## CRAB COVE VISITOR CENTER
*1252 McKay Ave./Central Ave., Alameda, 521-6887; W-Sun 10-4:30, Mar-Nov; free; free parking lot adjoins; picnic tables.*

Dedicated to helping people understand the richness of the area's marine environment, this tiny center has three-dimensional exhibits and a saltwater aquarium. Exhibits also explain the area's past as Neptune Beach—the "Coney Island of the West." Nature classes for families and children are often scheduled.

**Crown Memorial State Beach** is adjacent. Because the water tends to be warm and shallow, it is a great place for wading. But no life guards are on duty.

A **Sand Castle Contest** is held at the beach each June. You can stand in the sand and watch, or you can actually enter the whimsical contest in one of its various categories. The single rule is that you may use only materials found on the beach.

The **Elsie B. Roemer Bird Sanctuary** is located at the southern end of the beach. A saltwater marsh, it is an excellent spot to observe shorebirds and waterfowl.

## DUNSMUIR HOUSE AND GARDENS

*2960 Peralta Oaks Ct., 1 block east of Hwy 580 at the 106th Ave. exit, Oakland, 562-0328; Apr-Sept, Sun 11-3; house tours at 1, 2, & 3; adults $3, under 12 $2; picnic tables.*

Built as a summer home in 1899, this majestic estate is a pleasant surprise for those unfamiliar with it. Tour the grand 37-room Colonial Revival-style Victorian mansion, and then enjoy a picnic and walk on the nearly 40 acres of grounds.

It may be of interest to know that among the movies filmed here are the horror film *Burnt Offerings* and the James Bond thriller *A View to a Kill*.

Each December the grounds are transformed into a wonderland for the **Christmas at Dunsmuir** event. The house is decked out in appropriate finery; the greenhouse becomes a crafts salesroom; and food service is provided in the old horse stalls. Details change from year to year, so call for current information.

## LAKE MERRITT
*In Oakland.*

More than just a lake, this beautiful expanse of water is the hub of a variety of activities.

At night, a lovely "Necklace of Lights" circles the lake and makes for a beautiful sight.

### • Camron-Stanford House
*1418 Lakeside Dr./14th St., 836-1976; W 11-4, Sun 1-5; adults $2, under 13 free.*

Five rooms of this 1876 Italianate-style Victorian house have been restored and furnished in period style. Visitors gets a guided tour and the chance to view a short film on Oakland's history.

Each September a **Preservation Fair** is held. In the past there have been demonstrations of turn-of-the-century arts and crafts, exhibits providing information on renovating and restoring Victorian buildings, and special activities for children.

### • Children's Fairyland U.S.A.
For description see page 175.

### • Rotary Natural Science Center
*Bellevue Ave./Perkins St., 273-3739; daily 10-5; free.*

Exhibits here inform visitors about the Bay Area's natural history. Just about everyone is fascinated by the center's real beehive. Nature films are shown on Sunday afternoons at 1:30.

A tiny tots playground is nearby. So is the **Lake Merritt Waterbird Refuge**. Designated as a wildlife refuge in 1870, it is the oldest in the country. And it's full of hungry fowl.

### • Sailboat House
*568 Bellevue Ave., near Grand Ave., 444-3807; daily 9-3:30, later in summer; boat rentals $4-$10/hr.*

Row boats, paddle boats, canoes, and sailboats are among the many vessels available for rental.

The replica Mississippi sternwheeler *Merritt Queen* may be boarded here for a thirty-minute tour of the lake (daily in summer, Sat & Sun rest of year, hours irregular; adults $1, under 12 50¢). You can charter the whole boat, which holds up to 32 people, for only $12 per half-hour.

During December, the *Merritt Queen* totes carolers around Lake Merritt on **caroling cruises**. A songleader is provided to keep things organized. Reservations are necessary, and the fee is a reasonable $12 (day) or $20 (evening) per half-hour.

### LAKE TEMESCAL REGIONAL RECREATION AREA
*6500 Broadway/Hwys 13 & 24, Oakland, 652-1155; daily 8-dusk, swimming area May-Oct only; adults $2, 6-17 $1, 2-5 50¢, under 2 free; fee ($2) parking lot adjoins; picnic tables, food service in summer.*

Opened as a recreation area in 1936, this scenic 48-acre park offers swimming, fishing, jogging, and hiking. There is also a rose garden and two children's play areas. The swimming area on the 13-acre artificial lake is roped off, and there is a raft to swim out to.

### MARINE WORLD AFRICA USA
*Marine World Parkway/Highway 37, Vallejo, 707/644-4000; W-Sun, daily in summer, 9:30-5 in winter, to 5:30 in spring & fall, to 6 in summer; adults $19.95, 4-12 $14.95, under 4 free; fee ($3) parking lot adjoins; food service, picnic tables; stroller rentals ($4/ day).*

The exciting animal shows here feature killer whales, dolphins, sea lions, elephants, chimpanzees, tigers, and exotic birds. Then there is the spectacular Water Ski & Boat Show put on by handsome and beautiful

daredevil humans. Shows are scheduled several times during the day, so it's a good idea to look at the schedule when you arrive and plan you itinerary.

Visitors may walk through animal habitat areas to see the African animals and to ride an Asian elephant or Dromedary camel ($2). When in this section, don't miss the Prairie Crawl—a maze of tunnels with dome pop-outs where you can stare at the prairie dogs (and they at you).

One of the newest attractions, **Butterfly World,** is the only walk-through free-flight butterfly habitat in the western United States. A walk-in Lorikeet Aviary provides up-close observation of these brightly colored birds.

Younger children will especially enjoy the Whale-of-a-Time-World playground. It features a punching bag forest, giant climbing net, and Gentle Jungle petting area. Pony rides are available in the summer (75¢).

The really young ones will appreciate the darling dolphin-shaped strollers available for rent. (Note that there are diaper-changing facilities and water faucets in *all* the restrooms. Yes, even the *men's*!)

Consider taking the ferry. Red & White Fleet (800/445-8880 or 546-2896) uses high-speed catamaran ferries which depart from Pier 41 at Fisherman's Wharf in San Francisco. BART (707/648-4666 or 788-2278) also provides service.

## MILLER/KNOX REGIONAL SHORELINE
*841 S. Garrard Blvd., Richmond, 233-8051; daily 7:30-dusk; free; free parking lot adjoins; picnic tables.*

This 259-acre park has benches where you can sit and enjoy the spectacular bay view. A one-mile long bike/jogging trail circles a salt-water lagoon, and there are also hiking trails. Wind conditions usually permit kite-flying. In warm weather it's enjoyable to lounge in the sand at **Keller Beach** and sunbathe. The chilly, dirty water does not invite swimming.

## NILES CANYON RAILWAY MUSEUM
*Main St./Foothill Rd., Sunol, 462-4557; 1st & 3rd Sun of month, 10-4; by donation; free parking lot adjoins.*

Operating from 1967 to 1985 as the Castro Point Railway in Richmond, this railway museum lost it's lease there and reopened in 1988 down the line a bit. Volunteers spent over two years re-laying the rail on abandoned Southern Pacific Lines.

Now refurbished steam and wood-burning engines follow the original route of the circa 1869 Transcontinental Railroad. They hiss and chug through a woodsy gorge while pulling a variety of vintage cars. The four-mile round-trip takes about 45 minutes.

A "museum" displays old train cars and locomotives in the process of being meticulously restored by members of the Pacific Locomotive Association.

## OAKLAND ZOO
*9777 Golf Links Rd., 98th Ave. exit off Hwy 580, in Knowland Park, Oakland, 632-9525; daily 10-4; adults $2.50, 2-14 $1.50, under 2 free; fee ($2; free 1st M of month) parking lot adjoins; picnic tables, food service; strollers available to rent ($2/day).*

THREE KIDS GET ACQUAINTED

Besides the smallish main zoo, there is also a Baby Zoo where children can get right in there and feed and pet small animals.

The kiddie ride area includes an aluminum carousel, built in 1951 by the Allan Herschel Company, and a train ride around the zoo in either a scale model of the turn-of-the-century-style Jupiter or the 1940s-era Streamliner. The Skyfari chairlift offers a particularly good view of the outstanding African Veldt enclosure and its watering hole for giraffes, ostriches, and several species of crane.

It seems worth the cost of joining the zoo just to attend the annual member's night **Zoofari** gala each September. The event includes dinner, rides, and behind-the-scenes tours.

### OLD BORGES RANCH
*1035 Castle Rock Rd., in Shell Ridge Recreation Area, Walnut Creek, 934-6990; daily dawn-dusk; free; picnic tables.*

Dedicated to displaying the realities of rural life in early California, this 1,400-acre park operates as a working cattle ranch. All kinds of farm animals are in residence: goats, horses, pigs, sheep, rabbits, and approximately 100 head of cattle. Children can pump water and ring the ranch hand bell. There are two barns, a working windmill, and a blacksmith shop as well. The 1901 farm house will open for tours when renovation is completed in the summer of 1990. Friday evening campfires are also scheduled to begin then.

The area also has over 100 miles of hiking trails, a playground, and a children's catch-and-release fishing pond. (Bring your own fishing pole and bait; chicken livers are popular with the fish.)

Tuesday through Saturday you may drive around the ranch. On Sunday and Monday you must park your car at the ranch entrance and walk a short distance in.

### PICK YOUR OWN PRODUCE
In the Delta farming community of Brentwood you can have an old-fashioned good time picking your own produce. Picking fruits fresh from the farm will save you money and assure fresh, quality produce, and it's a wonderful experience for children and adults alike.

Dress in old clothing, and plan to get dirty. Pack a picnic lunch, and stop to eat at some enticing spot along the road or at a farm picnic area.

For a free brochure giving the details, send a long stamped, self-addressed envelope to: Harvest Time, P.O. Box O, Brentwood 94513. The brochure tells whether you may pick the produce yourself or whether it is already picked but for sale at low farm-to-you prices. You can call the farms directly for further information.

Of special note is the **Smith Family Farm** (625-3544). During October they have hayrides to their pumpkin patch. During December there are horse-drawn carriage rides to their Christmas tree cutting area. And during the summer visitors may make use of a shaded picnic area.

## SHADOW CLIFFS REGIONAL RECREATION AREA
*2500 Stanley Blvd., 1 1/2 miles east of Main St., Pleasanton, 846-3000; daily 7-5, sometimes earlier & later; fee ($2-$3) parking lot adjoins; picnic tables, food service in summer.*

Formerly a sand and gravel quarry, this park now offers swimming in a clear, 80-acre man-made lake surrounded by a sandy beach. Lifeguards are on duty in summer. Fishing is good (no permit needed for children under 16), and boats are available to rent. More facilities include **The Rapids Waterslide** (829-6230; additional fee), a horse/bike trail and hiking path, and a good kite-flying spot.

## SHOREBIRD NATURE CENTER
*160 University Ave./Seawall Dr., Berkeley, 644-8623; M-Sat 11-4; free; free parking lot adjoins; picnic tables.*

This small center has a 100-gallon aquarium. Over 45 programs are available for children and families; call for descriptions and reservations.

Marina tours are given on Saturdays from 1 to 3 p.m. Tot Walks are led from 10 to 11 a.m. Both require reservations.

## TILDEN NATURE AREA
Though this beautiful, well-developed park is quite familiar to most Berkeley residents, many other Bay Area residents remain unaware of its pleasures. Numerous picnic spots, tables, and barbecues are scattered throughout.

The **Environmental Education Center** (525-2233; Tu-Sun 10-5; free) is a good place to get oriented and obtain current information on the hours and prices of the various park attractions. Informative programs and naturalist-guided walks—many especially designed for families and children—are regularly scheduled. Exhibits stress local natural history, and there is a collection of animal skins and nature relics meant to be handled.

Just outside the center is the **Little Farm** (daily 8:30-5; free). This brightly-painted, well-maintained farm is home to cows, donkeys, sheep, ducks, chickens, goats, rabbits, pigs, and assorted other barnyard animals, plus a pond full of ducks.

The **Pony Rides** (527-0421; weekends 11-5 spring and fall, weather permitting, daily in summer; $1.50) are a little further away. Children 2 and older are strapped securely into a saddle with a back support and given an exciting ride in the pony wheel. Children 5 and older may ride on the fast track in a larger ring.

An antique **merry-go-round** (524-6283; weekends 10-5, summer daily 11-5; 50¢)—one of only four remaining classic carousels in northern California—is located in the center of the park. This delightful specimen was

built in 1914 by the Herschell-Spillman firm in New York. It was restored in 1978. Before it was installed in Tilden in 1948 it had been used at Urbita Springs Park in San Bernardino, at Ocean Beach in San Diego, and at Griffith Park in Los Angeles. In addition to horses, it sports an assortment of beautifully colored animals including a stork, a dragon, and a frog. Its large band organ, which operates like a player piano, is regarded as one of the finest examples of its kind.

Across the street from the carousel, the **Botanic Garden** (841-8732; daily 10-5; free) features native plants and makes an ideal spot for a leisurely, quiet walk. Free tours are given at 1:30 p.m. on weekends, June through August. A scenic 18-hole golf course (848-7373) is nearby.

**Lake Anza** (848-3385; daily May-Oct 11-6; adults $2, 6-17 $1, 2-5 50¢, under 2 free) is a wonderful, low-key swimming area. A snack bar is available, and lifeguards are usually on duty.

On the outskirts of the park, the **Redwood Valley Railway** (548-6100; weekends 11-6 weather permitting, daily in summer 11-5; $1) is a 15-inch gauge, coal-burning miniature train. Its scenic route includes a few tunnels and bridges.

**EAST BAY REGIONAL PARK DISTRICT**

In this section I've listed a few of the most popular parks in the East Bay Regional Park District. For information on the many other parks in this system, call 531-9300 extension 278. Ask for a sample copy of the monthly publication *Regional Parks Log* which tells what's happening. You might also want to ask for a copy of the free booklet describing each of the 46 parks in detail.

## — MISCELLANEOUS —

**ALAMEDA PENNY MARKET**

*791 Thau Way, Alameda, 522-7206; Sat & Sun 7-4:30; adults 50¢, under 14 free; free parking lot adjoins; food service.*

Held in the Island Drive-In, this flea market is a wonderful place to browse and collect bargains.

**AUDUBON CELLARS WINERY**

*600 Addison St./2nd St., Berkeley, 540-5384; tasting & tours M-F 12-6; free; picnic tables; strollers not permitted on tours.*

A winery in Berkeley? Yes, that's right. But don't expect to see vineyards. This winery buys its grapes from growers in the Sonoma and Napa valleys.

If the kids get antsy while you are tasting, you can sometimes purchase classy Vinet—grape juice varietals mixed with sparkling spring water—to quench their thirst.

**BERKELEY ICELAND**

*2727 Milvia St./Derby St., Berkeley, 843-8800; open daily, call for hours; $4.50/person, skate rental $1.50; free parking lot adjoins; food vending machines.*

With a rink measuring 100 by 200 feet, this ranks as one of the two largest ice skating rinks in the country. (The other is in Lake Placid, New York.)

Another ice skating rink, **Dublin Iceland**, is located in Dublin (829-4444). These rinks are unaffiliated.

**CHABOT OBSERVATORY AND PLANETARIUM**

*4917 Mountain Blvd./Observatory Ave., Oakland, 531-4560; most F & Sat evenings at 7; adults $2, children $1-$1.50.*

Public planetarium programs include science demonstrations, a film, and the chance to view the heavens through a large telescope—the only twenty-inch telescope in the country regularly available to the public.

Call for current program schedule.

## FORTUNE COOKIE FACTORY
*261 12th St./Harrison St., Oakland,  832-5552; M-Sat 9-5; 75¢ person.*

This bakery makes unusual fruit-flavored fortune cookies. They will allow you to insert messages of your own composition. Call for details.

Tours of the factory are available on a drop-in basis for small family groups; large groups should call ahead for an appointment. The fee includes a bag of cookies.

## MALIBU CASTLE
*8000 S. Coliseum Way/Hwy 17, Oakland, 569-4612 & 635-8419.*

For description see page 207.

## OAKLAND HARBOR BOAT TOURS
*444-3188; Thur at 10 & 12, May-Aug; free.*

Sponsored by the Port of Oakland, these tours board at **Jack London Square** and last a little over an hour. Reservations are necessary.

After the tour you can watch boats on the estuary and browse in the many shops lining the waterfront. Also, if you're lucky you might be here at the right time to watch a train pass slowly by on the tracks running down the middle of the street.

## RICHMOND PLUNGE
*1 E. Richmond Ave./Garrard Blvd., Richmond, 620-6820; call for hours and admission fees; free parking lot adjoins.*

Renovated to appear as it did when it opened in 1926, this plunge has a large indoor pool that measures 160 by 60 feet, ranges from $2^1/_2$ to 9 feet deep, and features two diving boards. There is also a wading pool measuring 30 by 30 feet, ranging from 1 to 2 feet deep, and sporting a fountain in the center. The pools are kept at 82 degrees. Caps are not required, but you do need to bring your own towels.

## TAKARA SAKE USA
*708 Addison St./4th St., Berkeley, 540-8250; tasting daily 12-6; free.*

One of only three sake factories in the United States (the others are in Hollister and Honolulu), Takara Sake welcomes visitors to sample several kinds of sake and plum wine in their spacious tasting room.

Though children may not taste, they are welcome. It might be a smart idea to bring along something for them to snack on. They might especially enjoy taking their shoes off and then sitting in the raised tatami room; a hole is cut in the floor for dangling feet.

An informative slide show on the history and making of sake is shown upon request.

## TELEGRAPH AVENUE
When people visit Berkeley they usually want to see this infamous location—home of the well-publicized '60s demonstrations and riots. "Tele" or "The Ave," as it is fondly referred to by locals, still looks much as it did then but is now usually a lot quieter. And now there are plenty of interesting shops and street vendor stalls. (Remember—this is where street art *began*).

Stop in at **Cody's** bookstore (#2454). Open long hours, it is a Berkeley institution and stocks obscure publications along with the latest bestsellers. Poetry readings are scheduled most Wednesday evenings, and there is a well-stocked kid's section. Then cross the street to **The Med** (#2475) for a cup of cappuccino and piece of super chocolate layer cake with rum custard filling; children like the soothing hot almond milk.

## WALNUT CREEK MODEL RAILROAD SOCIETY
*2751 Buena Vista Ave., in Larkey Park, Walnut Creek, 937-1888; open last F of month 8-10pm, also weekend before & after Thanksgiving (call for dates, days, & times), also usually last Sun in Apr; adults $1.50, 6-12 50¢, under 6 free; free parking lot adjoins; picnic tables, food service in Nov only; strollers not recommended.*

The large and elaborate layout of mountains, bridges, and towns measures 54 by 32 feet and has more than 4,300 feet of track. According to their brochure it is "the most mountainous and one of the largest exclusively HO scale lines in the United States." Society members demonstrate their trains and answer questions, and every hour on the half hour the lights dim and then flash to simulate nightfall and a storm.

## WEIBEL VINEYARDS
*1250 Stanford Ave., Mission San Jose, 656-2340; tasting daily 10-5, tours M-F 10-12 & 1-3; picnic tables.*

Located on the site of the old Leland Stanford Winery, this tasting room provides samples of sparkling and dessert wines. Children can try the non-alcoholic Champagnette. I always like to get a bottle of the red wine vinegar flavored with garlic to take home.

After selecting your wines, retire to the arbor-shaded picnic area for a leisurely lunch.

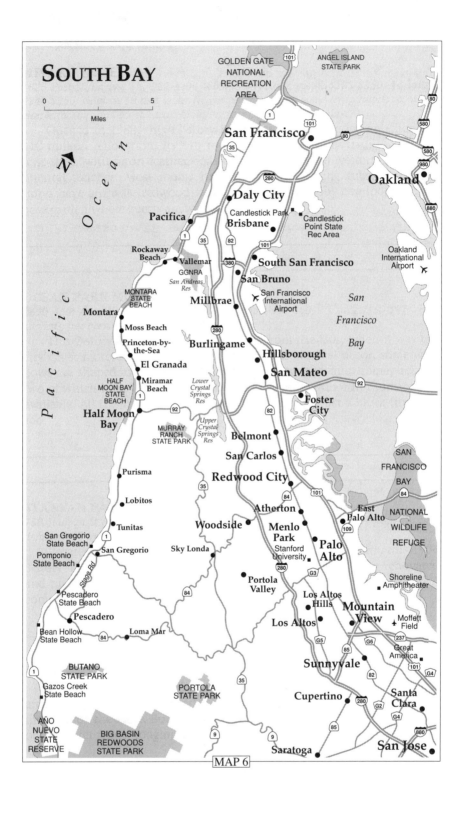

# SOUTH BAY

0        5
Miles

GOLDEN GATE
NATIONAL
RECREATION
AREA
101

ANGEL ISLAND
STATE PARK

80

1
101
580

**San Francisco**
35
80

580

980

**Oakland**

280
880

**Daly City**

**Pacifica**

Candlestick Park
**Brisbane**

Candlestick
Point State
Rec Area

Rockaway
Beach
**Vallemar**
GGNRA
San Andreas
Res

35
82
101

**South San Francisco**

**San Bruno**

Oakland
International
Airport

MONTARA
STATE
BEACH

**Montara**

**Millbrae**

San Francisco
International
Airport

*San*

*Francisco*

**Moss Beach**

280

*Bay*

**Princeton-by-
the-Sea**

**Burlingame**

**Hillsborough**

**El Granada**

**San Mateo**

HALF
MOON BAY
STATE
BEACH

**Miramar
Beach**

1

Lower
Crystal
Springs
Res

82

92

**Foster
City**

**Half Moon
Bay**

92

Upper
Crystal
Springs
Res

MURRAY
RANCH
STATE PARK

**Belmont**

**San Carlos**

SAN

FRANCISCO

BAY

**Purisma**

**Redwood City**

35

84

101

84

**Lobitos**

**Atherton**

East
**Palo Alto**

NATIONAL

**Tunitas**

**Woodside**

**Menlo
Park**

109

WILDLIFE

REFUGE

San Gregorio
State Beach

1

**San Gregorio**

Sky Londa

Stanford
University

**Palo
Alto**

Pomponio
State Beach

280

G3

Shoreline
Amphitheater

Stage Rd

**Portola
Valley**

**Los Altos
Hills**

**Mountain
View**

Pescadero
State Beach

84

**Los Altos**

Moffett
Field

**Pescadero**

Loma Mar

G5

G6

237

Bean Hollow
State Beach

84

Great
America

101

G4

BUTANO
STATE PARK

**Sunnyvale**

82

G4

1

35

Gazos Creek
State Beach

**Cupertino**

280

G2

**Santa
Clara**

AÑO
NUEVO
STATE
RESERVE

BIG BASIN
REDWOODS
STATE PARK

PORTOLA
STATE PARK

85

G4

880

9

9

**Saratoga**

**San Jose**

MAP 6

# South Bay

## Where To Eat

### ALLIED ARTS GUILD RESTAURANT

*95 Arbor Rd., Menlo Park, 324-2588; L M-Sat at 12, 12:30, 1, & 1:15, afternoon snack M-F 2-3:30; $; highchairs, booster seats; 100% non-smoking; free parking lot adjoins; reservations essential; no cards.*

This is the absolutely perfect spot to take Grandma for lunch when she is in town.

Originally a tearoom, this restaurant opened in 1932. In those days guild members prepared food in their homes and transported it to the premises for serving. Now a modern kitchen aids volunteers in preparing three-course luncheons which include a soup, hot entree with vegetable or salad, freshly-baked rolls, dessert, and choice of beverage. The menu is different each day, and all the recipes are for sale. One luncheon I enjoyed consisted of green vegetable soup, a colorful lemon-applesauce gelatin mold, tasty and tender turkey roulades stuffed with a cream cheese filling, tiny soft dinner rolls, and a rich brownie pie.

Peanut butter & jelly sandwiches and pizza are available for children, or they are welcome to share. My young daughter shared with me, and I also ordered her a refreshing glass of homemade fruit punch.

The afternoon snack consists of a dessert and beverage.

In warm weather an attractive patio is opened for dining; you must request it when you reserve.

Volunteers from the Palo Alto auxiliary of Children's Hospital at Stanford own and manage everything. Profits and tips are used to help support the hospital.

Allow time to wander through the attractive shops and peaceful gardens and courtyards scattered throughout the Spanish Colonial-style estate.

## BENIHANA OF TOKYO
*1496 Old Bayshore Hwy, Burlingame, 342-5202; 2074 Valco Fashion Park, Cupertino, 408/253-1221.*

For description see page 52.

## BROTHERS DELICATESSEN AND RESTAURANT
*1351 Howard Ave./El Camino Real, Burlingame, 343-2311; B, L, & D daily; $; high-chairs, booster seats, booths; free parking lot adjoins; reservations suggested; AE, MC, V.*

Transplanted Chicagoans and New Yorkers are always looking for a good deli out here. Even one that just comes close to what they were raised with is appreciated.

Brothers Deli comes close. My husband, a tough-to-please-when-it-comes-to-delis native Chicagoan, says it will do but "there are not enough old Jewish men and women sitting around talking in Eastern European accents to qualify as a truly great deli." But the corned beef in his sandwich was almost as lean as he remembered, and he was excited to see rice pudding on the menu.

Sitting in a comfortable booth in the noisy coffee shop-style dining room, I was pleased with my hot pastrami sandwich on rye—though I would have preferred dark rye and more Thousand Island dressing. But then I'm a native San Franciscan. I also enjoyed a generous chocolate phosphate.

To my daughter's satisfaction, her bagel was served with an overflowing cuplet of cream cheese and two smaller cuplets of butter and jam.

The extensive menu also offers many, many more sandwiches (including a hot dog, grilled cheese, and peanut butter & jelly), some hot plates and salads, a large variety of homemade soups (cold beet borscht, chicken noodle, matzo ball), and even a variety of hamburgers. There is something for everyone. Desserts include homemade strudel, a variety of cheesecakes (strawberry, chocolate, New York), and also regular cakes (poppyseed, German chocolate, carrot). Breakfast features omelettes, eggs, pancakes, corned beef hash, lox, and matzo brie.

Everything on the menu can be packed to go.

And believe it or not, this place is owned and operated by a *Chinese* couple!

## THE CASTAWAY
*Coyote Point Dr., San Mateo, 347-1027; L M-Sat, D daily, SunBr; $$; highchairs, booster seats, booths; children's portions; free parking lot adjoins; reservations suggested; AE, DC, MC, V.*

Though weekday lunch and dinner seem not as amenable to children, Sunday brunch here is perfect for families. There are numerous booths for tucking away wiggly kids, spacious tables with old-fashioned pressed-back oak chairs, and beautiful views of the Bay.

The buffet offers items such as eggs Benedict, quiche Lorraine, french toast, made-to-order omelettes, and Belgian waffles. Foods are served at various themed stations: a pasta bar; a seafood bar; a carving station with roast beef, ham, and turkey; an ice cream bar; etc.

Complimentary champagne is included (fresh-squeezed o.j. for the kids). Exotic drinks such as mai tais, banana and strawberry daiquiris, piña coladas, and strawberry Margaritas are available from the bar.

## CELIA'S
*504 Peninsula Ave., San Mateo, 343-5886; 423 University Ave., Palo Alto, 322-5900.*
For description see page 29.

## CHEF CHU'S
*1067 N. San Antonio Rd./El Camino Real, Los Altos, 948-2696; L & D daily; $$; high-chairs, booster seats, booths; take-out delivery; free parking lot adjoins; reservations suggested; AE, DC, MC, V.*

Chef Chu watches closely over his large kitchen staff and sees to it that excellence prevails. Impressive dishes include crisp fried won tons (served at room temperature with a blood-red sweet and sour sauce), Szechwan beef (deep-fried, tossed with a tasty sauce, and served over rice noodles), and a magnificent hot and sour soup fragrant with sesame oil. Children tend to enjoy the particularly good mu shu pork, served here with unusual square pancakes for wrapping. And then there's the lemon chicken, a beautifully presented dish consisting of deep-fried whole chicken breasts glazed with a lemon sauce and topped with a thin slice of lemon and a bright red maraschino cherry. Indeed, the menu is full of promising new pleasures to try on return visits.

A touch of elegance is provided by cloth-covered tables. In the evening cloth napkins are folded to resemble flowers and then tucked into glasses. Should there be a wait to be seated, the reception area has a large window providing interesting views of the busy kitchen.

## CHEVYS
*2907 El Camino Real, Redwood City, 367-6892.*
For description see page 136.

## COMPADRES MEXICAN BAR & GRILL
*3877 El Camino Real, Palo Alto, 858-1141.*
For description see page 29. At this branch children are weighed in and charged five cents per pound for a child's meal of tacos or enchiladas served with rice, beans, a kiddie kocktail, and ice cream!

## DAN'S PLACE
*Etheldore St./Virginia Ave., Moss Beach, 728-3343; D daily; $-$$; highchairs, booster seats; reservations suggested on weekends; MC, V.*

Judging from the outside you would probably be inclined to pass this

spot by, figuring it was just a local bar. But once people get through the bar in front to the restaurant in back, they find a large, casual dining hall. Tables are covered with red-and-white-checked cloths, and two walls of big windows look out over the ocean.

The clientele is basically townspeople who have patronized the restaurant for years. They come for the bargain family-style dinners which include a relish plate, soup or salad, pasta, entree (always fish plus a daily special), bread and butter, and coffee. A large a la carte menu includes seafood, fresh steamed clams in season, steaks, fried chicken, and veal and pasta dishes—all served with relishes, a choice of vegetable or pasta, and bread and butter. For an additional charge a complete dinner includes soup, appetizers, green salad, three marinated salads (cucumbers, beans, roast beef and potato), vegetable, ravioli, spaghetti, and coffee.

Children are welcome to share or split an order, and there are plenty of appropriate side dishes for them. If all else fails, consider chicken nuggets and fries which is available off the menu.

## DEMETRIS
*174 E. Third Ave./Ellisworth Ave., San Mateo, 340-9242; B & L M-Sat; $; highchairs, booster seats; no reservations; no cards.*

Whether you are eating in or out, orders are placed at the counter. If you are taking your order out for a picnic, ask the clerk to pack your selections to go. If you're eating in, select a table, and a server will deliver your order to your table when it is ready.

There are the usual deli items here, plus plenty of made-to-order sandwiches. You can also get gigantic arum sandwiches (rolled cracker bread stuffed with assorted goodies) and authentic homemade Greek spanakopita (spinach and Feta cheese wrapped in a triangle of flaky filo pastry).

With at least two day's notice, several picnic boxes are available. One includes a choice of barbecued chicken or ribs, either chile or baked beans, coleslaw, potato salad, and rolls or corn muffins with butter. Another includes a sandwich, soft drink, chips or salad, fruit, and a cookie or brownie. Yet another includes cold fried chicken, a drink, salad, fruit, and a cookie or brownie. If you really want to wow your family, especially if you have a BIG family, pre-order the sandwich measuring between four and six feet long.

The extensive breakfast menu includes ten kinds of omelettes, eggs Benedict, corned beef hash, regular egg items, and pancakes. There are also plenty of side orders that are sure to please kids: oatmeal, cream of wheat, donut, bagel and cream cheese, etc.

## DUARTE'S TAVERN
*202 Stage Rd., Pescadero, 879-0464; B, L, & D daily; $-$$; highchairs, booster seats, booths; reservations taken for dinner; AE, MC, V.*

Since 1894 diners having been coming here to enjoy drinks in the old-time bar and a homecooked meal in the cozy, casual coffee shop.

My favorite meal here is weekend breakfast, served until 3. The menu offers giant buttermilk pancakes (children may order a short stack) and outstanding omelettes (the artichoke—sauteed with garlic and olive oil—and the linguica—made with spicy Portuguese sausage) as well as the more usual breakfast items. Omelettes are available all day and come with chunks of fried unpeeled potatoes and sourdough toast.

Items available at both lunch and dinner include creamy artichoke heart soup, fresh artichoke hearts, fried oysters, homemade pies, fresh applesauce, and deep-fried prawns or chicken with fries. Hamburgers, grilled cheese, and peanut butter & jelly sandwiches are also available.

Dinner entrees include pork and lamb chops and grilled fresh fish. All are served with soup or salad, delicious mashed potatoes made from scratch, a fresh vegetable, and sourdough bread. Daily specials are posted on the wall.

Artichoke items are made with fresh artichokes from the nearby fields.

Reservations are essential for the very popular Friday, Saturday, and Sunday night prix fixe cioppino (seafood soup) feeds.

A walk through this tiny agricultural town takes you past colorful fields of straw flowers, an old-fashioned general store, and a 123-year-old church. For a lovely ride through the backcountry, take the quiet, winding road beginning in front of Duarte's and follow it seven miles north to San Gregorio, where the **Peterson and Alsford General Store** makes an interesting place to stop for picnic supples.

## EMIL VILLA'S HICK'RY PIT
*2310 Homestead Rd./Foothill Blvd., in Foothill Plaza, Los Altos, 408/720-8733; 980 E. Campbell Ave./Bascom Ave., Campbell, 408/371-2400.*

For description see page 140.

## FISH TRAP
*281 Capistrano Rd./Hwy 1, Princeton-by-the-Sea, 728-7049; L & D daily; $-$$; highchairs, booster seats; children's portions; free parking lot across street; no reservations; no cards.*

A view of the harbor and casual atmophere make this tiny roadside diner a pleasant stop for a quick meal. In addition to a rustic interior room, there is a glassed-in deck with heat lamps. Though there is sometimes a short wait to be seated, service is quick, encouraging a fast turnover.

Lunch is served until 5 and includes seafood items such as clam chowder, bouillabaisse, fish & chips, and calamari as well as hamburgers. The dinner menu additionally offers scallops, prawns, and steak—all served with a choice of homemade soup (usually a white clam chowder) or crisp salad, french bread, french fries or a baked potato, and a vegetable. The specialty of the house is rockfish fresh off the harbor fishing boats. It is available either broiled or dipped in batter and deep-fried tempura-style.

Children's dinners are a choice of fish & chips, calamari, prawns, or cheese bread.

## THE GOOD EARTH
*185 University Ave./Emerson St., Palo Alto, 321-9449; B, L, & D daily; $-$$; highchairs, booster seats, booths; separate children's menu; free parking lot adjoins; no reservations; AE, DC, MC, V.*

If your family has a tendency to turn up their noses at "natural foods," this comfortable restaurant is capable of changing their minds and maybe their habits. An impressive selection of food that is both tasty and nutritious is on the menu. The restaurant's aim is to eliminate overprocessed foods and refined sugar in favor of fresh fruits and vegetables.

Breakfast items include hot cakes with molasses-honey syrup and a variety of muffins. Omelettes, served with ten-grain toast, are available all day.

Salads include a Very Veggie (greens, cheeses, vegetables, marinated beans, mushrooms, chopped egg) and a Rainbow Supreme (fresh fruit served with a choice of cottage cheese, frozen or plain yogurt, or ice cream). Creative sandwiches include a very popular and extremely good cashew chicken, Charlie's almond tuna (with water chestnuts, celery, and chutney), and a planet burger (patty is made with vegetables, grains, nuts, and beans). Hot entrees include a walnut mushroom au gratin casserole and, for meat eaters, a country-style meatloaf made with organic beef.

Fruit shakes are made with high protein powder, honey, and frozen yogurt. They have enticing names like The Surfer (pineapple juice, coconut milk, banana) and Power Plus (carob powder, coconut milk, banana, nuts, and dates).

And the kids aren't left out. Their menu is decorated with games to keep them busy. Selections include a whole wheat tortilla pizza, a burrito, a miniature hamburger, and a grilled cheese sandwich.

Branches under the same ownership are in Cupertino at 20807 Stevens Creek Boulevard (408/252-3555), in Santa Clara at 2705 The Alameda (408/984-0960), and in Los Gatos at 206 North Santa Cruz Avenue (408/396-6868). Branches under separate ownership are in Berkeley (see p. 143) and Larkspur (see p. 213).

## HEIDI PIES

*1941 S. El Camino Real/20th Ave., San Mateo, 574-0505; B, L, & D daily; $; highchairs, booster seats; separate children's menu; free parking lot adjoins; no reservations; AE, MC, V.*

The selection of fresh homemade pies here is constantly replenished from the kitchen in back. Pie choices include fruit (raisin and gooseberry in addition to more common varieties), meringue (black bottom, banana), and specialty (German chocolate, pecan, cream cheese). My own favorite is the rich chocolate cream. The specialty of the house is hot apple pie, available plain or a la mode as well as with hot cinnamon sauce, whipped cream, or either cheddar or American cheese. Short order items, including a hamburger and grilled cheese sandwich, comprise the rest of the menu.

Between 2 and 4 p.m., coffee is only 30 cents when ordered with pie. Whole pies are available for take-out.

## HOBEE'S

*12 Bayhill Shopping Center, San Bruno, 588-9662; 4224 El Camino Real/Charleston, Palo Alto, 856-6124; 67 Town & Country Village/El Camino Real, Palo Alto, 327-4111; 2312 Central Expressway/Rengstorff, Mountain View, 968-6050; 21267 Stevens Creek Blvd., Cupertino, 408/255-6010; 920 Town & Country Village/Stevens Creek Blvd., San Jose, 408/244-5212.*

For description see page 144.

## HORKY'S
*1316 El Camino Real/Harbor Blvd., Belmont, 591-7177; L M-Sat, D daily; $$; high-chairs, booster seats; children's portions; no reservations; AE, DC, V.*

The menu here, in the format of a newspaper, informs diners that it takes ten to thirty minutes to prepare an order and encourages relaxation. It also relays the history of both the restaurant and its Mexican cuisine.

Appetizers include a cheese crisp (flour tortilla topped with melted cheese and green chilies) and nachos (tortilla chips topped with refried beans, melted cheese, and a spicy sauce). Among the more unusual entrees are an enchilada suprema de cangrejo (crab and picadillo sauce rolled in a tortilla and topped with melted Jack cheese, a green sauce, guacamole, sour cream, and more crab), mole poblano (boneless chicken cooked in a sauce of chocolate, chili, sesame, and other spices), camarones rancheros (prawns sauteed in a sauce of tomato, green chili, and capers), and nopales y chile con carne (chile made with cactus). Fried chicken and a hamburger are also available.

Desserts include Mexican hot chocolate and flan.

## LATE FOR THE TRAIN
*150 Middlefield Rd./Willow Rd., Menlo Park, 321-6124; B, L, & D Tu-Sat, SunBr; $$; highchairs, booster seats; 100% non-smoking; free parking lot adjoins; reservations suggested (not taken for SunBr); AE, MC, V.*

This formula-free restaurant features several different dining areas. Outdoor seating is particularly pleasant in good weather. An interesting collection of old-time sugar bowls and salt-and-pepper shakers decorate the tables.

Meals are made to order with organic, additive-free ingredients whenever possible, and very little red meat is used. At brunch delicious eggs piperade is a two-egg omelette served with a fantastic scone and sides of both delicious fried potatoes and a mixture of lightly sauteed bell peppers, onions, and tomatoes. The Lazy Susan (a choice of three: two eggs, fried potatoes, tabouleh, cottage cheese, fruit wedges, a small juice, toast, a scone) seems a good selection for children. Blintzes, whole grain pancakes, and various omelettes are also on the menu as are assorted sandwiches, salads, and hot entrees. Fresh-squeezed orange juice, continental coffees, and several champagne drinks round things out.

The lunch and dinner menus feature seafood, chicken, pasta, and vegetarian entrees.

Ask about half-price portions for children. Should your child become restless during any wait, head for the toy chest in the waiting area.

## THE MAGIC PAN
*70 Hillsdale Mall, San Mateo, 345-8557; 222 Oakridge Mall, San Jose, 408/629-3000; and 335 S. Winchester St., San Jose, 408/247-9970.*

For description see page 47.

## MARIE CALLENDER'S
*4710 El Camino Real/San Antonio Rd., Los Altos, 941-6989; L & D daily; $; high-chairs, booster seats, booths; children's portions; free parking lot adjoins; no reservations; MC, V.*

Pie is the name of the game here. Choose from standards (like apple, berry, and banana cream) as well as more unusual ones (like black bottom, rhubarb, and peanut butter). Fresh uncooked strawberry and peach are available in season. But in my opinion the sour cherry, available only around Valentine's Day and Washington's Birthday, is the best. Pies are made in the kitchen, crusts are light and flaky, and any can be purchased to take home.

The menu includes homemade chile and soups, several kinds of hamburgers, pot pies, croissant sandwiches, pastas, and a salad bar.

All this is enjoyed in an attractive setting of lace-covered windows and comfortable padded booths with beveled-glass partitions.

Branches are in Milpitas at 333 Abbott Street (408/263-PIES), in San Jose at 780 South Winchester Boulevard (408/243-9018), and in Sunnyvale at 751 East El Camino (408/245-3710). Another branch is in Pleasanton (see p. 150).

## MAX'S OPERA CAFE
*1250 Old Bayshore, Burlingame, 342-MAXS; 711 Stanford Shopping Center, Palo Alto, 323-MAXS.*

For description see page 49.

## MIRAMAR BEACH INN
*131 Mirada Rd., off Hwy 1, 3 miles north of Half Moon Bay, 726-9053; L M-F, D daily, Sat & SunBr; $$-$$$; highchairs, booster seats, booths; children's portions; reservations suggested; MC, V.*

Situated across the street from the ocean in a somewhat isolated spot, this casual restaurant offers expansive views and is especially nice for Sunday brunch. The a la carte menu then offers a variety of seafood and egg combinations as well as eggs Benedict and sourdough french toast. An all-you-can-eat buffet, which includes champagne, is also available.

The lunch menu has salads, hot sandwiches (including several hamburgers), omelettes, and homemade chowder with garlic bread. The pricier dinners include seafood, steak, and pasta and come with salad, fresh vegetables, rice pilaf, and bread and butter. Many customers stick around for the live rock music which begins at 10 p.m. on Friday and Saturday nights; the cover is half-price with dinner.

Smaller portions are available for children, and the price is adjusted according to age and appetite. A grilled cheese sandwich will be made upon request.

After brunch, visit the beach behind the rocky breakfront in front of the restaurant to take a walk, sunbathe, or build a sand castle. Look closely and you may even see a flock of brown pelicans bobbing on the surf and diving for food.

## PASAND
*3701 El Camino Real/Lawrence Expressway, Santa Clara, 408/241-5150.*
For description see page 153.

## PINE BROOK INN
*1015 Alameda de las Pulgas/Ralston Ave., Belmont, 591-1735; L M-Sat, D Tu-Sun, SunBr seatings at 10:30, 12:15, and 1:45; $$; highchairs, booster seats, booths; children's portions; free parking lot adjoins; reservations essential; AE, MC, V.*

Because it is located in a shopping center, I was surprised that this restaurant is both unusual and exceptional. The treehouse effect in the main dining room, which is perched overlooking a nursery and has large windows framed with hanging plants, is enhanced by a huge pine tree growing right through cut-outs in the floor and ceiling.

After being seated, brunch diners are offered a choice of drinks—coffee, orange juice, milk, and champagne (two refills are included). Water arrives in fancy goblets and is given further flair with a floating slice of lemon. Then comes a basket full of hot muffins and sweet rolls, and also dishes of fresh fruit adorned with fresh flowers. Service is fast and attentive. When you're ready, it's off to the hot buffet to fill your plate with sausage, bacon, ham, roast beef, fried chicken, scallops and shrimp in a brandy sauce, smoked fish, spinach souffle, scrambled eggs with mushrooms, crepes stuffed with apples, hash-browned potatoes, eggs Benedict, french toast, blueberry pancakes, assorted salads—and more!

If your children are small eaters, ask your server to determine a fair charge based on what the child actually eats. When you've finished eating, you can all play "restaurant critic" by filling out the form soliciting your comments and suggestions.

Brunch usually is a noisy time, when the classical music playing in the background can barely be heard above the din—a perfect situation for families. The lunch and dinner atmosphere is quieter. These menus include a hamburger and hot dog (bratwurst) for children. Adult specialties include sauerbraten, several schnitzels, and fresh fish.

The **Carlmont Nursery**, located adjacent to the restaurant, is pleasant for after-brunch browsing. **Twin Pines Park**, located four or five blocks east on Ralston Avenue, has a playground, nature trail, and picnic area.

## PIZZA & PIPES
*821 Winslow St./Broadway, Redwood City, 365-6543; L & D daily; $; highchairs; metered parking lot adjoins; reservations accepted; no cards.*

The huge Wurlitzer theater pipe organ housed here was transplanted from the Fifth Avenue Theatre in Seattle, Washington, where it was used in the 1920s and '30s as the sound accompaniment to silent movies.

When it is being played (Tu-Sun 6:30 to closing), all conversation is drowned out by lively renditions of "The Mickey Mouse Club Theme," "Chattanooga Choo Choo," and other all-time favorites. Kids love it. Some sing along, while others jump out of their seats to view the movement of the glass-encased pipes. This is definitely the place to go when your children are cranky and ill-behaved. If they don't actually change their mood and have a good time, at least you won't be able to hear them.

Incidentally, the pizza is quite good. You can choose from the more common types as well as the likes of a Canadian bacon, with either pineapple or tomatoes, and a vegetarian. I was told by the manager, "We make anything." Sandwiches, nachos, garlic and cheese bread, and a salad bar are also available. Drinks include beer, wine, and soft drinks.

Branches are in Daly City at the Serramonte Shopping Center (994-2525) and in Santa Clara at 3581 Homestead Road (408/248-5680).

### THE POT STICKER
*3708 S. El Camino Real/37th Ave., San Mateo, 349-0149; L & D daily; $$; highchairs, booster seats; free parking lot adjoins; reservations suggested; AE, DC, MC, V.*

With cloth-covered tables and carpeted floors, this popular restaurant provides a quiet refuge from the busy street on which it is located.

The Chinese Mandarin-style cuisine served here is lightly spiced, has very little sauce, and is heavy on the vegetables—especially celery. The menu has many expected items such as hot and sour soup, sizzling rice soup, Mongolian beef, and princess chicken (small chicken cubes sauteed with chopped celery and peanuts and just a tad of hot bean sauce), as well as exotic items made with beef tripe and beef tendon. And, of course, potstickers.

Though kids probably won't be too fond of Hunan crispy whole fish, it is a dramatic item served with hot sauce. Clay-baked beggar's chicken and boneless Peking duck, cooked in a special oven, must be ordered two days in advance.

Two branches are in San Francisco (see p. 57).

### RUSTY PELICAN
*1094 N. Wolfe Rd., Cupertino, 408/255-6240.*
For description see page 153.

### SANTINI'S RESTAURANT
*2214 El Camino Real/22nd Ave., San Mateo, 341-5794; D Tu-Sun; $$; highchairs, booster seats, booths; children's portions; free parking lot adjoins; no reservations; MC, V.*

The choices on the menu here can be a bit overwhelming. There are nine spaghetti dishes, nine veal dishes, seventeen pizza combinations, and a wide variety of pastas, seafood, and steak. Complete dinners are available as well as a la carte portions.

My husband describes the informal atmosphere as typical of a Chicago neighborhood Italian restaurant—vinyl tablecloths and a blaring jukebox, practically unheard due to the din of happy diners.

## SCOTT'S SEAFOOD GRILL & BAR
*2300 E. Bayshore Rd., Palo Alto, 856-1046; 185 Park Ave., San Jose, 408/971-1700.*
For description see page 155.

## STAGECOACH RESTAURANT
*3062 Woodside Rd., Woodside, 851-8010; B & L daily, D W-M, Sat & SunBr; $-$$; highchairs, booster seats, booths; children's portions; free parking lot adjoins; reservations suggested; AE, MC, V.*

Though Woodside feels very rural, it is located just a few miles from bustling El Camino Real. It has been called the "horsiest community in the United States." It seems there are more horses per capita here than in any other community in the country! The four hitching posts located outside this restaurant's front door seem to back up that claim, and on weekends there are often horses and wagons "parked" there. For those of you arriving in the modern replacement for the horse, there are also plenty of parking spaces.

The mellow atmosphere inside is comfortable and unpretentious and accentuated with soft music and old oak furniture. At Sunday brunch choices include omelettes, french toast, huevos rancheros, and eggs Benedict—all served with a choice of bacon or sausage, fresh-squeezed orange juice, unlimited champagne, and coffee, tea, or milk. At lunch there are salads, sandwiches (including a grilled cheese), and twelve kinds of hamburgers as well as an assortment of hot entrees. Dinners are predominantly seafood but include steaks, veal, chicken, and pasta. Children's dinners are a choice of spaghetti, prawns, or hamburger.

Quality is high. All dressings, soups, and sauces are house-made, and vegetables are fresh and cooked to order.

This is a pleasant stop prior to visiting the backcountry reached by following Woodside Road.

## TACO BELL
*5200 Coast Hwy/Linda Mar Blvd., Pacifica, 355-0591; L & D daily; $; highchairs, booths; children's portions; free parking lot adjoins; no reservations; no cards.*

This restaurant is mentioned here because of its exceptional oceanfront location. The attractive redwood building in which it is located overlooks the ocean. When it gets crowded inside, it's just a few steps to a beach picnic. Free entertainment is provided by always-present surfers.

## T.G.I. FRIDAY'S

*3101 S. El Camino Real/Hillsdale Blvd., San Mateo, 570-4684; L M-F, D daily, Sat & SunBr; $-$$; highchairs, booster seats; separate children's menu; free parking lot adjoins; no reservations; AE, DC, MC, V.*

Where can a mom go for lunch with two giggly 10-year-old girls in tow? Where will the noise level cover their sometimes best-left-unheard comments, and where will the menu be a match for their strange appetites? Those were the questions.

Friday's fern bar was the unexpected answer. After we three were comfortably seated at a table covered with a cheerful red-striped plastic cloth, the girls were each given a box of crayons and their own coloring book menu. From what qualifies as the most extensive children's menu I've yet come across, they both chose a kid-sized shake and grilled cheese.

The sandwich was made with American cheese and white bread—the way they like it—and was served with a side of sizzling fries and garnish of apple wedges. One kid additionally polished off a cherry coke. But I had to finish the other's chocolate coke which was declared, unfairly in my opinion, "Gross." Other choices on the inexpensive children's menu include a hot dog, hamburger, peanut butter & jelly sandwich, and spaghetti.

While the girls got sillier, I sipped my tasty Tom Collins—made from scratch at the massive bar dominating the restaurant's center. My plate of chicken fingers (battered, deep-fried strips of chicken breast) was served with a bacon-mustard dipping sauce and sides of fries and coleslaw. The vast adult menu additionally offers everything from a french dip sandwich to a hamburger to a chimichanga to blackened filet mignon.

As we left, the girls each holding their parting gift of two helium-filled balloons, I kidded our cute young waiter, "I bet you're glad we're going." He replied sweetly, "I've had worse. Last weekend I had a toddler who liked to throw glasses."

I asked the girls what they had liked best. "Him," they agreed with overwhelming preteen enthusiasm. I second that emotion.

Branches are in San Bruno at 1250 Grundy (952-8443) and in San Jose at 10343 North Wolfe Road (408/257-2050). Another branch is in San Francisco (see p. 61).

## THE VILLAGE GREEN

*89 Portola Ave., El Granada, 726-3690; B, L, & tea Thur-Tu; $; highchairs, booster seats; 100% non-smoking; no reservations; MC, V.*

A touch of England is purveyed in this tiny, cozy, and cheery enclave just off busy Highway 1. Tables are covered with green floral cloths and pink napkins, and the nearby ocean can be glimpsed through lace-framed windows.

Breakfasts are big (the "farmhouse": half a grapefruit or glass of juice, cold cereal, toast, pot of tea or coffee, and choice of three: eggs, bacon, sausage, and fried tomato, potato, or bread) or small (the "light": an egg and toast). Something in between is also available. Lunch includes traditional items like Cornish pasties, Welsh rarebit, and crumpets with toasted cheese.

Tea items are available all day. Cream tea includes two scones, jam, and wonderful sweet clotted cream. The tea plate consists of assorted finger sandwiches, savories, and sweets. (A tea plate I enjoyed here was filled with cucumber and cream cheese sandwiches, an excellent rich shortbread, jam tart, slices of toasted orange bread, a portion of a banger, bits of crumpet, a delicious warm scone, and a slice of moist milk chocolate cake with jam filling.) Of course both are served with a pot of tea (or coffee) covered with a perky cozy. Each table has its own jar of tart homemade lemon curd.

Truthfully, I brought my family to this spot with trepidation. It turned out the children fit in splendidly, and they even liked the food. Perhaps that is because English food is categorized as being bland—the kind most kids like best.

### YET WAH
*1026 Foster City Blvd., in Marlin Cove Shopping Center, Foster City, 570-7888.*
For description see page 65.

---

## — PICNIC PICK-UPS —

---

### BROTHERS DELICATESSEN AND RESTAURANT
*1351 Howard Ave./El Camino Real, Burlingame, 343-2311.*
For description see page 190.

### DEMETRIS
*174 E. Third Ave./Ellisworth Ave., San Mateo, 340-9242.*
For description see page 193.

### EL FARO
*435 El Camino Blvd., South San Francisco, 589-6289.*
For description see page 65.

### FIREHOUSE NO. 1 BAR-BE-QUE
*1420 Burlingame Ave./El Camino Real, Burlingame, 864-7816; M-Thur 11:30-9, F & Sat 12-10, Sun 12-9; pre-packed picnic boxes by reservation; beer, wine; B, L, & D in sit-down area; AE, MC, V.*

Pork and beef ribs, hot links, and chicken are prepared over an oak fire, imparting a smoky flavor. Sauces are one alarm (mild), two alarm (medium), or three alarm (hot). Hamburgers, sandwiches, and salads are also available, as are sides of coleslaw, potato salad, beans, chile, corn muffins, and corn-on-the-cob. The proprietor promises "the best bar-b-que in the whole damn town!"

# What To Do

---

## — PERFORMING ARTS —

---

### PALO ALTO CHILDREN'S THEATRE
*1305 Middlefield Rd., Palo Alto, 329-2216; adults $2, under 18 $1.*

The seasonal productions here appeal especially to children and are performed by child actors ages 8 through 18. In the past they have included such favorites as *The Tales of Beatrix Potter* and *Charlotte's Web*. Summer productions are usually staged outside in an adjacent garden. Call for current schedule.

Hot dogs, chips, and milk are sold for pre-theater dining, and picnics are encouraged.

---

## — MUSEUMS —

---

### BARBIE HALL OF FAME
*460 Waverley St./University Ave., Palo Alto, 326-5841; Tu-F 1:30-4:30, Sat 10-12 & 1:30-3:30; adults $2, under 12 $1.*

Opened in 1984 on Barbie's 25th birthday, this unusual museum is packed with over 7,000 dolls and accessories. It is the largest Barbie collection open to the public and is 90% complete. (The missing dolls are all newer ones.) When my 10-year-old daughter and her friend entered the museum, they shrieked, "Oooh, this is cool!"

### PALO ALTO JUNIOR MUSEUM
*1451 Middlefield Rd./Embarcadero, Palo Alto, 329-2111; Tu-F 10-12, 1-5, Sat 10-5, Sun 1-4; free; free parking lot adjoins.*

Opened in 1934, this was the first junior museum on the West Coast. Exhibits are of the hands-on variety, especially fun for young children. Special programs, movies, and one-day workshops are scheduled regularly. Call for details. An outdoor mini-zoo houses local animals such as raccoons, pelicans, ravens, and crows.

---

## — OUTDOORS/PARKS —

---

### AÑO NUEVO STATE RESERVE
*New Year's Creek Rd./Hwy 1, Pescadero, 879-0595; tours Dec-Mar; reservations necessary; tickets $2, 800/444-7275; fee ($3) parking lot adjoins.*

Huge elephant seals return to this beach each year to mate and bear their young. Docent-guided tours, lasting 2½ hours and covering three miles, take visitors close enough to observe the seals basking in the sun or sleeping. Usually that is the extent of the activity seen, but occasionally one of the weighty bulls roars into battle with a challenging male.

Though the seals look fairly harmless, they are unpredictable and can be dangerous. Males are especially irritable. That is why there is a law dictating that visitors may get no closer to a seal than twenty feet. Parents must be especially careful to keep a good hand on children, as they have more trouble than adults in judging distance.

The season runs something like this. The males arrive in early December. (This is when most of the battles occur.) The females arrive in January, and the babies begin to arrive in late January. (Birthing is sometimes observed.) Mating occurs in February, when the population peaks. Then the seals begin to leave.

This site is one of only two mainland breeding colonies in the world for the northern elephant seal.

Dress warmly, wear comfortable shoes, and don't forget your binoculars and camera. Do bring snacks and drinks for the kids; there is no food service and no water. Note that strollers are impractical on the sandy dunes.

## BEACHES
*On Hwy 1, 879-0832; $2/person.*

Fall is one of the best times to visit the spectacular unspoiled beaches in this area. Warm, clear weather then invites oceanside sunbathing and picnicking. Be careful, though, about going in the water as tides can be dangerous. Check with a ranger station or lifeguard before swimming.

### • San Gregorio State Beach
*Approximately 40 miles south of San Francisco; free parking lot adjoins; picnic tables.*

This picturesque beach is very popular, and its parking area fills early on weekends.

### • Pomponio State Beach
*1.8 miles south of San Gregorio; picnic tables.*

### • Pescadero State Beach
*1 mile south of Pomponio; free parking lot adjoins; picnic tables.*

Children may enjoy sliding on the sand dunes located at the north end. They can also wade in a creek and explore tide pools.

**Pescadero Marsh Natural Preserve**, a refuge for waterfowl and wildlife, is located adjacent. Marked trails are available for hiking. Docent-led nature walks are scheduled; call for details.

## COYOTE POINT PARK
*Coyote Point Dr., San Mateo. Park: 573-2593; sunrise to sunset; $3/car; picnic tables. Museum: 342-7755; W-F 10-5, Sat & Sun 1-5; adults $2, 6-17 $1, free on F. Both: free parking lot adjoins.*

This park boasts a barbecue area, several playgrounds, inviting grassy areas, an 18-hole golf course, a rifle range, and a beach with bathhouse. During summer lifeguards are on duty. As if all this isn't enough, it's also located on a descent route for the San Francisco International Airport, making it a wonderful place to just sit and watch planes landing.

Surrounded by an aromatic grove of eucalyptus trees, the architecturally stunning **Coyote Point Museum** aims to educate visitors about local ecology and the environment. Live colonies of ants, termites, and bees may usually be viewed along with multi-media displays. A **Live Animal Center**, with caged native animals and animal dioramas, is a short walk away.

## FILOLI ESTATE
*Canada Rd., Woodside, 364-2880; guided tours Tu-Sat, Feb-Nov; $6/person; no children under 12; reservations required; free parking lot adjoins.*

Under the protection of the National Trust for Historic Preservation, this 654-acre country estate features a 43-room (not counting closets, halls, and bathrooms) modified Georgian mansion. It was built in 1917 by architect Willis Polk for the William Bowers Bourn II family. Now it is best known as the Carrington home shown at the beginning of TV's *Dynasty*.

Tours of the sixteen acres of mature formal gardens include such delights as two herbal knot gardens, a garden designed to resemble a stained-glass window at Chartres Cathedral in France, and a practical cutting garden.

### JAMES FITZGERALD MARINE RESERVE
*At end of California Ave., off Hwy 1, Moss Beach, 728-3584; daily, sunrise-sunset; free; picnic tables.*

The tidepools are excellent here. Naturalist-led walks are scheduled several times each month, as low tides permit. Call for upcoming schedule.

### PALO ALTO DUCK POND
*2775 Embarcadero Rd., Palo Alto. Duck Pond: sunrise-sunset; free; picnic tables. Nature Center: 329-2506; Thur-F 2-5, Sat & Sun 1-5; free. Both: free parking lot adjoins.*

This is one of the Bay Area's best spots to feed ducks and birds. Located in a quiet, unpopulated area away from town, it usually has a hefty number of hungry ducks and seagulls—even a few swans. Plenty of unusual migrating birds are usually mixed in for added color.

Wooden park benches are available for resting. A small airport located nearby provides plane-watching.

The adjacent **Lucy Evans Baylands Nature Interpretive Center** has exhibits which orient visitors to the area. Workshops, films, and slide shows are scheduled regularly. During daylight hours, visitors may walk over the 120-acre salt marsh on a raised wooden walkway. Naturalist-led walks are scheduled on weekends.

---

# — MISCELLANEOUS —

---

### ACRES OF ORCHIDS
*1450 El Camino Real/Hickey Blvd., South San Francisco, 871-5655; daily 8-5, tours at 10:30 & 1:30; free; free parking lot adjoins.*

One of the largest orchid nurseries in the world, this family-owned business began small in the 1890s. Now it incorporates approximately 800,000 square feet of green houses.

Reservations for the hour-long tours are not necessary. Participants see a variety of orchids and learn about how they are propagated and cared for. Some are actually quite easy to grow and would make a good project for children.

Plants are available for purchase, and free assistance is given in choosing the best variety for your particular home environment.

## GREAT AMERICA

*Hwys 101 & 237, in Santa Clara, 408/988-1800; from 10 daily June-Aug, Sat & Sun Mar-May & Sept-Oct; tickets $18.95, 3-6 $9.45, under 3 free; fee ($3) parking lot adjoins; food service; strollers available to rent ($2/day).*

There's no question about it. The thrill rides at this 100-acre theme park are spectacular, and the four roller coasters are great shocking fun. Then there are the Yankee Clipper and Logger's Run flume rides, the double-decker carousel, and the Sky Whirl—the world's first triple-arm Ferris wheel. Smurf Woods features special rides and activities for children under 12. The largest indoor movie screen on the West Coast and three live shows round out the fun.

## MALIBU CASTLE

*320 Blomquist St./Seaport Blvd., Harbor Blvd. exit off Hwy 101, Redwood City, 367-1905; daily 11am-10pm; prices vary; free parking lot adjoins; food service.*

This kiddie wonderland has three 18-hole miniature golf courses, sprint cars, baseball batting cages, a huge video gameroom, and two racing car courses. As if that isn't enough, there is also a fast-food restaurant serving the things kids love best: pizza, hamburgers, and hot dogs.

A branch is located in Oakland (see p. 185).

## NASA AMES RESEARCH CENTER
*Hwy 101/Moffett Blvd., Moffett Field Naval Air Station, near Mountain View, 604-6497. Visitor Center: M-F 9-4:30; free; free parking lot adjoins; picnic tables. Tours: call for schedule; reservations must be made at least 2 weeks in advance.*

All ages are welcome at the Visitor Center, where informational displays are available on the space program and on aeronautical research. There are models of wind tunnels and planes of the future as well as a real Apollo spacesuit. A retired U-2 spy plane may be viewed in the parking lot.

However, children must be at least 9 for the tour. Depending on this aerospace laboratory's current research activities, the tour may include seeing the world's largest wind tunnel, centrifuge operations, research aircraft, and/or flight simulation facilities. Each begins with a half-hour orientation.

## STANFORD UNIVERSITY CAMPUS
*In Palo Alto.*

### • Guided Tours
*723-2560 or 723-2053; daily during school year at 11 & 2:15, call to confirm.*

Led by students, these hour-long tours leave from the information booth at the main entrance to the **Quadrangle**.

### • Hoover Tower Observation Platform
*723-2053; M-F 10-11:45 & 1-4:30, Sat & Sun 10-4:30, call to confirm; adults $1, under 13 50¢, families $2.50.*

This tower stands 285 feet tall and affords the opportunity to orient yourself to the campus layout. The 35-bell carillon plays daily at noon and 5. A museum at the base honors Stanford graduate, and former President, Herbert Hoover.

Tours of the **Medical Center** (723-4000) and **Linear Accelerator** (926-2204) are available by appointment. Call for details.

### • Stanford University Museum of Art
*723-3469; by donation; picnic tables.*

Severe earthquake damage has temporarily closed this museum. It may remain closed into 1991. Call before visiting. When open, it offers some interesting California Indian exhibits. The adjacent one-acre **Rodin Sculpture Garden** is open all day, every day, and tours are still being given on Wednesdays and Saturdays. Call for times. Together the museum and garden hold the world's second-largest collection of Rodin sculpture. (The largest is in Paris.)

## SUNSET MAGAZINE GARDEN
*Willow Rd./Middlefield Rd., Menlo Park, 321-3600; M-F 8-4:30; free.*

Behind-the-scenes tours of the editorial offices and test kitchens are offered at 10:30, 11:30, 1, 2, and 3. Visitors are welcome to tour on their own the seven acres of landscaped gardens surrounding an impressive 1.3-acre lawn.

## WHALE-WATCHING TOURS
*Board in Princeton-by-the-Sea.*
    For more information see page 112.

## THE WINTER LODGE
*3009 Middlefield Rd./Oregon, Palo Alto, 493-4566; daily 3-5:30, Sept-Apr, call for other sessions; admission $4, under 4 free, skate rental $1; free parking lot adjoins; picnic tables, vending machines.*

An *outdoor* ice skating rink in Palo Alto? Well, it's not on a frozen lake. Indeed, it's located in a nicely manicured residential section of town. But it is removed from traffic and surrounded by tall eucalyptus trees. And it's the only outdoor rink in the Bay Area. Designed for families and children, the rink measures about two-thirds the size of an average indoor rink, making it too small for competitive skating.

Weather does affect the skateability of the ice. In warmer weather a tarp is used to protect the ice from mid-day heat. An overhang allows skaters protection when it rains.

A Family Barbecue is scheduled one Sunday evening each month from 6 to 9. Families bring their own dinner supplies; the rink management provides heated coals, condiments, chips, punch, and coffee. Families can skate and snack throughout the evening.

Other ice skating rinks located on the Peninsula include **Belmont Iceland** at 815 Old Country Road in Belmont (592-0532), **Golden Gate Ice Arena** at 3140 Bay Road in Redwood City (364-8090), and **Ice Capades Chalet** at 2202 San Mateo in the Fashion Island shopping center in San Mateo (574-1616).

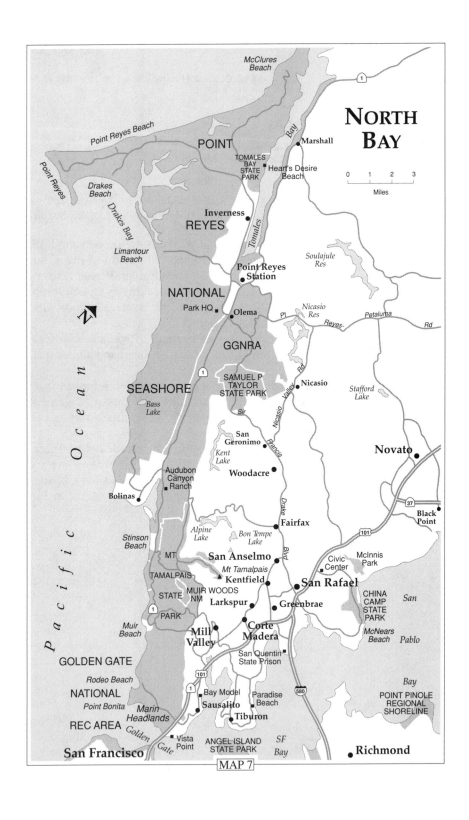

NORTH BAY

McClures Beach

Point Reyes Beach

POINT

Bay

Marshall

TOMALES BAY STATE PARK

Heart's Desire Beach

Point Reyes

Drakes Beach

Drakes Bay

Inverness

REYES

Tomales

0   1   2   3
Miles

Limantour Beach

Soulajule Res

Point Reyes Station

NATIONAL

Park HQ

Olema

Pt

Nicasio Res

Petaluma

GGNRA

Reyes

Rd

SEASHORE

SAMUEL P TAYLOR STATE PARK

Nicasio

Stafford Lake

Bass Lake

Sir

Valley

Rd

Novato

San Geronimo

Francis

Kent Lake

Woodacre

Audubon Canyon Ranch

Bolinas

Drake

Black Point

37

Stinson Beach

Alpine Lake

Bon Tempe Lake

Fairfax

101

Pacific Ocean

MT

San Anselmo

Blvd

Civic Center

McInnis Park

TAMALPAIS

Mt Tamalpais

Kentfield

San Rafael

STATE

MUIR WOODS NM

Larkspur

Greenbrae

CHINA CAMP STATE PARK

San

PARK

Muir Beach

Mill Valley

Corte Madera

McNears Beach

Pablo

GOLDEN GATE

San Quentin State Prison

Rodeo Beach

NATIONAL

Point Bonita

Marin Headlands

101

Bay Model

Paradise Beach

580

Bay

POINT PINOLE REGIONAL SHORELINE

Sausalito

REC AREA

Golden Gate

Vista Point

Tiburon

ANGEL ISLAND STATE PARK

SF Bay

San Francisco

Richmond

MAP 7

# North Bay

## Where To Eat

### BUBBA'S DINER

*566 San Anselmo Ave./Tunstead, San Anselmo, 459-6862; B & L daily, D F-Sun; $; booster seats, booths; children's portions; 100% non-smoking; free parking lot adjoins; no reservations; MC, V.*

The '50s diner lives on at this unpresumptious, extremely casual spot. Children should be comfortable either in one of the overstuffed booths or on a swivel-stool at the long counter. They also should be comfortable with the menu, which is basically sandwiches and exceptionally good hamburgers. Flavorful sirloin hamburger meat is ground in the kitchen, char-broiled to order, and served on onion rolls with all the usual trimmings plus a side of homefried potatoes.

Good side orders for children with small appetites are homemade applesauce, buttermilk biscuits, and bagels with cream cheese. Drinks include thick milkshakes (made the old-fashioned way in metal containers), cherry cokes, and New York egg creams. And then there are the pies—huge berry and apple pies and a rich fudge-walnut topped with whipped cream. The breakfast menu is served until 3 p.m. and includes the predictable items as well as house-made corned beef hash, challah french toast, lox scrambled with eggs and green onions, and create-your-own omelettes.

### THE CANTINA

*541 E. Blithedale Ave./Camino Alto, in Blithedale Plaza, Mill Valley, 381-1070; L M-Sat, D daily, SunBr; $$; highchairs, booster seats, booths; free parking lot adjoins; no reservations; AE, MC, V.*

It is not unusual in Marin County to find a very good restaurant located in a shopping center. This restaurant is an example. Popular at lunch, it becomes ridiculously crowded at dinner, when waits can be quite long. A variety of tangy Margaritas and fresh fruit daiquiris may be ordered, with or without alcohol, to help pass the time.

The predictable Mexican items and combination plates are on the large menu, as are a few more unusual ones. Green enchiladas topped with a tart tomatillo sauce are good, but deep-fried chimichangas topped with guacamole are outstanding. Chicken mole, fajitas, sandwiches, hamburgers, and steaks are also on the menu. At brunch you can get an omelette, huevos rancheros, or huevos gringo-style with either ham or bacon. Children might like the Mexican pizza or cheese crisp.

The patio is choice for lunch on warm days. In the evening it is open for drinks only. Mariachis entertain Tuesday through Saturday from 7 to 10 p.m.

## CELIA'S

*1 Vivian Way, San Rafael, 456-8190.*

For description see page 29.

## CHEVYS

*302 Bon Air Shopping Center, Greenbrae, 461-3203.*

For description see page 136.

## CHEZ MADELEINE

*10905 Hwy 1, Point Reyes Station, 663-9177; D Tu-Sun; $$; highchairs, booster seats; free parking lot adjoins; reservations suggested; MC, V.*

Would you believe I found a French restaurant that has both escargot and a hamburger on the menu? One that will also make a grilled cheese sandwich for a kid upon request? Chez Madeleine has been doing this for years.

Current owners Chuck (the chef) and Kristi (the hostess) Edwards are the parents of a 7-year-old. They took over a few years ago and are carrying on the tradition of serving families that was established by the prior owners.

My meal began with a wonderful, light celery soup topped with red bell pepper purée. My husband's began with French onion soup. So she could eat with us, our daughter was served her cheeseburger and sizzling french fries at this time. While she was busy picking sesame seeds off the bun, we poured Chateau Lacarelle Beaujolais into our glasses.

While the kid nibbled like a bunny at her burger, her daddy and I chowed down like rabbits our perfect, crisp green salads.

For my entree I chose the daily special—a brochette of impeccably fresh salmon, scallops, and prawns with beurre blanc. It was served with rice and a sweet carrot purée. My husband had grilled veal sweetbreads and chicken livers, served with homemade mashed potatoes and a four-onion marmalade. We were both pleased. Having quit after eating less than half of her burger, our child was quite content to draw pictures on her placemat.

When dessert time rolled around, she miraculously recovered her appetite and was ready to eat again. Lacking any courage or convictions this particular evening, I allowed her to order a classic crème au caramel. Her dad had the same but I, thinking ahead, had fifteen minutes before ordered a Grand Marnier soufflé. Lucky me.

Chez Madeleine features a casual, noisy atmosphere. It reminds me of French restaurants I have happily happened upon in the French countryside. Children blend into such an atmosphere and seem a real part of it. This night there was a toddler in a highchair and several other children looking to be about age 8 and older. Everyone was enjoying themselves.

## EMIL VILLA'S HICK'RY PIT
*205 Strawberry Town and Country Village, Mill Valley, 388-6442.*
For description see page 140.

## THE GOOD EARTH
*2231 Larkspur Landing Circle, Larkspur, 461-7322.*
For description see page 194.

## GUAYMAS
*5 Main St., Tiburon, 435-6300; L & D daily; $$; highchairs, booster seats; reservations suggested; AE, DC, MC, V.*

A perfect example of the gustatory plenty we experience here in the Bay Area, Guaymas serves up unusual, upscale regional Mexican fare.

In pleasant surroundings of bleached-wood furnishings, adobe-style decor with colorful semitropical decorative touches, and sweeping views of San Francisco, diners choose from an assortment of imaginative, sophisticated menu items. There are none of the expected tacos and enchiladas. Instead there is a large selection of tantalizing seafood items.

On warm days you can sit out on the deck by the water and enjoy a Margarita: Americano-style—sweet and with ice, or Mexican-style—tart and without ice. You can order from ten different tequilas and ask for a complimentary sangrita chaser—a blend of tomato and orange juices spiked with chilies. And there are, of course, a variety of Mexican beers. Non-alcoholic beverages include fruit-flavored Penafiel mineral waters and agua frescas—described on the menu as "refreshing water made from pods, flowers, grains or fruits."

Each table receives a complimentary basket of tiny soft corn tortillas with both red and green salsas for dipping. I especially enjoyed an appetizer of little "crisp corn tortillas topped with guacamole, marinated shrimp, cilantro" served three to a portion. A salad item which worked well for my highly selective daughter consisted of "thin slices of jicama, cucumber, and fresh fruit in season with lemon-chile dressing"—hold the dressing.

More adventuresome diners might want to start with "fresh cactus strips, onions, fresh cheese with cilantro-chile vinaigrette." The restaurant is widely praised for its chunky guacamole served with freshly-made chips.

Tamales, made with fresh corn masa, make a very interesting main dish. I tried an assortment which included a "chicken tamale with green and red chile sauce in a corn husk," a pork version with "guajillo chile sauce in a banana leaf," and a green corn masa version "stuffed with cactus, plantain, salsa cruda, steamed in a green corn husk and topped with fresh Mexican cream."

Spit-roasted meats are a kitchen forte. "Thinly pounded veal with peanut-serrano chile sauce" was a presentation of tender meat with a delicate grilled flavor. Next time I want to try the butterflied "giant shrimp marinated in lime juice and cilantro," which looked quite tempting on the open kitchen's gourmet "beach barbecue" grill.

I find it surprising there are no children's portions, since children and families dine here in herds. You might want to order for them from the appetizers or, if you have two young children, have them share a dish. Just ask your server, and the kitchen will split an item. Promising selections include "corn tortilla turnovers filled with a variety of fresh ingredients" (known popularly as quesadillas), pollo en mole—"half chicken with sauce of chocolate, chiles, fruits and spices," and "bullfighter's skewers of marinated chicken and beef" meant to be rolled into the warm corn tortillas they are served with—just like tacos.

Children, and everyone else, can easily be satisfied come dessert. A creamy coconut custard flan was our personal favorite, but you can also get a spectacular "fritter with 'drunken' bananas and vanilla ice cream," "avocado and lime pie," and assorted Mexican cookies.

## JERRY'S FARM HOUSE
*10005 Hwy 1, Olema, 663-1264; B Sat & Sun, L & D Tu-Sun; $$; highchairs, booster seats; children's portions; free parking lot adjoins; reservations suggested; AE, MC, V.*

This is the perfect dinner stop after an outing at Point Reyes. Good homecooked food and a casual, unpretentious atmosphere keep it very busy.

Complete dinners include a choice of green salad or homemade soup, a baked potato with plenty of butter and sour cream, a steamed fresh vegetable, two big baking powder biscuits which are simply wonderful with honey, and coffee or tea. Pan-fried fresh seafood entrees include a delicate filet of petrale sole, delicious fresh scampi, and fresh oysters from nearby Johnson's Oyster Farm—all served with a very good homemade tartar sauce. Barbecued chicken, steak, and daily specials are also on the menu. Children's portions of all dinners are half-price.

A lighter luncheon menu of salads, oyster stew, vegetable soup, chile, hamburgers, and both grilled cheese and peanut butter & jelly sandwiches is available all day. Those delicious biscuits are available as a side order.

"Everything has been the same here for thirty years, and it'll be the same thirty years from now," the owner's son has assured me. Thank goodness some things don't change.

## LA GINESTRA
*127 Throckmorton Ave./Miller Ave., Mill Valley, 388-0224; D Tu-Sun; $$; highchairs, booster seats, booths; free parking lot adjoins; no reservations; no cards.*

Named for the Scottish broom flower which is native to both Mount Tamalpais and Sorrento, Italy (and which locally, unfortunately, is considered a pesty weed), this very popular and casual restaurant specializes in Neapolitan cuisine.

The ample menu includes a large selection of pastas, pizzas, and veal dishes as well as a garden-fresh minestrone soup, a good cannelloni, and an excellent eggplant Parmesan. All are cooked to order and served with french bread and butter. Veal, chicken, and seafood entrees are served with a choice of ravioli, spaghetti, french fries, or fresh vegetables. Fried or sauteed fresh squid are always on the menu along with spaghetti with zucchini, gnocchi (potato dumplings) a la Napolentana, and saltimbocca Sorrentine. Stuffed whole sea bass is available when the catch permits.

Children's portions will be prepared upon request. When we dine here, we usually order a small pizza, which has an excellent crust, for the children to share.

For dessert there is a rich homemade cannoli and a frothy zabaglione made with white wine.

During peak dining times on weekends there can be a fifteen- to twenty-minute wait. It can be pleasantly passed in the adjoining bar where opera arias sometimes play enchantingly in the background.

## LE CROISSANT
*1143 4th St./B St., San Rafael, 456-7669; B & L daily; $; no reservations; no cards.*

An interesting menu and use of fresh ingredients make a visit to this simple lunch counter well worthwhile. The usual breakfast items are available along with crumbly-good corn muffins, made fresh in the kitchen, and a variety of continental coffees. Orange juice, grapefruit juice, and lemonade are fresh-squeezed and unsweetened.

Lunch features a variety of interesting sandwiches, including an excellent grilled Swiss on rye, a frankfurter on a french baguette, and an excellent hamburger—all served with a side of very good french fries or homemade potato salad. The wonderful jams, soups, and desserts—even the mayonnaise—are all made from scratch.

Though this restaurant is basically arranged to accommodate individuals and couples, a family might be seated in the front at one of the few tables for four, or at the long lunch counter where you can watch the kitchen activity from a swiveling stool. As wonderful as it is, this gem might best be skipped if you have children under age 3 with you.

## MAYFLOWER INNE
*1533 4th St./E St., San Rafael, 456-1011; L M-F, D daily; $; highchairs, booster seats; children's portions; free parking lot adjoins; reservations suggested; MC, V.*

For those of you who have been to England and grown fond of the cozy pubs, this restaurant offers the chance to experience a similar ambiance closer to home. And a visit to Marin County sure beats the airfare to England.

Our waitress greeted us with, "Hello, lovies," and handed us a menu offering large portions of traditional bland-but-hearty English cuisine: steak and kidney pie, Cornish pasties (beef stew wrapped in a crescent pie pastry), bangers (English sausages), and fish & chips.

Children's portions of fish & chips and bangers & chips are available. When dining here with our fish-hating children, we have composed a meal from appetizers—a sausage roll (sausage baked in a pastry), Scotch egg (a hard-boiled egg rolled in sausage meat and bread crumbs and then deep-fried), and a side order of chips.

Drinks include assorted English ales and beers on tap, a ginger beer for kids, and, of course, tea. Dessert is a choice of fresh rhubarb pie, sherry trifle (a pudding), or chocolate cake.

To really enjoy your visit here, you need to take your time and relax in the English manner. Remember, in England pubs are social institutions. Patrons visit to unwind and enjoy the facilities and actually *talk to each other!* Before, during, or after your meal you can enjoy a friendly game of darts or Ping-Pong or even pinball. Call for the current schedule of entertainment and dart competitions.

## PASAND
*802 B St., San Rafael, 456-6099.*
For description see page 153.

## THE PELICAN INN
*On Hwy 1, Muir Beach, 383-6000; L, tea, & D Tu-Sun; $$; highchairs, booster seats; children's portions; free parking lot adjoins; no reservations; MC, V.*

What a pleasure it is to drive the backroads to this cozy establishment—an authentic reconstruction of an actual 16th century English Tudor inn. Its casual and friendly pub atmosphere absorbs families comfortably. Seating is available both outside on a patio and inside in a rustic, dark dining room furnished with several long communal tables and a number of more private individual ones. Candles add to the cozy feeling but don't shed much light. On cold, foggy days a fireplace often warms the interior, and upbeat classical music cheers the heart.

The limited lunch menu changes daily and consists of homemade traditional English pub fare like bangers and mash (mashed potatoes made from scratch), shepherd's pie, and usually a soup and a salad plate. And you'll be glad to know that everything seems more carefully prepared and tasty than the fare of this type I remember being served in England. Children may share an order with a sibling or a parent. Ales and beers complement the food, and a variety are on tap. Children may like the ginger beer.

Unfortunately, the relatively expensive dessert tray is hard to resist. Choose from pecan pie, warm English trifle (delicate custard mixed with raspberry jam and chunks of white cake), and, on occasion, semi-sweet chocolate mousse.

The simple afternoon tea consists of an assortment of tea snacks and, of course, tea.

Several snug rooms, complete with canopied beds, are rented out upstairs, but unfortunately none are really suitable for families.

## THE RICE TABLE
*1617 4th St./G St., San Rafael, 456-1808; D Thur-Sun; $$; highchairs, boosters seats; reservations suggested; AE, MC, V.*

The Indonesian islands were once also known as the "Spice Islands," as this area is where many spices originate. During their domination of these islands, the Dutch served some of the best native dishes at huge feasts called "rijstaffel" or "rice table." This cozy, nicely decorated restaurant serves a West Java version of this elaborate dinner along with some a la carte items. The kitchen is family-run and the dishes served are secret family recipes.

The rice table dinner begins with shrimp chips and several dipping sauces, green pea vegetable soup, deep-fried lumpia (like spring rolls), both a cabbage and bean sprout salad with peanut sauce dressing, both white and saffron-yellow rice, fried rice-noodles, pickled vegetables, and roasted coconut. Then come marinated pork and chicken satays, shrimp sauteed in butter and tamarind, a mild chicken curry, beef sauteed in soy sauce and cloves, and a great dessert of fried bananas sprinkled lavishly with powdered sugar. Two other versions of the dinner—one with less dishes and one with more—and several less elaborate Indonesian meals are also available. A small amount is charged for children to share the dinner and be served their own soup, salad, rice, and dessert.

Looking for "hot?" One entree touted as "hot" here is suggested for "real cowboys and dragon-slayers only; no 'too hot' complaints accepted!"

Beer, which goes beautifully with Indonesian food, is available along with an Indonesian-style coffee, tamarind juice, and several kinds of teas.

Any leftover food can be packaged to take home.

## SAM'S ANCHOR CAFE
*27 Main St./Tiburon Blvd., Tiburon, 435-4527; L M-F, D daily, Sat & SunBr; $-$$; highchairs, booster seats; separate children's menu; no reservations; AE, MC, V.*

Sitting outside on the deck here, watching the boats and seagulls, is truly a sublime experience. It is especially a treat when the sun is shining (don't forget your sunglasses, visors, and sunscreen), and Tiburon tends to be sunny, but it is also wonderful when the fog rolls in.

Dress is casual, and a typical weekend morning finds jet-setters and celebrities dining happily right alongside everyday people. Singles make their connections here at brunch while parents relax and unwind with Sam's famous Ramos gin fizz. Cranky sounds from children don't travel far, but seem instead magically absored into the natural atmosphere (air).

Though the reasonably-priced brunch menu has a variety of egg dishes, sandwiches, and salads, my family always seems to order the same thing—a burger with fries and a fizz.

The children's menu, available only at lunch and dinner, is served with crayons and offers a choice of a hamburger, hot dog, spaghetti, or fish & chips.

Be prepared. At times the wait to get in at Sam's can reach two hours.

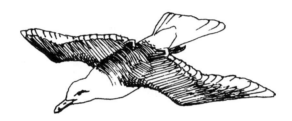

## STATION HOUSE CAFE
*Main St./Third, Point Reyes Station, 663-1090; B, L, & D daily; $$; highchairs, booster seats, booths; children's portions; 100% non-smoking; free parking lot adjoins; reservations suggested; MC, V.*

The dress of the clientele here is casual, most being on their way to or from spending a day with nature on the Point Reyes peninsula. Families fit into the cheerful ambiance well and will appreciate the large, varied, and continuously-changing menu.

Choose from sandwiches (including a grilled cheese, a hot dog, and a made-to-order peanut butter & jelly), hamburgers (using ground chuck made from Niman-Schell organically-grown beef), light and inexpensive entrees (a quiche, very good fish & chips, and a satisfying chicken and sausage pot pie), and pricier daily specials which usually include fresh fish and local oysters. Reasonably priced desserts include a homey tapioca pudding, several ice cream sundaes, Cocolat truffles, apple and pecan pies, and occasional specials.

Here all stages of hunger can actually be satisfied at the same table. Most of the ingredients used are fresh, and everything is generally quite good.

Wonderful, too, for tired families is the fact that service is fast and unpretentious. Occasionally there is live music on weekends.

## TAQUERIA MEXICAN GRILL

*1001 Sir Francis Drake Blvd./College, Kentfield, 453-5811; L & D daily; $; highchairs; free parking lot adjoins; no reservations; no cards.*

Nestled under tall redwoods, this attractive fast-food restaurant features tile floors, massive wooden benches and tables, piñatas, and a jukebox playing Mexican tunes. All help set the mood for the burritos, chimichangas, and tacos which are the menu mainstays. Fillings are a variety of meats accented with fresh beans and a sauce of chopped fresh tomatoes and cilantro. Hamburgers and tostadas are also on the menu. Guacamole may be purchased to nibble on while you wait for your order to be prepared.

Branches are in Danville, Walnut Creek, and Concord (see p. 158).

## TONY ROMA'S

*347 Corte Madera Town Center, off Hwy 101, Corte Madera, 927-7414; L & D daily; $$; highchairs, booster seats, booths; separate children's menu; take-out delivery; free parking lot adjoins; no reservations; AE, MC, V.*

In a clubby atmosphere featuring oak trim, green tabletops, and lots of mirrors, diners here are presented with a choice of ribs: baby backs, St. Louis-style, Carolina honeys, Cajun-style, and beef. The menu also offers barbecued shrimp and chicken, grilled halibut, and steak.

All entrees are served with a tasty coleslaw and a choice of sweet ranch-style beans, a baked potato with sour cream, or french fries. Lighter appetites can be satisfied with a hamburger, sandwich, or salad.

The children's menu is presented with crayons and offers a choice of deep-fried chicken fingers, barbecued chicken, a burger, and ribs. All are served with french fries and cole slaw. Do turn the menu over to select one of the children's specialty drinks.

A menu describing interesting adult specialty drinks is also available. However, if you order a regular drink (iced tea, soft drink, juice, milk), you get complimentary refills.

## TONY'S SEAFOOD

*18863 Hwy 1, Marshall, 663-1107; L & D F-Sun;, $; highchairs, booster seats; free parking lot adjoins; no reservations; no cards.*

Many restaurants in this area offer oyster specialties. My family especially enjoys this one because it is very casual and has facilities for children. In addition, there are many window tables with relaxing views of Tomales Bay.

The house specialty is oysters barbecued in the shell. They are available as an appetizer. Deep-fried oysters are available as a complete meal, with a green salad and fries made from fresh potatoes. Fresh fish specials change with the day's catch, and a hamburger and grilled cheese sandwich are also on the menu. Beer, which seems to go especially well with oysters, is available from the bar.

## YET WAH
*2019 Larkspur Landing Circle, Larkspur, 461-3631.*
For description see page 65.

---

# — PICNIC PICK-UPS —

---

## LET'S EAT + SWEET THINGS
*1 Blackfield Dr., in Cove Shopping Center, Tiburon; Let's Eat, 383-FOOD; Sweet Things, 388-8585; open M-F 10-7, Sat 9-7, Sun 10-6; pre-packed picnic boxes by reservation; free parking lot adjoins; sit-down area, no table service; MC, V.*

For picnic fare stop at Let's Eat and choose from a continuously changing menu of delicious salads—perhaps a wild rice with smoked cheese and grapes, or a flavorful Mexican chicken sprinkled generously with cilantro. My child was happy as a meadowlark with a simple fresh fruit mix. Sandwiches are made to order. A "Panhandle pastry" is sometimes available. I enjoyed an exquisite example made with Jack cheese, artichokes, chicken, and mild chilies—heated to the perfect temperature before I left the shop. A large variety of non-alcoholic drinks are available, as are pâtés and chocolate truffles. All picnics are packed with the appropriate utensils and plates.

Get dessert a few doors down at Sweet Things. My daughter's quickly eaten Fanny Annie cupcake consisted of devil's food with a cheesecake-like filling. My own slice of tasty, weighty carrot cake was packed attractively upon a doily-covered paper plate. A variety of interesting cookies also beckon. Dare you even ask about the Fallen Angel Torte or the Black Magic Cake?

## LLUNCH WITH A LLAMA
*Camelid Capers, 669-1523; Apr-Nov; adults $40, children 6-12 $25, under 6 free; bring-your-own picnic $25/$10.*

Not sitting on his hand at a llama auction a few years back was how it all began for Jerry Lunsford. Totally enthusiastic about his new responsibility, he soon began offering llama-chaperoned picnic hikes at Point Reyes National Seashore.

Because the llamas set the pace—and they definitely are not in any hurry—my family's five-mile picnic hike with Jerry along the **Palo Marin Trail** was leisurely. My 9-year-old daughter was so busy leading "her" llama that she never complained of being tired.

In a clearing by **Bass Lake**, a picnic was spread before us upon colorful cloths. Katrina Anderson, Jerry's girlfriend and partner, had obviously been busy the day before. We started with salmon pâté and a tangy hummus cracker spread. Then two kinds of aram sandwiches appeared—roast beef and vegetarian.

About this time my daughter started complaining. "Yuck," she unabashedly exclaimed. Katrina was ready with a jar of homemade huckleberry jam and peanut butter.

We adults then got back to a potato salad made with Peruvian purple potatoes grown in our caterer's own garden. Another salad was made with quinoa—a type of Peruvian grain now grown in the highlands of Colorado. Dessert was creamy homemade vanilla ice cream and brownies.

While we leisurely feasted, llamas Zephyr and Zarro hummed contentedly and munched on alfalfa carried in for them on Jerry's back.

## MARIN FRENCH CHEESE COMPANY
*7500 Petaluma-Point Reyes Rd., Petaluma, 707/762-6001; sales room daily 9-5, tours daily 10-4 on the half-hour (less frequently in winter); beer, wine; free parking lot adjoins.*

To get here exit Highway 101 at the Central exit in San Rafael and follow Third Street west to Sir Francis Drake Boulevard. Stay on Sir Francis Drake west, through the towns of San Anselmo and Fairfax, on into the scenic countryside populated with horse ranches. After Woodacre and before the town of San Geronimo, turn right onto Nicasio Valley Road. Follow this quiet country road through the redwoods to the Petaluma-Point Reyes Road and turn right (east). Follow this road until you reach the cheese factory, located on the left side of the road.

The Thompsons have operated this family cheese factory since 1865 and have perfected the art of making Camembert cheese. They also make good Brie, schloss, and breakfast cheeses. Tours take visitors through the factory and explain how these special cheeses are produced. Cheeses are sampled at the end.

Picnic supplies are available in the adjoining store where these special cheeses are on sale along with salami, french bread, sandwiches, crackers, soft drinks, juices, and ice cream. Two large grassy areas, one with a large pond, beckon for picnics. Some picnic tables, shaded from the sun by colorful umbrellas, are also available.

## MILL VALLEY MARKET/KAYSER PASTRIES
*12 Corte Madera Dr./Throckmorton, Mill Valley, 388-3222; M-Sat 7-7, Sun 9-6; prepacked picnic boxes by reservation; beer, wine; metered parking lot adjoins; no cards.*

Family-owned since 1929, this small but well-stocked market has everything you need for a fabulous picnic. The *San Francisco Chronicle* reports that it carries "80 kinds of honey, 50 brands of green olives, 72 vinegars, 152 salad dressings, 280 types of soup, 311 jams and preserves, 110 mustards and more . . ."

The bakery—where you can get fresh breads, cookies, streudels, cakes, pies, and stuffed sausage rolls—is tucked in the back adjacent to a liquor shop.

## SWEDEN HOUSE BAKERY

*35 Main St./Ark Row, Tiburon, 435-9767; M-F 8-5, Sat & Sun 8:30-6; pre-packed picnic boxes by reservation; beer, wine; B & L in sit-down area; parking lot across street, free M-F; no cards.*

My family likes to stop here and pick out a dessert pastry from the tantalizing selection. There are chocolate tortes, fruit tarts, raspberry shortbread, and chocolate chip cookies—all made on the premises. Open-face sandwiches, on either German six-grain or sweet, orangey Swedish Limpa bread, make unusual picnic fare. Soups and salads are also available.

Should you decide to dine in, try the small, sunny outdoor deck. It has a great view of the bay.

# What To Do

## — HISTORIC SITES —

### MARIN COUNTY HISTORICAL SOCIETY MUSEUM
*1125 B St., San Rafael, 454-8538; W-Sun 1-4; free.*

Situated in a Victorian built in 1880, this museum is filled with area memorabilia. It is located in **Boyd Park**, a pleasant spot with picnic tables, barbecues, a playground, and a tennis court.

### MISSION SAN RAFAEL ARCHANGEL
*1104 Fifth Ave., San Rafael, 456-3016; daily 11-4; free.*

Reconstructed in 1949, this was the next-to-last mission built in California's chain of 21. Visitors may take a self-guided tour. A tiny museum, with displays of mission furniture and old photos of its reconstruction, adjoins.

### OLD ST. HILARY'S CHURCH
*Esperanza/Centro West, Tiburon, 435-1853; W & Sun 1-4, Apr-Oct; free; free parking lot adjoins.*

When the spring wildflowers are blooming, stop at this 1888 Carpenter's Gothic church for an educational visit. Local wildflowers are displayed and labeled for easy identification. Two rare wildflowers, which can be found nowhere else in the world, grow in the surrounding fields: the Black Jewel and the Tiburon Paintbrush. See if you can identify them. Wildflower tours are available by prior arrangement.

## — PERFORMING ARTS —

### KIDSHOWS
*Marin Center, Civic Center, San Rafael, 472-3500.*

For description see page 168.

## — MUSEUMS —

### BAY AREA DISCOVERY MUSEUM
*428 Corte Madera Town Center, next to World Savings, Corte Madera, 927-4722; W-Sun 11-5, admission $1, under 2 free; free 1st Thur of month 5-8pm; free parking lot adjoins.*

This activity-oriented, hands-on museum is like an indoor playground. It's perfect for a rainy day. The small space is packed with big ideas: an Underwater Adventure Tunnel, which is big enough for parent and child to crawl through together; a Space Maze, where kids can build their own enclosure; a Colorforms Wall, where younger children can create endless designs; a Discovery Theatre, where kids can choose from an assortment of costumes, put on make-up, and perform on stage. Special programs and children's workshops are scheduled each month.

This museum is scheduled to move to East Fort Baker, in Sausalito near the Golden Gate Bridge, in December of 1990. It will be greatly expanded. Call for directions before you visit.

---

# — OUTDOORS/PARKS —

---

## AUDUBON CANYON RANCH
*4900 Hwy 1, 3 miles north of Stinson Beach, 868-9244; mid-Mar to mid-July, Sat & Sun 10-4, weekdays by appt; by donation; free parking lot adjoins; picnic tables.*

Each spring pairs of Great Blue Herons and Great Egrets nest in the tops of this ranch's tall redwood trees. Situated on picturesque Bolinas Lagoon, it is also home to approximately sixty other species of bird. Here these birds are offered protection and a chance at survival, and the public is offered the chance to view them during their nesting period.

A self-guided trail leads to Henderson Overlook, where telescopes are available for closer viewing and a naturalist is on hand for interpretation. Picnic tables are located in a grassy area below, and a nearby converted dairy barn houses natural history displays.

## BLACKIE'S PASTURE
*On Greenwood Beach Rd., off Paradise Dr., Tiburon; free parking lot adjoins.*

When picnic weather hits, it's a good idea to have the perfect picnic spot in mind. This just might be it.

Park your car and walk a short distance east to an expanse of grass overlooking the bay known as **McKegney Green**. Bring bikes for the bike-trail running the three miles into town.

(Blackie was a legendary local horse, beloved by children in the area who would feed him goodies from their lunchbags on the way to school. His former pasture is actually paved over and is now the parking lot. However, his charming gravesite was spared and can be visited at the edge of the lot.)

## MARIN DISCOVERIES
*927-0410.*

This non-profit environmental education organization puts out a quarterly catalogue of classes and field trips. Most take place in Marin County, and there are always some aimed specifically at families. Past family-oriented classes have included Stepping Out With Toddlers, Backpacking With Tots, Family Tidepooling, and Family Full Moon Hike.

## MARIN HEADLANDS
*Alexander Ave. exit off Hwy 101, just north of Golden Gate Bridge, Sausalito, 331-1540; daily 8:30-4:30; free; free parking lot adjoins; picnic tables.*

Start an outing here with a stop at the Visitor Center. Information on local animal and plant life is available, and you can also get a closer look at the ocean through a telescope and pick up a trail map.

Outside the center, **Rodeo Beach** awaits to soothe your soul. Seagulls abound, as do some more rarely-seen birds. Don't forget to bring your stale bread and binoculars. The rocky sand draws the eye for beachcombing, and visitors are permitted to carry away a few of their favorite finds. (No plant life may be removed.)

Free ranger-led walks and nature programs are scheduled regularly. Many are family-oriented. Call for a free schedule.

As you leave, follow McCullough Road to Conzelman Road. This leads past some of the old bunkers and gun batteries which attest to the area's military past. Further down, several twists in the road allow for magnificent views of the Golden Gate Bridge, and behind it San Francisco. You may want to stop to take your picture on what appears to be the edge of the earth. Follow this road back to Highway 101.

The lovely old **Point Bonita Lighthouse** (the last on the Pacific Coast to be automated) schedules free two-hour tours each Saturday and Sunday at 1. Sunset walks are scheduled the first and third Wednesday of each month. Full moon walks are also scheduled. Call for more information.

The mostly-dirt half-mile trail to the lighthouse has one section, about a block long, which can be scary. Be prepared to keep a good grip on small children. The walk is not recommended for children under 4. Consider putting toddlers in a backpack. The trail includes climbing down a short but steep set of stairs, going through a tunnel, and crossing a 120-foot suspension bridge. Visitors are encouraged to dress warmly and wear sturdy shoes.

Remember that this lighthouse is still in use. When the fog rolls in, the horns blow. Do bring plugs or cotton to protect everyone's ears.

Should you want to spend the night in this area, the **Golden Gate Hostel** offers inexpensive lodging. Sleeping facilities are dormitory-style bunkbeds; one family room is available by reservation. A kitchen is available for food preparation, and there are laundry facilities, a place to store bikes, and even a tennis court! For more information call 331-2777.

## MUIR WOODS NATIONAL MONUMENT
*Hwy 1/Panoramic Hwy, Mill Valley, 388-2595; daily 8-sunset; free; free parking lot adjoins; food service.*

Redwood trees have a life span of 400 to 800 years but have been known to live beyond 2,000 years. They are found only in a 540-mile long by 30-mile wide strip of the northern California coast.

This magnificent virgin redwood forest is located only seventeen miles north of San Francisco. The woods envelope 560 acres with six miles of walking trails. The easy Main Trail is paved and has interpretive exhibits. The seven unpaved trails are a bit more challenging but lead away from the crowds (over one million people visit each year!).

Junior Ranger Discovery Packs are full of tools which assist in teaching children about the park. They may be borrowed from the Visitor Center.

No matter what time of year, visitors should bring along warm wraps. The dense forest lets in very little sunlight, and the weather is usually damp, foggy, and cold.

Picknicking is not permitted.

## OLD MILL PARK
*Throckmorton Ave./Old Mill Rd., Mill Valley; picnic tables.*

Sheltered by the old growth of a redwood grove, this park offers idyllic stream-side picnicking. A rustic sun-speckled playground area has tables, some of which are inside a circle of giant redwoods.

## POINT REYES NATIONAL SEASHORE
*Located off Hwy 1 west of Olema, 663-1093; daily; free; free parking lot adjoins; picnic tables.*

Known for its beaches and hiking trails, this area has plenty of interesting things for visitors to do.

Many activities are clustered around the Park Headquarters. A Visitors Center houses a working seismograph and a variety of nature displays.

A short walk away **Kule Loklo**, a replica Miwok Indian village, has been re-created using the same tools and materials as the Indians themselves originally used. Demonstrations of weaving, arrowhead-making, and other crafts are sometimes scheduled.

The **Morgan Horse Ranch**, where pack and trail animals for the national parks are raised and trained, schedules feeding times at 8 a.m. and 4 p.m.

Trails beginning near the headquarters include the self-guided **Woodpecker Nature Trail**, the mile-long self-guided **Earthquake Trail** which follows the San Andreas fault, and the popular 4.4-mile **Bear Valley Trail** which winds through meadows, fern grottos, and forests before ending at the ocean.

Point Reyes has over 70 miles of equestrian trails, and horses may be rented at two nearby stables. Or bring your bikes.

Further away from headquarters is the **Point Reyes Lighthouse,** where it is claimed winds have been recorded blowing at 133 miles per hour—the highest rate in the continental U.S. The bottom line is it gets might windy, cold, and wet at this scenic spot. The lighthouse, reached by maneuvering 300 steps down the side of a steep, rocky cliff, is a popular spot in winter for viewing migrating grey whales.

Wide, level **Drake's Beach** is a good spot for taking a walk. **Drake's Beach Cafe** (669-1297) is open there daily from 10 to 6. Though prices are inexpensive, the food is exceptional: homemade soup, old-time hot dogs with sauerkraut, juicy hamburgers on wholewheat buns, grilled fish, barbecued oysters, organic salads. The peanut butter & jelly sandwich is made with homemade jam, the chocolate chip cookies with wholewheat flour, and the lemonade with fresh lemons.

A visit to the scenically situated **Johnson's Drakes Bay Oyster Company** (1717 Sir Francis Drake Blvd., Inverness, 669-1149; Tu-Sun 8-4:30; free parking lot adjoins) allows viewing the various stages of the oyster farming process. Oysters are available for purchase. Once we bought a raw oyster cocktail to enjoy on the spot and were surprised to find that one of our kids was actually enthusiastic. I was less so.

### RICHARDSON BAY AUDUBON CENTER & SANCTUARY
*376 Greenwood Beach Rd./Tiburon Blvd., Tiburon, 388-2524; W-Sun 9-5; adults $2, children $1.*

The eleven acres that comprise this wildlife sanctuary reflect grassland, coastal brush, freshwater pond, and marsh habitats. Birds and animals are sheltered and fed here. A self-guided nature trail leads to a rocky beach and to a lookout spot with sweeping views of Richardson Bay and San Francisco. Guided nature walks begin on Sundays at 9 and 1.

The 1876 **Lyford House,** the oldest Victorian home in Marin County, is open on Sundays from 1 to 4.

### SLIDE RANCH
*2025 Shoreline Hwy, Muir Beach, 381-6155; call for schedule; adults $10, children $8, under 2 free; free parking lot adjoins; picnic tables; strollers not recommended.*

Perched dramatically on the ocean side of Highway 1 near Muir Beach, this ranch offers the city-slicker a chance to get back to the land . . . a chance to learn about a self-sustaining rural lifestyle through exposure to frontier arts . . . a chance to slow the pace.

During Family Days programs, children and adults learn together about things like cheesemaking, composting, and papermaking. Though the program varies according to the season and the ages of participants, a typical day begins with smiling staff members greeting visitors in a fragrant grove of eucalyptus. A visit to the sheep pen usually follows, giving-children the chance to "pet a four-legged sweater." Then, turning the tables, children who really just want to be kids can don a sheepskin and wander disguised among the goats—who tend to stare quizzically and then run. A picnic lunch, nature walk, and visit inside the chicken pen round out this family experience. Reservations are necessary.

## SWIMMING BEACHES

### • Heart's Desire Beach
*In Tomales Bay State Park, off Hwy 1 near Pt. Reyes, 669-1140; 8-sunset; fee ($3) parking lot adjoins.*

The setting is lovely, and access is available to the warm bay waters for swimming and wading.

### • Paradise Beach
*On Paradise Dr., 1 mile from Tiburon, 435-9212; daily 7-sunset; fee ($3-$5) parking lot adjoins; picnic tables.*

This sheltered nineteen-acre site boasts a large lawn area and barbecues. Fishing is permitted from a pier, and no license is required. The beach is small, quiet, and nice for wading. Note that on warm days the small parking lot fills early.

### • Stinson Beach
*Off Hwy 1, Stinson Beach, 868-0942; free parking lot adjoins; picnic tables, food service.*

This seems to be everyone's favorite beach. It is magnificent and offers a little taste of the southern California beach scene. Lifeguards are on duty during the summer. Since the weather here is often different from everywhere else in the Bay Area, you might want to call and check the conditions before leaving (868-1922).

## A WALK WITH MRS. TERWILLIGER
*Terwilliger Nature Education Center, 50 E. Camino Dr./Granada, Corte Madera, 927-1670; fee varies.*

No childhood is complete without a nature walk led by Elizabeth Terwilliger. This well-known Marin County naturalist prefaces her walks with a hands-on introduction to some of nature's casualties. Then the unusual Mrs. T opens your family's eyes to the beauty of nature. A walk with her is "something special"— as she is fond of saying about nature's wonders— and something you won't soon forget.

(Note that Mrs. Terwilliger is not my mother. At least not *this* Mrs. Terwilliger. We are not related.)

## — MISCELLANEOUS —

### CALIFORNIA MARINE MAMMAL CENTER
*Marin Headlands, Sausalito, 331-7325; daily 10-4; free; free parking lot adjoins; picnic table.*

Marine animals which are injured, sick, or orphaned are cared for here until they are ready to be released back into their natural habitat. Docent-led tours are available on weekends, self-guided tours during the week.

## SAUSALITO

This warm and sunny town is popular with both regular tourists and local tourists. People come from everywhere to enjoy strolling the main street: Bridgeway. There are plenty of restaurants and boutiques, and the view across the bay to Tiburon and San Francisco is superb.

Don't miss a stop at the **Village Fair** (777 Bridgeway, 332-1902; daily 10-6). This unusual indoor shopping center houses 35 shops and features a curvy, steep "Little Lombard" path to the upper floors. Located on the top floor, the **Cafe Madrona and Bakery** serves up moderately priced homemade sandwiches, soups, and pastries and offers great views.

Picnic supplies can be picked up in several stores along Bridgeway. Then just cross the street and find a spot to sit on the rocks for some invigorating al fresco dining. Free entertainment is provided by boats and seagulls.

### US ARMY CORPS OF ENGINEERS BAY MODEL VISITOR CENTER
*2100 Bridgeway, Sausalito, 332-3870, 332-3871; Tu-Sat 9-4; free; free parking lot adjoins; picnic tables.*

Located on the site of the shipyard where World War II Liberty Ships and tankers were built, this is a working hydraulic scale model of the Bay Area and Delta estuary systems. As big as two football fields, it was built to simulate bay water conditions for research. A computerized slide show and interpretive displays help make this complex scientific instrument understandable.

The model operates irregularly; call for upcoming dates. An audio tour is available in English, Spanish, French, German, and Japanese.

### THE WILDLIFE CENTER
*76 Albert Park Lane/B St., San Rafael, 454-6961; Tu-Sun 9-5; free.*

Injured animals are caged here while being nursed back to health. When recovered, they are returned to their natural habitat.

Signs in the center's tiny exhibit room say "please touch."

A park, with a playground and small stream, is nearby.

# Catered Birthday Parties

After planning and executing seemingly countless birthday parties, I find that my enthusiasm for doing it all by myself is waning. There is definitely something to be said for having someone else do the preparation and cleanup.

At the following establishments everything but the inviting is done for you, and in many cases the cost is only slightly higher than what it would be if you did it all yourself! Best of all, when the party is over, you get to go home and leave the mess for someone else to deal with.

Unfortunately, however, many of the fast-food chain franchises are starting to drop these parties as their business increases. Call your local outlet for details. Prices and provisions will vary because franchise owners decide individually what to offer at their facility.

And be sure always to call for reservations several weeks in advance. As you can imagine, this kind of party is popular.

**BERKELEY RECREATION DEPARTMENT**
*644-8517; maximum of 15 children; $85, $100, & $150.*

Ever progressive, this city's recreation department offers three party options. Plan A includes a decorated cake, punch, ice cream, hats, and noise makers, plus decorated plates, cups, napkins, and utensils. Plan B adds hot dogs. Plan C allows up to 30 people. Each includes a party room and an assistant to help with set-up, serving, and outdoor games. Special themes may be arranged. Locations are Live Oak Center, Frances Albrier Park, Willard Park, and James Kenney Park.

Non-residents may also book these parties at no additional fee. Do check with your local recreation department to see if they offer such a program.

231

## BURGER KING
*No minimum; maximum of 15 children; $4/child, birthday child free.*

A party at the franchise in Alameda (523-4810) includes a hamburger or cheeseburger, french fries, soft drink, a decorated cake, decorated plates and napkins, all utensils, balloons and decorations, and someone to oversee some party games.

## CHILDREN'S FAIRYLAND
*(See p.175); 452-0584; minimum of $72 for 8 children, each additional child $9.*

Parties include admission for each child and their adult companion, invitations, a decorated cake, ice cream, punch, blow-outs, and hats, plus decorated tablecloth, napkins, plates, cups, and utensils. The birthday child is announced at the day's puppet show and given a "magic key" to the storyboxes.

Adults may not participate in the eating unless they are each paid for. However, you are welcome to bring along separate snacks for them, and the snack stand sells coffee. A homemade coffeecake sounds good.

There are two party areas. One has brightly-colored carousel animals decorating the perimeter. The other has a Cinderella theme, with a big pumpkin decorating the table and a slipper slide into the sandbox.

## CHUCK E. CHEESE
*In Hayward, Concord, Marinwood, and San Jose; maximum of 10 people; $61.03.*

You may have heard this chain also referred to as Pizza Time Theatre. Its true name seems impossible to pin down. The locations above offer a party package. The San Jose location (408/267-8600) includes one large and one medium pizza with two toppings, two pitchers of soda and refills, 87 tokens for video games, hats, balloons, and decorated napkins, plates, cups, and utensils. The birthday child also receives a mini-pizza and a t-shirt.

## FARRELL'S
*In Daly City, Foster City, Fremont, San Pablo, and San Jose; 4 parties, 2 with a 10-child minimum, 2 with no minimum; $5.95/child.*

Farrell's *is* fun for everyone—especially children. And parties here are downright exciting. The Clown Party includes: choice of hamburger, hot dog, grilled cheese sandwich, peanut butter & jelly sandwich, or peanut butter & banana sandwich; large french fries; all the soda they can drink; clown sundae; favors of party hats, balloons, noise makers, candy, and blow-outs. Several more parties are available. Call for details.

Note that this restaurant's name is scheduled to be changed.

## MALIBU CASTLE
*(See p. 207); minimum of 6 children; no maximum; $6.95 & $8.95/child.*

The least expensive Golf Party includes pizza, a soft drink, popcorn, ice cream, and the party set-up of tablecloth, napkins, cups, and plates. Each guest also gets five game tokens and one round of miniature golf. The more expensive Sprint/Golf Party includes all of that plus two sessions in the sprint racing cars (children must be at least 4' 6" to ride).

### McDONALD'S
*Minimum of 10 children; $53.50 + $5 each additional child.*

Parties at the Richmond franchise (233-7824) include invitations, choice of hamburger or cheeseburger, regular french fries, regular soft drink, a decorated Ronald McDonald chocolate cake, vanilla ice cream, hats, favors, helium-filled balloons, and all necessary plates, cups, and spoons. A trained hostess oversees party games and gives kids a tour of the kitchen.

Some locations also have a McDonaldland Park featuring McDonald-land characters in the form of play equipment.

### PIZZA HUT
*In Castro Valley, Foster City, Hayward, Oakland, San Jose, San Leandro, & South San Francisco.*

The franchise in San Leandro (351-3555) offers a package for $4.85 per person for a minimum of eight. For every four guests it includes a large pizza with three toppings, a pitcher of soft drinks, hats, blow-outs, balloons, favors, and decorated tablecloths, plates, cups, napkins, and utensils.

### SAN FRANCISCO CHILDREN'S ZOO
*(See p.102); 753-7114; minimum of 10 people, no maximum; $7.50/person.*

Parties include a decorated cake with candles, ice cream, apple juice, napkins, plates, cups, and utensils. Favors, a ticket for the merry-go-round, and admission to both the Children's Zoo and the regular zoo are included. For $2 more per person, a box lunch of a hot dog and potato chips is added. Parties are held in a brightly-colored outdoor area.

### SAN FRANCISCO SCHOOL OF COOKING
*(See p. 20); 474-3663; minimum of $210 for 20 children, each additional child $10.50.*

Children cook their own party food here. They make a mess and have a ball. First they help prepare the cake batter. While it bakes, they design their own individual pizzas. While those bake, they frost and decorate the cake. They eat the pizza, then the cake. Then they go next door to the San Francisco International Toy Museum (see p. 84) to play. They receive favors, and then return to the kitchen for some games.

What do the adults do during this "No Parents Allowed" event? They are welcome to stay and watch from the back of the room. Or they may leave and go shopping. Some parents have been known to bring their own cheese, crackers, and wine.

The party lasts about three hours.

A similar party is available at Le Meridien Hotel (see p. 20).

### SHAKEY'S PIZZA PARLOR
*At the Shakey's in Hayward (783-5441)*

The management provides birthday groups with complimentary balloons. The birthday child is also given a free mini-pizza with one topping and a medium soft drink. Appropriate eats for the rest of the group may be ordered a la carte. No cake is provided, but celebrants are welcome to bring their own.

### YOUNG PERFORMERS THEATRE
*(See p. 81); 346-5550; minimum of 12 children + 2 adults; $10 & 15/person.*

The It's Your Party package includes a decorated cake and candles, fresh fruit, apple juice, favors, and decorated napkins, plates, cups, and utensils. Each guest also receives admission to the current production. The Ultimate Party also includes a party helper to lead games and a backstage tour.

Special theme parties are also available throughout the year: Mad Hatter Tea Party, Pirate Treasure Hunt Party, Magic Party, Dracula Party, Wind in the Willows Party, Be an Artist Party. Call for details.

# Birthday Programs Minus Catering

Many places offer wonderful birthday programs but no catering. This is more work for you in that you must round up the refreshments yourself. But you still get to leave the mess behind.

### BAY AREA DISCOVERY MUSEUM
*(See p. 223); minimum of 5 children, maximum of 12; $10/child.*

This party includes table decorations and paper goods, party favors, and free admission to the museum. The birthday child is given a special gift, and an assistant is usually available to help.

### THE ELEPHANT'S TRUNK
*15100 Hesperian Blvd., San Leandro, 481-1583; mimimum of 10 children; $5.95-$9.95/child.*

Three parties are available in the Elephant Party Room of this children's store. The Basic Party Package includes 90 minutes of supervised activities and the paper goods for the table: tablecloth, plates, cups, cutlery. Each child gets a craft item, a birthday button, and a free gift coupon. The birthday child gets special surprises. The Fancy Party Package adds a helium balloon and loot bag for each child. The Deluxe Party Package adds party invitations, a centerpiece which may be taken home, and a $1 store gift certificate for each child.

You provide the food. Discounts are available on frozen yogurt and soft drinks from the **Cotton Cow Cafe** located next door.

## EXPLORATORIUM
*(See p. 92); 561-0302; maximum of 13 children; $45; Sundays only.*

A room is made available for the party celebration. You bring any decorations or food. A guided tour follows your feast.

This program is available to members only. A family membership for one year is $40. Benefits include free admission for the family and one guest for the entire year, free admission to over 80 other science museums world-wide, a subscription to their quarterly magazine, a monthly newsletter telling about special events, and invitations to member's parties, previews, and receptions. What a great birthday present this would make!

## GHIRARDELLI CHOCOLATE MANUFACTORY
*(See p. 34); minimum of 10 people; $30 minimum.*

The birthday child must be 12 or under and is given a free sundae. You purchase from the menu for everyone else. This program is being revised. The plan is to offer a complete package. Call for current details.

## LAWRENCE HALL OF SCIENCE
*(See p. 171); 642-5134; maximum varies from 15-25 people; $45-$55.*

Among the large selection of science-oriented workshops available to entertain celebrants are Hot Stuff (volcanoes), Tin Can Cameras, and Blowing Birthday Bubbles (January through April only).

Parties are held in the cafeteria. You bring all food and paper goods. Because there is no place to store it, ice cream is not permitted. If you would like to arrange for hot dogs or sandwiches and drinks, call the cafeteria staff at 644-3171. The cost is approximately $2 to $3 per person.

## SAN FRANCISCO CHILDREN'S ART CENTER
*Fort Mason Center, Bldg. C, San Francisco, 771-0292; 10 children/$110, $7/additional child to maximum of 15.*

Party includes a special room, an art teacher, and appropriate materials for a project. You supply food, set-up, and decorations.

## TERWILLIGER NATURE EDUCATION CENTER
*(See p. 228); 927-1670; maximum of 15 children; $50; Fridays only.*

During the first hour, a staff naturalist makes a presentation. During the second hour, you may stuff yourselves among the already-stuffed animals and birds at the center. Refreshments are provided by you.

## THE WINTER LODGE
*(See p. 209); 493-4566; minimum of 15 skaters; $4.50/skater.*

For a private or semi-private party, you bring your party paraphernalia to set up in an outdoor picnic area or indoor club house. For an additional $5 fee, you can bring the makings and use the rink's barbecue facilities.

You can also have a simpler skating party, during regular public sessions, and use the vending machines to provide hot chocolate and candy for snacks. This runs $4 per skater with a minimum of ten skaters.

# Annual Events

### CHINESE NEW YEAR CELEBRATION & PARADE
*In San Francisco; 391-2000; free.*

First held in 1851 and held again every year since, this very popular event is composed of a beauty pageant, an outdoor carnival in China-

town, and the famous **Golden Dragon Parade** featuring the spectacular block-long golden dragon.

For information on **Chinese New Year Walks,** see page 70.

Depending on the lunar calendar, this event is sometimes held in February or March.

## ZOO RUN

For description see page 102.

## — FEBRUARY —

## DINOSAUR DAYS

For description see page 171.

## ORCHID SHOW
*In San Francisco, at Fort Mason Center; 441-5706; adults $5, under 12 $3.*

Thousands of gorgeous blooming orchid plants are on display at this stunning show, said to be the largest of its kind held on the West Coast. Many plants are entered for judging and show only, but hundreds more are available for purchase. Lectures by international orchid experts are scheduled. Sponsored by the San Francisco Orchid Society.

This event is sometimes held in March.

## — MARCH —

## BOUQUETS TO ART

For description see page 83.

## BREAKFAST WITH THE EASTER BUNNY
*In selected Emporium and Macy's stores.*

Dates and details vary from year to year and store to store. Call the one nearest you one month before Easter for further information.

## SAN FRANCISCO INTERNATIONAL FILM FESTIVAL
*In San Francisco; 567-4641; tickets $6.50.*

Known for honoring the finest in cinematic achievement, America's oldest film festival presents recent world productions. Some programs are free, and family films are usually included.

## ST. PATRICK'S DAY PARADE
*In San Francisco; 467-8218; free.*

This traditional parade has been held annually for over 80 years.

**WHITE ELEPHANT SALE**
*In Oakland; 273-3401; free.*

This mammoth rummage sale, which claims to be northern California's largest, offers just about anything you can imagine—plus things you can't! Proceeds benefit the Oakland Museum.

— APRIL —

**CHERRY BLOSSOM FESTIVAL**

For description see page 108.

**WILDFLOWER SHOW**

For description see page 173.

— MAY —

**BOOK SALE**
*In San Francisco, at Fort Mason Center; 558-3857; free.*

The largest book sale in the West is presented each year by Friends of the San Francisco Public Library. Many children's titles are available. All books left on the last day sell for half-price.

During the rest of the year, bargains are available at the library's **Book Bay** store (771-1076) in Building C at Fort Mason. Children's titles are usually plentiful, and there are often records and tapes.

**EXAMINER BAY TO BREAKERS**
*In San Francisco; 777-7770; entry fee.*

The world's largest, and perhaps zaniest, footrace is usually routed through the Financial District, up the Hayes Street hill, and on through Golden Gate Park to the Great Highway. Outrageous get-ups are de rigueur and in the past have included everything from a set of crayons to Humphrey the Whale. Children are welcome; parents have been observed running with babes in arms and/or strollers.

**LEONARD J. WAXDECK BIRD CALLING CONTEST**
*In Piedmont, at Piedmont High School; 420-3644.*

Mr. Waxdeck, a biology teacher, also teaches some of his students to mimic the calls of various birds. The students demonstrate their expertise each year in this contest. In the past, the winners have been invited to appear with Johnny Carson on *The Tonight Show.*

Attendance is by invitation only. To secure an invitation, write to Mr.

BAY TO BREAKERS FOOTRACE

Waxdeck at Piedmont High School, 800 Magnolia Avenue, Piedmont 94611. Include a stamped, self-addressed envelope. Tickets are limited. In this situation, like so many others, the early bird gets the worm.

## MOTHER'S DAY ROSE SHOW
*In San Francisco, San Francisco County Fair Bldg. in Golden Gate Park; 564-9968; free.*

See a splendid variety of climbing, mini, and old garden roses at this show—the largest in northern California.

## MOUNTAIN PLAY
*In Mill Valley, in the natural amphitheater atop Mt. Tamalpais; 383-1100; adults $14, children under 18 $10, under 3 free.*

Presented annually since 1913, the plays here have run the gamut from the obscure, to Shakespeare, to well-known Broadway musicals. It is traditional to arrive early to select a stone to sit upon and then relax and enjoy a picnic lunch. A snackbar dispenses tasty food items, too. Experienced play-goers also bring sun lotion and visors as well as down jackets.

In the old days people came on burros, by stagecoach, or on the old Mount Tamalpais Scenic Railway, known also as the "Crookedest Railroad in the World." Now free shuttle buses are available. After the performance,

audience members may choose between riding the buses back down the moutain or participating in a memorable four-mile hike down to the **Mountain Home Inn.** The hike is easy enough for most children 5 and older to participate in. Buses pick up hikers at the inn and take them the rest of the way down the mountain.

## NIGHT TOUR AT THE ZOO

For details see page 103.

# — JUNE —

## CABLE CAR BELL RINGING CHAMPIONSHIPS
*In San Francisco, at Union Square; 392-4880; free.*

Competition is held in both pro and amateur divisions. The previous year's champion defends his title, and amateurs (who include some well-known Bay Area personalities) ring on behalf of non-profit organizations.

Judges are selected from among the area's musical and theatrical elite.

## FATHER'S DAY KITE FESTIVAL
*In San Francisco, at the Marina Green (foot of Scott St. between Fort Mason and the St. Francis Yacht Club); 652-4003; free.*

Past competitions have included the Littlest Kite That Flies, Kid's Kite Catch, and Most Beautiful Handmade Kite. Demonstrations of fighter kites and synchronized stunt kites are usually scheduled.

## GREAT SAN FRANCISCO BIKE ADVENTURE
*In San Francisco; 863-1444; registration fee $12, under 16 $4.*

Bicycle a fifteen-mile route through the city at a relaxed pace. Roads are closed to car traffic. Note that this is not a race, and all ages are welcome. Proceeds benefit American Youth Hostels.

## SAND CASTLE CONTESTS
*In San Francisco, at Aquatic Park; 775-LEAP; free.*

Sponsored by Learning through Education in the Arts Project, the entertaining LEAP contest pits professional architects against one another. Observers are welcome.

For a description of an amateur contest held at Crown Memorial State Beach, see page 176.

## STERN GROVE MIDSUMMER MUSIC FESTIVAL
*In San Francisco, at 19th Ave./Sloat Blvd.; 398-6551; free.*

This program features the finest of Bay Area performing arts and has occured each summer since 1938. Held in the Grove's natural outdoor amphitheater, it is the country's oldest continuous free summer music festival.

Surrounded by eucalyptus and redwood trees, viewers are treated to a mixed bag of music and dance. One week it's the San Francisco Opera, the next it's an ethnic dance troupe. The festival continues through mid-August.

It is traditional to bring a picnic lunch and the Sunday paper and to spend the pre-performance time indulging in food, drink, and relaxation. If you run short of food and drink, a stand sells snacks. Don't forget a blanket to sit on. Dress for warm weather, but bring wraps in case it turns chilly.

In several large, open areas adjoining the amphitheater, children can romp and play and run off steam before the performance and during intermission. Bring balls and appropriate toys.

If you plan to attend with a large group of people, picnic tables are available by reservation through the Recreation and Park Department after 9 a.m. on the Monday before the performance (666-7035).

Year-round, the city's newly restored **croquet lawns** are available here for play. For more information, call 776-4104.

### UNION STREET SPRING FESTIVAL
*In San Francisco, on Union St. between Gough & Fillmore Sts.; 346-4561; free.*

At this super street fair hundreds of artists and craftspeople display and sell their work in stalls lining the street. Outdoor cafes are set up in the middle of each block, and ongoing entertainment is scheduled.

Don't miss the Waiter's Race in which competing waiters must open a bottle of wine, pour two glasses, and carry it all on a tray up the Laguna hill to Green Street and then back again to Union. The first one back with everything intact wins.

---

# — JULY —

---

### COMEDY CELEBRATION
*In San Francisco, in Golden Gate Park; 543-3030; free.*

Bring a blanket, a picnic, and a smile. Laughs are provided by local professional comedians. In the past participants have ranged from upstarts—who just naturally seem to try harder—to such established luminaries as Robin Williams, Bob Goldthwait, and Father Guido Sarducci. Content of the ongoing program is appropriate for the entire family.

### FOURTH OF JULY FIREWORKS AND FESTIVITIES
*In San Francisco, Crissy Field (next to The Presidio); 777-7120; free.*

Beginning in the early afternoon, a variety of music and entertainment is presented continuously. A special children's stage is always scheduled. A highlight is the Sixth Army's traditional 50-cannon salute to the nation. The celebration culminates with a fireworks spectacular after sunset. Sponsored by the *San Francisco Chronicle*.

### MARIN COUNTY FAIR
*In San Rafael, Civic Center Fairgrounds; 499-6400; adults $6, children $4, under 4 free.*

Five days of fun include evening performances by big name entertainers and a low-level fireworks display. All entertainment and carnival rides are included in the admission fee. A special Children's Day is always scheduled.

### TROLLEY FESTIVAL
*In San Francisco, along Market Street; 923-6162; adults 85¢, 5-16 25¢.*

Vintage electric trolley cars from around the world join San Francisco's own historic streetcar fleet during this popular festival. Cars run every ten minutes from 10 to 6, originating at the Transbay Terminal (1st and Mission Streets) and ending at Castro and Market Streets. Trolleys may be boarded and deboarded every block along the two-mile route. Usually the festival continues into September.

# — AUGUST —

### SAN FRANCISCO COUNTY FAIR FLOWER SHOW
*In San Francisco, County Fair Bldg. in Golden Gate Park; 753-7090; adults $3, under 12 free.*

Take time to smell the flowers. This largest of all judged flower shows in the West features the home-grown entries of Bay Area non-commericial horticulturists and amateur gardeners. Along with plants native to the area, there are displays of carniverous plants, Bonsai trees, and tropical species. Educational demonstrations and a plant auction are also scheduled.

### RENAISSANCE PLEASURE FAIRE
*In Novato, off Hwy 37 at Black Point Forest; 892-0937; adults $12.50, 3-11 $5, under 3 free.*

Visitors experience an authentic re-creation of an Elizabethan village as it would have appeared over 400 years ago during a Harvest Festival. Actors, musicians, jesters, jugglers, acrobats, dancers, puppeteers, and mimes dressed in Elizabethan costume are on hand to provide authentic period entertainment. Exotic food and drink, quality crafts, and appropriate diversions are purveyed throughout.

Visitors are encouraged to dress in Renaissance costume. Indeed, it

has been described as "the largest costume party in the world."
The faire usually runs into September.

## — SEPTEMBER —

### CLIO AWARDS
*In San Francisco, Palace of Fine Arts Theatre, Bay St./Lyon St.; 864-3018; tickets $7.*
See the best TV commercials and print ads from the past year. Winners are selected for creativity from among entries from around the world. It is promised there will be no interruptions of commercials for a program.

### INTERNATIONAL STREET PERFORMERS FESTIVAL
*In San Francisco, at Pier 39; 981-PIER; free.*
San Francisco's best street performers do their stuff along with some internationally renowned entertainers.

### KQED OLD-FASHIONED ICE CREAM SOCIAL & TASTING
*In San Francisco, Concourse Exhibition Center, 7th St./Brannan St; 553-2200; adults $12, children 10 and under $7; strollers not permitted.*
At the world's largest ice cream festival, ice cream manufacturers from

around the country scoop up samples of their sinful, sublime, and even silly flavors while a Dixieland band plays in the background. In addition to ice cream, there are usually sherbet, gelato, sorbet, glacé, and dipped bars available for unlimited sampling.

And keep in mind that ice cream is a healthier food than you might think. It's high in protein, calcium, and vitamins A and B-2. Maybe it's even less fattening than you think. A typical half-cup serving has 128 calories—less than a danish (274) or a slice of apple pie (404).

Proceeds benefit public television station KQED.

## MICHAELMAS FAIRE
For description see page 75.

## PRESERVATION FAIR
For description see page 177.

## SUKAY CONCERT
*In San Francisco; 441-5706; tickets $10-$14, children half-price.*

This San Francisco-based quartet plays high-spirited, joyous Andean music. They play both new and traditional music using over 25 native instruments from Bolivia, Ecuador, and Peru. The interesting instruments include panpipes, flutes, drums, rattles, and one made from an armadillo shell.

As for their appeal to children, one 9-year-old girl who had been told to be very still wrote to the group saying she couldn't help herself, "giggles keep escaping from my feet."

In addition to this annual concert, they often appear in town when not touring. Call for current schedule.

---

# — OCTOBER —

## COLUMBUS DAY CELEBRATION
*In San Francisco; 467-8218.*

San Francisco's is the only Columbus Day celebration in the country which includes a re-enactment of Columbus' landing in San Salvadore. When landing at Aquatic Park, the person acting as Columbus wears a handmade Italian replica of the great navigator's clothing. The **Blessing of the Fishing Fleet** takes place the next day at Fisherman's Wharf, and the **Columbus Day Parade** usually takes place the next weekend.

## FESTIVAL OF THE SEA
For description see page 85.

THE BLUE ANGELS' FLEET WEEK SHOW

## FLEET WEEK
*In San Francisco; 981-8030; free.*

To celebrate the anniversary of the Navy's birthday, the City of San Francisco throws a gigantic birthday party each year and the public is invited. In the past there have been demonstrations of high-speed boat maneuvering, parachute drops, and a fly-by of World War II vintage aircraft. The Blue Angels, the Navy's precision flight demonstration team, also perform in a breathtaking culmination.

Viewing is best from Crissy Field, the Marina Green, Aquatic Park, Pier 39, and the Marin Headlands.

As part of the celebration, all Navy ships moored at the piers are usually opened for public visits.

## GRAND NATIONAL RODEO, HORSE, & STOCK SHOW
*In San Francisco, at Cow Palace; 469-6058; admission charge.*

This is the largest such show held west of the Mississippi. The rodeo and horse show are scheduled each evening in the arena. Ticketholders are invited to come early to enjoy a variety of related activities: dairy animal auctions; judging contests; displays of unusual breeds of livestock including tons of premium steers, wooly sheep, and prime swine. For kids there are hayrides and a special White Line Tour which takes them (and their parents) in to see the baby animals.

## HALF MOON BAY ART & PUMPKIN FESTIVAL
*In Half Moon Bay; 726-9652; free.*

This festive event includes pumpkin carving and pie-eating contests,

arts and crafts booths, a variety of pumpkin foods, and ongoing entertainment. Children are invited to wear costumes and participate in the parade.

Nearby pumpkin patches, brightly-colored with their seasonal loot, are open for picking.

## JACK-O-LANTERN JAMBOREE
For details see page 175.

## SAN FRANCISCO FAIR
*In San Francisco; 557-8758; adults $4, under 5 free.*

This urban version of the traditional county fair features continuous entertainment, exhibits galore, food booths operated by well-known restaurants, and a wine pavilion (separate admittance fee) featuring tasting and demonstrations. Pre-registration is required for the outrageous contests, which include Fog Calling, The Impossible Parking Space Race, and Operatic Lip Synching.

---

## — NOVEMBER —

---

## DICKENS CHRISTMAS FAIR
*In San Francisco, at Pier 45, Fisherman's Wharf; 800/52-FAIRE, 892-0937; adults $12.50, 3-11 $5, under 3 free.*

See *A Christmas Carol* brought to life at this re-creation of Christmas in Victorian London. It provides the opportunity for the grumpiest Scrooge to get into the spirit of the season.

Visitors can play unusual games such as Lace-A-Lady, purchase fine and unusual yuletide gifts, and feast on authentic period food and drink such as plum pudding and hot buttered rum.

Entertainment is continuous and includes parades, melodrama performances, and caroling contests. There is even dancing with Mr. and Mrs. Fezziwig and their guests at their celebrated party. And if all this isn't enough, Her Majesty Queen Victoria and her consort Prince Albert always attend.

Visitors are encouraged to dress in period costume.

The fair runs through mid-December.

## INTERNATIONAL TAIKO FESTIVAL
*In Berkeley, U.C. Campus, Zellerbach Hall; 642-9988.*

In ancient Japan, taiko drums were relied upon to get rid of evil spirits and to bring on the rain. Now the throbbing sounds and colorful performers provide thrilling entertainment but little rain.

DICKENS CHRISTMAS FAIR

**OXFAM FAST FOR A WORLD HARVEST**
For description see page 260.

**TEDDY BEAR FILM FESTIVAL AND PARADE**
For description see page 169.

**WALNUT CREEK MODEL RAILROAD SOCIETY "BIG SHOW"**
For description see page 186.

---

## — DECEMBER —

---

### A CHRISTMAS CAROL

*In San Francisco, Geary Theatre; 749-2ACT; tickets $10-$32. Clift Hotel: 495 Geary St., 775-4700.*

After thirteen years of presenting Dickens' popular seasonal ghost tale, the American Conservatory Theatre has it down pat.

The sentimental story, which celebrates the rebirth of the human spirit and the death of indifference, is sure to rekindle any lagging Christmas enthusiasm. (Do take any grumpy holiday Scrooges you may know.) And ACT's lively, colorful production enhances it with a musical score of carols, songs, and dance.

It is interesting to note that Dickens' story is credited with actually reviving the celebration of Christmas, which at the time his book was published in 1843 had slipped to the status of a quaint, almost obsolete, custom. It is also considered responsible for some English social reform. Fortunately for all of us, his story still manages to wake up the spirit of human kindness.

Following all performances, which run about two hours with no intermission, members of the cast appear in costume at a **Meet-the-Cast Party**. Don't miss this opportunity to introduce your children to these legendary characters and collect an autograph or two.

After a matinee performance, what could be more appropriate than tea at the elegant Clift Hotel? Located just down the block from the theater, the hotel provides a sumptuous **Christmas Carol Tea** in its elegant **Redwood Room**. Guests are treated to a long buffet table laden with scones and crumpets and cakes and cookies and pies and tarts and tortes and fruits and roasted chestnuts and even candy canes and gingerbread men.

Tea is served at table, along with special children's drinks like hot chocolate and spiced cider. The regular High Tea menu is also available. Reservations are recommended.

## BREAKFAST WITH SANTA

*In San Francisco, Hyatt Regency; 788-1234.*

Ever wonder what Santa eats for breakfast? Find out, and thrill your young children at the same time. The food and excitement should be adequate to see you all through a busy morning of shopping after.

These special breakfasts take place at **Mrs. Candy's Restaurant** in the magnificent Atrium Lobby of the Hyatt Regency. Adults order from the regular breakfast menu; children order from a special menu designed for the event. Santa visits everyone, and no reservations are necessary. Kids are usually given a favor. Don't forget your camera.

Similar events, which require reservations, occur each year in selected Emporium and Macy's stores. Since dates and details vary from year to year and store to store, you will need to call the one nearest you in mid-November for further information.

## CAROLING CRUISES
For description see page 178.

## CATHEDRAL CHOIR CHRISTMAS CONCERTS
For description see page 75.

## CHRISTMAS AT DUNSMUIR
For description see page 177.

## THE CHRISTMAS STAR PLANETARIUM SHOW
For description see page 91.

## CHRISTMAS TREE FARMS
*800/952-5272.*

Isn't it time you chopped your own? This year provide your children with the memorable experience of an envigorating trek through the woods to choose the family Christmas tree. This is also a way to be sure your tree is fresh and won't lose most of its needles before you get it home.

Call for a free list of Christmas tree farms located in your county.

See also page 182.

## DRIVE-BY NATIVITY SCENE
*In El Cerrito, 944 Arlington Ave.; weather permitting, Dec 12-26; lit 6-10 pm; free.*

For almost 40 years Sundar Shadi has turned his hillside yard into a gigantic nativity scene for Christmas. Among the hundreds of life-size props are sheep, donkeys, camels, goats, shepherds, the Three Wise Men, and a pink angel. Mr. Shadi makes all the figures himself, and his wife makes the clothing. Carols are broadcast over loudspeakers as cars drive slowly by. Mr. Shadi sets up the display each year as a gift to the community.

He spends the rest of the year turning his yard into blooming Persian carpets and floral tributes to various organizations. The best time to view this effort is in June. Special theme displays may also be viewed the week before Halloween and from Palm Sunday through Easter.

## FUNGUS FAIR
*In San Francisco, County Fair Bldg. in Golden Gate Park; 753-7090; adults $2.50, under 12 $1.50.*

Thinking about eating that wild mushroom growing in your yard? Play it safe and have it identified first by a knowledgeable expert at this unusual fair. You can also view hundreds of kinds of wild fungi, including a number of poisonous varieties, and get tips on cultivating and cooking edible varieties. Sponsored by the San Francisco Mycological Society.

## GOLDEN GATE PARK CHRISTMAS TREE LIGHTING
*In San Francisco, in Golden Gate Park; 666-7107; free.*

San Francisco's official Christmas tree, a 100-foot Monterey Cypress located at the east entrance to Golden Gate Park, is lit each Christmas with over 3,000 lights. The Mayor is usually present to flip the switch. Santa also makes an appearance, and the audience is led in singing carols.

## GUARDSMEN CHRISTMAS TREE SALE
*In San Francisco, Fort Mason Center; 775-6852.*

Claiming to have the largest enclosed Christmas tree lot in northern California, the Guardsmen sell approximately 10,000 trees each year. They are famous for having the best selection of Noble Firs but also stock a variety of other trees, including Douglas Fir, Frazer Fir, and Scotch Pine.

Just visiting the lot is a thrill; it looks like a small forest. And on rainy days, since the lot is enclosed, you don't get wet.

Trees range from two to sixteen feet, cost from $7 to $435, and are tax-deductible. Garlands, wreaths, holly, mistletoe, and decorations are also on sale.

All proceeds are used to send underpriviledged Bay Area children to summer camp.

## THE NUTCRACKER
*In San Francisco, War Memorial Opera House; 621-3838; tickets $5-$40.*

The San Francisco Ballet has been presenting its delightful and festive version of *The Nutcracker* since 1944, when it blazed the path for all subsequent U.S. Nutcrackers by dancing the first full-length production. It has always been an extravagant interpretation, with hundreds of thousands of dollars worth of scenery and handmade costumes.

Each performance features the company's principal dancers—plus 30 to 40 children from the Ballet School, a spectacular growing Christmas tree, and a cannon that uses real gunpowder and makes a loud, smoke-producing boom. (The cannon once not only boomed but self-destructed!)

**Sugar Plum Parties** follow some matinee performances. They are held in the downstairs cafeteria. Guests are served sugary goodies (cookies, candy, soda), and the costumed cast members are available for autographs. Proceeds benefit the Ballet School. (Purchase party tickets at the same time you purchase your Nutcracker tickets.)

## PETER AND THE WOLF CONCERT
For description see page 81.

## PICKLE FAMILY CIRCUS HOLIDAY SHOW
For description see page 80.

## SANTA PARADE
*In Oakland, along Broadway between 10th & 20th Sts.; 764-3332; free.*

This grand parade includes floats, costumed characters, marching bands, and Santa himself. After the parade, everyone is invited to the

THE NUTCRACKER

downtown Oakland Emporium store (sponsor of the event) to enjoy free entertainment and meet Santa.

## THANK SANTA
For details see page 175.

## UNION SQUARE WINDOW DISPLAYS
*In San Francisco.*

Each year the biggest department stores (Macy's, I. Magnin, and Saks Fifth Avenue) treat the public to elaborate window decorations. Some feature moving mechanical displays.

Take time to walk completely around the square. It's also usually worth going a block further down to 250 Post Street to see the Gump's display.

It's also nice to visit **Bayberry Row**, located on the seventh floor of Macy's. It is a commercial, but beautiful, Christmas wonderland, and Santa is there. The lobby of the St. Francis Hotel is also worth a walk-through.

Street entertainers, vendors, and carolers provide further diversion.

## VICTORIAN TEA

For description see page 164.

# Appendixes

## — APPENDIX I —

### *The Big Yellow House Meets Suzie*

*The following true story was originally published in* Parents' Press. *The names have not been changed to protect the guilty. The restaurant chain no longer exits.*

"It looks just like I thought it would," enthused Mommy as Daddy parked in front of The Big Yellow House restaurant in surburban Dublin. "But somehow I expected it to be out in the country—not tucked between two modern buildings."

The children, dressed in their Sunday Best, stepped onto the parlor scale for their preliminary weigh-in. Twenty-two-month-old Suzanne weighed in free. (She stubbornly refused to stand on the scale, and the manager was experienced enough with children to know not to push her.) Eight-year-old David weighed in at $1.95.

While this was going on, Daddy had cleverly found himself a comfortable stuffed chair in the bar and had ordered a Margarita for himself and a piña colada for Mommy. Served in heavy Mason jars (the kind in which Grandma used to put up preserves), the drinks seemed low in alcohol—certainly not enough to fortify the innocent parents for what was to come.

"Meyers, party of three plus a highchair," blared the loudspeaker.

The family jumped up and followed the hostess up the imposing lobby stairway to a table on the second floor.

"I want to sit here by the railing," shouted David above the dining din.

Mommy apprehensively assented, discounting thoughts of utensils and food dropping over the edge onto waiting patrons.

The appetizer course arrived as soon as the family was seated. David dug into the cheddar cheese spread and slathered it onto a cracker. Mommy quickly prepared a similar cracker for Suzie, who was already beginning to show signs of restlessness. Suzie gulped it down and grabbed for more. "She likes it," observed Mommy. "Maybe she'll eat well tonight."

"Don't eat too much now," warned Daddy. "There's lots more food coming."

"When are they going to bring Daddy's surprise?" David asked Mommy in his normal, boisterous voice.

257

"Shh. Later," she whispered back.

The young waitress cued Daddy, who was getting suspicious, "Act surprised."

In a few minutes she reappeared with an iron pot of steaming minestrone soup. Daddy ladled out servings while Mommy cooled Suzie's portion with ice water. Before Mommy had even tasted hers, Suzie had decided it was quite delicious and was handing her bowl back and demanding more.

"This hot cornbread is just like I make," said Mommy approvingly. "Here. Try some with honey butter."

"I have to go to the bathroom," said David urgently. Daddy accompanied him while Mommy dished up yet another bowl of soup for little Suzie.

"I want the Thousand Island dressing," David said when the waitress brought a large bowl of salad and a selection of dressings.

"I think I'll try the Italian," said Mommy as Daddy drowned his crisp greens with the house sour-cream-and-herb. Meanwhile Suzie had ingested the interiors of her cherry tomatoes and neatly ejected the exteriors onto her makeshift napkin-bib. "Oh, oh. It looks like Suzie's done eating now, and we haven't even gotten to the main course."

After the salad was removed, things made a turn for the worse. Suzie became restless and decided to go full-swing into her Terrible Twos behavior, never minding that she still had two months to go until such behavior was official. She sweet-gurgled Mommy into giving her the last bit of the piña colada and then hurled the empty Mason jar into the air. It landed under the chair of a startled lady at an adjoining table. Mommy quickly apologized and, curious, asked, "How do you manage to keep your little girl so quiet?"

The lady smiled and replied, "She's not her usual self today. She's toned down, because she's not feeling well."

"Oh," said Mommy, disappointed that she was not to learn The Secret of Raising Well-behaved Children.

"Yuck," said David when the main course of pork roast and fried chicken arrived. "I don't have to eat any of that, remember? You promised I could eat only what I wanted, and I just want applesauce."

"You should at least taste everything," chided Daddy. "Here. I'll bet you'll enjoy these reconstituted mashed potatoes. Have some gravy, too. Umm," Daddy continued," this pork roast is so tender and tasty—it's as good as Grandma's! And the fried chicken is crispy and juicy—just the way I like it."

Tempted by that last enthusiasm, David tentatively tasted a drumstick. "It's better than the Colonel's," he sarcastically commented but continued to eat.

Suzie was now out of her highchair and caterwauling while hanging onto the stair railings and pulling down the decorations. Mommy was holding Suzie's dress straps with one hand and attempting to eat with the other. Icy stares came from two nearby tables where couples without children were dining serenely.

"I have a tummyache from bunky Suzie's crying," moaned David. "She's a t—d."

"David, don't call your sister names," scolded Daddy, slightly intimidated by the potential fireworks of the situation.

"My tummy hurts, too," agreed Mommy, "but I just can't stop eating this delicious pork roast." Never one to let impending disaster stand between her and a good meal, she added, "Should we ask for another portion? You know, the fixed price of $5.95 includes seconds."

"No," said Daddy emphatically as he viewed screaming Suzie rolling around on the rug next to Mommy's feet. "I think we'd better get out of here as quickly as possible."

Just as Daddy reached the panic point, the staff assembled and began singing "Happy Birthday." The hostess handed a truly surprised Daddy a complimentary hunk of moist lemon birthday cake topped with whipped cream. "Oh, no!" exclaimed Daddy earnestly. "What's this?"

"Can I have some?" David callously asked before Daddy had a chance even to sample his cake.

"Next year surprise me with a birthday dinner at home," Daddy muttered as the family got into the car.

"Poor baby," soothed Mommy. "Really though, the food was so good and such a bargain, let's come back again next year," she enthused, displaying her fortunately short memory. "Suzie will be in the Terrific Threes stage then, and we should be able to eat more and enjoy it more."

"I'm hungry," piped up David as they drove away. "What can I have for a snack when we get home?"

Take heart. They actually do grow up.

SUZIE

---

## — APPENDIX II —

---

## *A Family Fast: Oxfam Fast for a World Harvest*

When you have plenty to eat every day and, in fact, can be very choosey about what you eat, it can be hard to relate to incapacitating hunger. Most of us living in this land of plenty have never really experienced hunger—except maybe by choice during a diet.

That's why I think Oxfam's annual Fast for a World Harvest is such a worthwhile program.

Oxfam America describes itself as "a nonprofit, international agency that funds self-help development and disaster relief in poor countries in Africa, Asia, Latin America, and the Caribbean." The organization was founded in England in 1942; its name is derived from Oxford Committee for Famine Relief.

How does fasting aid a world harvest you might wonder. "It provides a symbolic way to participate in the struggles of the poor and hungry around the world," replies an Oxfam representative. "Fasters express solidarity with victims of the silent holocaust of hunger, and actively support life-giving international development."

The Oxfam Fast is held each year on the Thursday before our Thanksgiving holiday. This seems a particularly good time to reflect upon the relative abundance we enjoy—compared to many Third World people—as a matter of course. Oxfam asks that participating fasters contribute to the cause the amount of money saved from their food budgets by fasting.

When I first heard about this fast, I encouraged my own family to participate. My children were already sensitive to the issue of hunger from having seen the reports on the terrible famine in Ethiopia. My teen, who was in a growth stage where he had a large appetite, wasn't anxious to stop eating for a day. My youngest was interested and full of questions.

Upon reflection, I think it was a good idea to start talking about the fast approximately a week in advance. This gave us all plenty of time to adjust to the idea and become supportive.

Oxfam points out that there are a number of ways to fast. They don't recommend that children, who are still growing, eat nothing. So in our family we decided to have only juice (and coffee or tea for the adults) for breakfast. For lunch the children were to decide for themselves what to eat. They each chose to eat much less than normal and proudly announced that they had rejected sweets. My husband and I stuck to liquids.

At dinner I made a pot of rice, and we drank water. The dinner was most enlightening. It really brought home what was missing from our table . . . what we take for granted. And we realized that we were still eating much more than many less fortunate people.

During dinner we tallied what we had saved by fasting. Each of us estimated the cost of what we would have normally eaten during this period. We rounded it off, and for dessert we wrote out a check to Oxfam.

If you would like to participate in the Oxfam Fast for a World Harvest this year, call the San Francisco office at 863-3981 and ask for a free Family Fast Packet. It contains supportive education aids for you to use with your family.

## — APPENDIX III —

## *Books for Further Exploration*

### ABOUT THE SAN FRANCISCO BAY AREA

• *For Children*
    *\*The Cable Car and the Dragon* by Herb Caen (Chronicle Books, ©1972). Written by San Francisco's favorite newspaper columnist, this delightful story takes place one foggy evening when a bored cable car and an equally bored dragon from the Chinese New Year's parade get together for some fun on the city's famous hills.
    *Elephants on the Beach* by Irene Brady (Charles Scribner's Sons, ©1979). This book tells the story of an artist's day on the beach sketching the huge elephant seals at Año Nuevo. Their habits are described along with those of other animals sharing the same habitat. The book is appropriately illustrated with sketches and makes an informative before- and after-visit story for children.
    *Humphrey, The Lost Whale* by Wendy Tokuda and Richard Hall (Heian International, Inc.). Humphrey was an adventurous whale who got lost in the San Francisco Bay in 1985. He captured everyone's heart as he tried to get back to the ocean. This is the story of his trip in and out of the bay. The authors, a husband and wife team, are both journalists who covered the Humphrey story at work.
    *\*Kidding Around San Francisco* by Rosemary Zibart (John Muir Publications, ©1989). Written especially for children, this easy-to-read book gives information on the city's history and sightseeing highlights. Child-friendly restaurants, stores of interest to young shoppers, and a calendar of special events are also included. Recommended for ages 8+.

• *For Parents*
    *Bargain Hunting in the Bay Area* by Sally Socolich (Wingbow Press, ©1989). This book tells you "where to save 20% to 70% on almost anything one can buy." Special sections are devoted to children's new and used apparel and toys.
    *The Bay Area At Your Feet; There, There: East San Francisco Bay At Your Feet; Golden Gate Park at Your Feet,* all by Margot Patterson Doss (Don't Call It Frisco Press, ©1988, 1978, 1978). Detailed information for wonderful Bay Area walks to enjoy at your own pace.
    *Bay Play: A Complete Guide to the Best Children's Activities in the Bay Area* by Susan Andrews (Conari Press, ©1989). This helpful resource covers children's summer and after-school programs in the Bay Area.

*Berkeley Inside/Out* by Don Pitcher (Heyday Books, ©1989). This "complete guide to understanding and enjoying Berkeley," will be of interest to both visitors and long-time residents. It covers restaurants, attractions, and lodgings and provides historical and political insight.

*The Best of the Bay Area for You and Your Child* by Susan D. Waldman, Ph.D. (Firestone Press ©1989). This reference book is chock-full of resources parents of young children want to know about.

*The East Bay Out* by Malcolm Margolin (Heyday Books, ©1988). Using a personalized approach, this author details the beauties of the forty-plus parks contained in the East Bay Regional Park District. Special emphasis is given to history and natural attractions.

*Exploring Point Reyes* by Phil Arnot & Elvira Monroe (Wide World Publishing/Tetra, ©1989). A general guide with detailed trail maps, black and white photos, and information on both wildlife and sights.

*\*Family Bike Rides: A Guide to Over 40 Specially Selected Bicycle Routes in Northern California* by Milton A. Grossberg (Chronicle Books, ©1981). Detailed descriptions of bike routes include sightseeing suggestions and maps, plus such valuable information as where to park your bike safely and where to stop for refreshments. All routes are short, level, scenic, and off main roads.

*Playgrounds of the Peninsula* by Ava Zelver Everett (Tioga Publishing, ©1988). Children just can't get in enough time at playgrounds. This guide, complete with helpful maps, tips you to well-equipped playgrounds sprinkled from San Mateo to Cupertino.

*San Francisco by Cable Car* by George Young (Wingbow Press, ©1984). The author, a former cable car conductor, is now a professional tour guide. He describes the city's cable car lines and how to use them for sightseeing.

## EATING IN RESTAURANTS

### • For Children

*Eating Out* by Helen Oxenbury (Dial Books for Young Readers, ©1983). If you've ever lived through a disasterous experience with your kids in a restaurant, you're bound to get a chuckle out of this short story. It makes dinner at home look very good, even when you're too tired to cook.

*Frog Goes to Dinner* by Mercer Mayer (Dial Books for Young Readers, ©1974). This is a darling children's book depicting a restaurant disaster worse than any I've personally witnessed. If you've ever wondered what would happen if a little boy smuggled a frog into a fancy restaurant, here is a possible answer. You and your children are bound to get a giggle out of this one.

**• For Parents**

*The Fast Food Guide: What's Good, What's Bad, and How to Tell the Difference* by Dr. Michael Jacobson and Sarah Fritschner (Workman Publishing, ©1986). The authors dissect menu items from seventeen major fast-food chains, identifying those which are least, as well as those which are most, nutritious. They tell who uses food dyes, MSG, and other potentially hazardous additives.

## CHILDREN'S COOK BOOKS

Teaching children to cook is an important part of their education, but it seems the subject is no longer taught in school. So we parents must do this ourselves at home.

It is important to grab opportunities for teaching when they arise. A few attractive cookbooks can help inspire interest in most children.

I have found that one of the most important ingredients in a successful cooking lesson is time. Before you begin, make sure there are no time pressures. Best of all, plan your lesson so that just you and your child are home.

*Dinner's Ready Mom* by Helen Gustafson (Celestial Arts, ©1987). Written by a working mother, this cookbook is designed to help children ages 8 to 14 get dinner on the table. Recipes for wholesome, complete meals are easy to follow, and there's space for you to write in your own family's favorite recipes.

*The Fun of Cooking* by Jill Krementz (Alfred A. Knopf, ©1985). An inspiring coffee table kind of book, this is filled with wonderful black and white photos showing an assortment of kids preparing "their" recipes. Liz makes chocolate waffles. Sarah makes hamburger pie. Muffie makes homemade granola. And Jason makes doggie biscuits.

*\*Kids Cooking: A Very Slightly Messy Manual* by the editors of Klutz Press (Klutz Press, ©1987). The recipes in this built-for-abuse book have all been approved by a panel of "vegetable-leery taste-testers." Recipes included range from Tuna Wiggle to Darrell's "Forget-the-Cookies-Just-Give-Me-That-Batter" Chocolate Chip Cookie Recipe. A set of sturdy color-coded plastic measuring spoons are included.

*My First Cook Book* by Angela Wilkes (Alfred A. Knopf, ©1989). This oversize book is particularly nice for young children because it uses step-by-step color photographs to illustrate each recipe. Life-size photos show each ingredient, making it easy for children to check their work. Child-pleasing recipes include Speedy Pizzas, Fruit Fools, and Silly Sundaes. Yum.

*\*Science Experiments You Can Eat* by Vicki Cobb (Harper & Row, ©1972). What makes popcorn pop? How does jelly jell? Why does bread

rise? Experiment in your kitchen with these 39 easy and delicious science experiments and then eat the results!

You may have trouble finding some of these books in your local bookstore. (Note that those with an asterisk in front are available through *The Family Travel Guides Catalogue*, see page 282.) Some are out of print and no longer available except through your library or, if you're lucky, a bookstore that specializes in used books. For current information, call the publisher:

Alfred A. Knopf (Random House) 800/638-6460
Celestial Arts (Ten Speed Press) 415/845-8414
Charles Scribner's Sons 800/257-5755
Chronicle Books 800/445-7577
Conari Press 415/527-9915
Dial Books for Young Readers (E.P. Dutton) 212/725-1818
Don't Call It Frisco Press 415/488-0401
*The Family Travel Guides Catalogue* 415/527-5849
Firestone Press 415/346-3823
Harper & Row 800/237-5534
Heian International, Inc. 415/471-8440
Heyday Books 415/549-3564
John Muir Publications 505/982-4078
Klutz Press 415/857-0888
Tioga Publishing 415/965-4081
Wide World Publishing/Tetra 415/593-2839
Wingbow Press 800/999-4650
Workman Publishing 800/722-7202

# Indexes

## ALPHABETICAL INDEX

### A
abacus, 147
Academy of Sciences, 89
*A Christmas Carol*, 249, 251
Acres of Orchids, 206
Adventure Playground, 174
African Veldt enclosure, 181
African Waterhole exhibit, 90
Alameda Penny Market, 184
Alamo Square, 77
    tour, 114
Alcatraz Island, 68
Alexander Lindsay Junior Museum, 171
Allan Herschel Company, 181
Allied Arts Guild Restaurant, 189
Allyne Park, 77
*Alma*, 88
American Carousel Museum, The, 93
American Property Exchange, The, 126
American Youth Hostels, 242
Anchor Steam beer, 79
Andean music, 247
Anderson, Katrina, 220
Angel Island State Park, 95
Año Nuevo State Reserve, 203
antique toys, 84
Anti-gravity Mirror, 92
Apollo spacesuit, 208
aquariums, 90, 91, 175, 182
Aquatic Park, 96, 106, 247
Ardenwood Historic Farm, 163
art classes, 82, 84
art deco architectural tours, 113
Arthur Menzies Garden of California
    Native Plants, 101
Arturo's, 131
Asian Art Museum, 83
Audubon Canyon Ranch, 224
Audubon Cellars Winery, 184
*A View to a Kill*, 177
A Walk With Mrs. Terwilliger, 228
Ayala Cove, 95

### B
baby food grinder, 10
Baby Zoo, 181
Baez, Joan, 127
Baker Beach, 96
*Balclutha*, 85
Ballantyne, Sheila, 3
Barbie Hall of Fame, 203
BART, 5
baseball batting cages, 207
Basic Brown Bear Factory & Store, 105
basketball court, 102
Basque Hotel, 25
Bass Lake, 220
Batliner, Arnold, 121

Battery Chamberlin, 96
Bay Area Discovery Museum, 223, 234
bay cruise, 89
Bay to Breakers, 239
Bayside Boat & Breakfast, 126
Beach Blanket Babylon, 78
Bear Valley Trail, 226
Bears to Go, 106
Bed & Breakfast International, 126
beehives, 102, 177, 205
belly dancer, 32
Benihana of Tokyo, 52, 131, 190
Benkyo-Do Co., 52
Berkeley Iceland, 184
Berkeley Recreation Department, 231
Berkeley Rose Garden, 175
Berkeley Shakespeare Festival, 167
Berkeley Thai House, 13
Bertola's, 132
Best Western Kyoto Inn, 123
Bette's Ocean View Diner, 132
Bette's To Go, 133
Biblical Garden, 101
bikerides, 95, 96, 224, 242
Bill's Place, 25
Birdman of Alcatraz, 68
bird sanctuaries, 176, 177, 205, 224, 227
*Birds, The*, 111
Black Diamond Mines Regional Preserve, 164
Black Jewel, 223
Blackie's Pasture, 224
Blessing of the Fishing Fleet, 247
Blue and Gold Fleet Bay Tours, 112
Blue Angels, 247, 248
Blue Danube Coffee House, 48
boat rentals, 101, 177, 182
Book Bay, 239
book sale, 239
Botanic Garden (Tilden Nature Area), 183
Botanical Garden (U.C. Berkeley), 165
Bouquets to Art, 83
Bourn II, William Bowers, 206
Boyd Park, 223
Bread & Honey Tea Room, The, 26
Breakfast with Santa, 252
Breakfast with the Easter Bunny, 238
Brennan's, 133
Brothers Delicatessen and Restaurant, 190
Brothers' Bagel Factory, 161
Bubba's Diner, 211
Bubble Festival, 92
Bufano sculptures, 91, 127
Buffalo Paddock, 97
bumper cars, 109
Burger King, 232
*Burnt Offerings*, 177
butterfly garden, 102
Butterfly World, 179
By the Square, 117

## C

Cable Car Bell Ringing Championships, 242
Cable Car Charters, 113
Cable Car Museum, 93
cable cars, 93, 114, 242
Cactus Taqueria, 134
Cadillac Bar, 26
Cafe de Young, 83
Cafe Madrona and Bakery, 230
Caffe Giovanni, 134
Caffe Roma, 27
California Academy of Sciences, 89
California Marine Mammal Center, 229
California Palace of the Legion of Honor, 81
California Pizza Kitchen, 120
California Tidepool exhibit, 91
Calzone's, 27
camel ride, 179
Camelid Capers, 220
Camp Hyatt, 122, 123
Campanile, 165
campsites, 95
Camron-Stanford House, 177
C & H Sugar refinery, 151
Candlelight Fort Tours, 73
Cannery, The, 105
Cantina, The, 211
Capone, Al, 68
Capp's Corner, 28
Caravansary, 65
carillons, 73, 165, 208
Carlmont Nursery, 198
carniverous plants, 165, 244
caroling cruises, 178
carousels, 93, 97, 102, 110, 175, 181, 182, 207
Carroll, Diahann, 127
Carson, Johnny, 239
Carter, President Jimmy, 118
Cartoon Art Museum, 82
Cartwright, The, 116
Casa de Eva, 135
Castaway, The, 190
Castro Point Railway, 180
C. A. Thayer, 87
Cathedral Choir Christmas Concerts, 75
Cathedral Hill Churches tour, 114
Celia's, 29, 135, 191, 212
Chabot Observatory and Planetarium, 184
Chamber of Horrors, 95
Chancellor Hotel, 117
chantey sings, 87
Che Sun Tong Co., 71
cheese factory, 221
Chef Chu's, 191
Cherry Blossom Festival, 108
Chevys, 29, 136, 191, 212
Chez Madeleine, 212
children's art show, 83
children's books, 83, 239
Children's Fairyland U.S.A., 175, 232
Children's Playground, 97
Children's Zoo, 102, 233
China Beach, 96
China Station, 137
Chinatown, 68
   walks, 113
Chinese Culture Center, 68
Chinese Culture Foundation, 70
Chinese medicinal herb garden, 165

Chinese New Year celebration & parade, 237
Chinese New Year walks, 70
Chinese temples, 71
Christ Was an Ad Man, 128
Christmas at Dunsmuir, 177
Christmas Carol Tea, 251
Christmas foods, 33
Christmas Star, The, 91
Christmas tree farms, 253
Chuck E. Cheese, 232
Chung, Henry, 41
circuses, 79, 80
City Guides, 114
City Hall tour, 114
Claremont Resort Pavilion Room, 137
Cliff House, 63
   Visitors Center, 71
Clift Hotel, Four Seasons, 117
CLIO Awards, 245
Cocolat, 67
Codornices Park, 175
Cody's bookstore, 186
Coit Tower, 72
   tour, 114
Colonial museum, 76
Colorforms Wall, 224
Columbus Day celebration and parade, 247
Comedy Celebration, 243
Compadres Mexican Bar & Grill, 29, 106, 191
Compass Rose, The, 30
concerts, 81, 247
Concord Pavilion, 167
Conservatory of Flowers, 98
cookie-decorating parties, 33
Cookies North Beach, 28
Corn Popper, The, 106
Cost Plus Imports, 105
Coyote Point Museum and Park, 205
Crab Cove Visitor Center, 175
crepes, 47
Crogan's Bar and Grill, 138
crookedest street in the world, 73
croquet lawns, 243
Crown Memorial State Beach, 175

## D

Dan's Place, 191
Danville Hotel Restaurant & Saloon, 139
darts, 216
Dashiell Hammett Tour, 114
daVinci, Leonardo, 71
Declaration of Independence, 77
Demetris, 193
de Young Memorial Museum, M.H., 82
Dial-A-Story, 5
Dianda's Italian-American Pastry, 45
Dickens, Charles, 251
Dickens Christmas Fair, 249
Dinky transportation toys, 84
Dinner Is Served, 19
Dinosaur Days, 171
dinosaurs, 84, 167, 171
Discovery Room, 90
Discovery Theatre, 224
Disney merchandise, 110
Doidge's Kitchen, 30
Doing and Viewing Art class, 82
dolls, 84, 111, 173, 203
Dominguez Mexican Bakery, 60
donkey engine, 88

Doors of Paradise, 73
double-decker bus tours, 113
dragon hedge, 100
Drake's Beach, 227
    Cafe, 227
Drive-by Nativity Scene, 253
Duarte's Tavern, 193
Dunsmuir House and Gardens, 176
Dutch Kitchen, 121
*Dynasty*, 206

**E**
Eagle Cafe, 31
earthquake, simulated, 110
Earthquake Trail, 226
East Bay Regional Park District, 184
East End tour, 101
Edison, Thomas, 120
Edwards, Chuck and Kristi, 212
Edy's, 139
elephant ride, 179
elephant seals, 90, 204
Elephant's Trunk, The, 234
elevator, glass, 121, 122
El Faro, 65, 161, 202
Elizabethan village, 244
El Machino, 136
El Mansour, 31
Elsie B. Roemer Bird Sanctuary, 176
El Sombrero, 32
Elvis's cape, 37
Embarcadero Center, 122
    garage, 64
Emil Villa's Hick'ry Pit, 140, 194, 213
Environmental Education Center, 182
*Eppleton Hall*, 88
Equestrian Center, 98
Esprit Factory Outlet, 105
eternal flame, 108
Eugene O'Neill National Historic Site, 164
*Eureka*, 86
Examiner Bay to Breakers, 239
Exploratorium, 92, 235

**F**
factory outlets, 106
Familiar, 112
Family Days, 227
Fantasia, 32
Fantasy Forum, 168
F.A.O. Schwarz, 110
Far East Cafe, 33
Far Side Gallery, The, 90
Farallon Islands excursions, 112
Farrell's, 232
fasting, 260
Fatapple's, 140
Father's Day Kite Festival, 242
Fenton's Creamery, 141
Fern Dell, 101
ferries, 5, 95, 179
Ferris wheels, 82, 175, 207
Festival of Lessons, 75
Festival of the Sea, 85
Fezziwig, Mr. and Mrs., 249
Fierstein, Fred, 174
Filbert Street steps, 72
Filoli Estate, 205
Findley's Fabulous Fudge, 106

Firehouse No. 1 Bar-be-que, 202
Fish Trap, 194
fishing pond, 181
flea market, 184
Fleet Week, 248
Fog Calling Contest, 249
Fondue Fred, 142
Fong, Edsel Ford, 58
food stalls, 165
footraces, 102, 239
Ford, Harrison, 37
Fort Funston, 96
Fort Point National Historic Site, 73
Fortune Bakery, 70
fortune cookie factories, 70, 185
49-Mile Drive, 115
Foucault pendulum, 90
Four Seasons Clift Hotel, 117, 251
Fourth of July fireworks and festivities, 243
fragrance garden, 101
French Room, 33
Friends of the San Francisco Public Library, 239
Fuchsia Garden, 101
Fuddruckers, 142
Fudge Alley, 143
Fungus Fair, 253
Funtasia, 109
F.W. Woolworth Co., 111

**G**
Galaxy Sandwich Shop, 171
G.B. Ratto & Co. International Grocers, 161
Gem and Mineral Hall, 90
Gentle Jungle, 179
Geology Department, U.C. Berkeley, 167
*Geo. Shima* wheelhouse, 88
Ghiberti, Lorenzo, 73
Ghirardelli Chocolate Manufactory, 34, 106, 235
Ghirardelli Square, 106
Ghirardelli's, 106
Giant Camera Obscura, 71
gold displays, 78, 90
Golden Gate Bridge, 73, 94, 112, 225
Golden Gate Fortune Cookies Company, 70
Golden Gate Hostel, 225
Golden Gate International Exposition, 94
Golden Gate Model Railroaders, 84
Golden Gate Park, 96
    Christmas tree lighting, 253
Golden Turtle, 35
Goldthwait, Bob, 243
Gonzales, George, 93
Good Earth, The, 143, 194, 213
Goosebumps, 106
Gorilla World, 102
Grace Cathedral, 73
    Choir of Men and Boys, 75
    tour, 114
Grace Marchant Garden, 72
Gramma's, 143
Grand National Rodeo, Horse, &
    Stock Show, 248
Gray Line Tours, 113
Great America, 207
Great China Art Co., 71
Great San Francisco Bike Adventure, 242
Greater Tuna, 79
Greens, 36
Guardian, The, 174
Guardsmen Christmas tree sale, 254

Guinness Museum of World Records, 94
Gunne Sax outlet, 106
Guaymas, 213

**H**

Haas-Lilienthal House, 75
Hagiwara, Makoto, 100
Haight-Ashbury tour, 114
Half Moon Bay Art & Pumpkin Festival, 248
Hallidie, Andrew, 115
Hammett, Dashiell, 114, 120
Handlery Union Square Hotel, The, 118
hang-gliders, 96
Harbin Manchurian, 37
Hard Rock Cafe, 37
Harvest Time, 181
Heaney, Frank, 68
Heart's Desire Beach, 228
Heidi Pies, 195
Hello Kitty, 52, 111
Help At Home, 19
Henderson Overlook, 224
herb garden, 165
herb shops, Chinese, 71
herbal knot gardens, 206
*Hercules*, 88
Heritage Walk, 70
Herron, Don, 114
Herschell-Spillman, 97, 183
historic houses, 75-77, 163, 164, 176, 177,
   205, 223, 227
Historic Market Street tour, 114
Hitchcock, Alfred, 111
Hobee's, 144, 195
Hofmann, Hans, 173
Holiday Inn Union Square, 118
Hollywood Movie Classics, 170
Holmes, Sherlock, 118
Holocaust Memorial, 81
Homemade Express, 18
Hong Kong Tea House, 38
Hoover, President Herbert, 208
Hoover Tower Observation Platform, 208
Horky's, 196
Hornblower Dining Yachts, 39
horseshoe courts, 101
hostels, 128, 225
Hotel Diva, 118
Hotel Union Square, 120
House of Prime Rib, 39
houseboat, 88
Hoyle, Geoff, 81
Hunan, 40
Hunan Restaurant, 144
*Hunchback of Notre Dame, The*, 75
Huntington Falls, 101
Hyatt Regency San Francisco, 121, 252
Hyde Park Suites, 126
Hyde Street Pier, 85

**I**

Ice Creamery, The, 145
ice skating rinks, 184, 209
Impossible Parking Space Race, 249
Indian village, 226
Insect Zoo, 102
International Street Performers Festival, 109, 245
International Taiko Festival, 249
Isobune, 52

**J**

Jack London Square, 185
Jackson Square/Portsmouth Square tour, 114
Jack-O-Lantern Jamboree, 175
Jade Villa, 146
Jagger, Mick, 118
James Fitzgerald Marine Reserve, 206
Japan Center, 51, 106
Japanese Tea Garden and Teahouse, 98
   tour, 101
Japantown tour, 114
Jerry's Farm House, 214
Jewels in the Bay exhibit, 94
Jewish museum, 171
Jil's Restaurant, 20
John Hinkel Park, 167
John Muir National Historic Site, 164
Johnson, Sterling, 93
Johnson's Drakes Bay Oyster Company, 214, 227
Jones, Indiana, 37
Josephine D. Randall Junior Museum, 84
Joy Luck, 146
Judah L. Magnes Museum, 171
Julia Morgan Theatre, 168
Jupiter train ride, 181
Just Desserts, 41
Justin Herman Plaza, 122

**K**

Kabuki Hibachi, 52
Kayser Pastries, 221
Keller Beach, 180
Kelly, George "Machine Gun", 68
Kensington Park Hotel, 120
Khan Toke Thai House, 41
Kidshows, 79, 168, 223
Kinderzimmer, 111
King George Hotel, The, 120
King of China Restaurant, 42
King Tsin, 146
King Yen, 147
Kintetsu Building, 51
Kirin, 42
Kite Shop, The, 106
kite-flying spots, 106, 180, 182, 242
Kow Loon Pastry, 15
KQED Old Fashioned Ice Cream
   Social & Tasting, 245
Kule Loklo, 226
Kuleto's, 121
Kushitsuru, 52

**L**

Lace-A-Lady, 249
La Cuchina, 43
La Ferme Beaujolaise, 66
La Ginestra, 215
Lake Anza, 183
Lake Merritt, 177
   Waterbird Refuge, 177
Lakeside Delicatessen, 161
Lake Temescal Regional Recreation Area, 178
Lane Heung Bakery, 70
La Nouvelle Patisserie, 106
La Palma Market, 61
Larkey Park, 186
La Rondalla, 43
Larry Blake's, 148
Laserium, 91

La Taqueria, 44
Late for the Train, 196
La Val's, 148
La Victoria Bakery and Grocery, 60
Lawrence, Ernest Orlando, 171
Lawrence Hall of Science, 171, 235
Le Croissant, 215
Le Meridien Hotel, 20
Legion of Honor, California Palace of the, 81
Leonard J. Waxdeck Bird Calling Contest, 239
Leon's Bar-B-Q, 45
Let's Eat, 220
Levi Plaza, 72
Liberty Ships, 89, 230
lighthouses, 68, 149, 225, 227
lily pond, 165
Lincoln Park, 81
Linear Accelerator, Stanford, 208
Little Farm, 182
Little Joe's, 45
Little Lombard, 230
Live Animal Center, 205
L.J. Quinn's Lighthouse, 149
llamas, 220
Lloyd Lake tour, 102
llunch with a llama, 220
Logger's Run, 207
Lombard Street, 73
Lorikeet Aviary, 179
Lori's Diner, 120
Lowie Museum of Anthropology, 166
Lucca Delicatessen, 66
Lunsford, Jerry, 220
Lyford House, 227

**M**
macaws, 29, 128
Machine Gun Kelly, 68
Macy's Electronics Department, 111
Made to Order, 161
Madonna, 118
Magic Concert, 127
Magic Pan, The, 47, 196
magic paraphernalia, 110
Maiko, 150
Mai's Vietnamese Restaurant, 47
Make-A-Circus, 79
Malibu Castle, 207, 232
*Maltese Falcon, The*, 114, 120
Mama's, 48
Mansion Hotel, The, 127
Marie Callender's, 150, 197
Marin County Fair, 244
Marin County Historical Society Museum, 223
Marin Discoveries, 224
Marin French Cheese Company, 221
Marin Headlands, 225
Marina Yacht Harbor, 93
Marine World Africa USA, 178
Maritime Museum, 85
Martinez Adobe, 164
Max's Diner, 49, 150
Max's Opera Cafe, 49, 150, 197
Maybeck, Bernard, 92
Mayflower Inne, 216
maze, 175
McDonald's, 50, 233
McFerrin, Bobby, 81
McGovern, George, 127

McKegney Green, 224
Med, The, 186
Medical Center tour, Stanford, 208
Mee Mee Bakery, 70
Meet-the-Cast Party, 251
Mels Drive-In, 50
Mermaids Seafood Bar, 120
Merritt Queen, 177
merry-go-rounds (see "carousels")
Mexican Museum, The, 82
M.H. de Young Memorial Museum, 82
Michaelmas Faire, 75
Midnight Mass, 75
Mid-Winter Exposition, 100
Mifune, 51
Mikado, 52
Mike's Chinese Cuisine, 52
Mill Valley Market, 221
Miller/Knox Regional Shoreline, 180
Mindscraper, 110
mines, 164
miniature golf, 207
Miramar Beach Inn, 197
misfortune cookies, 70
Misono, 52
Mission Dolores, 77
Mission Murals tour, 114
Mission Rock Resort, 53
Mission San Jose de Guadalupe, 164
Mission San Rafael Archangel, 223
missions, 77, 164, 223
Miwok Indian village, 226
Miyako Hotel, 124
modern art museum, 83
Momentum Machine, 92
Mongolian firepot dinner, 37
Monkey Island, 102
*Monterey Clipper*, 88
Monterey Market, 162
Montgomery Street tour, 114
Moon-viewing Garden, 101
Morgan Horse Ranch, 226
Morrison Planetarium, 91
Mother's Day Rose Show, 240
Mount Livermore, 95
Mount Tamalpais Scenic Railway, 240
Mountain Home Inn, 241
Mountain Lake Park, 102
Mountain Play, 240
Mrs. Candy's Restaurant, 252
Muir, John, 164
Muir Woods National Monument, 226
MUNI, 5
Muriel's Doll House Museum, 173
Musee Mecanique, 71
Museo Italo-Americano, 83
Museum of Paleontology, 167
music boxes, 110
Music Tracks, 110

**N**
Nantucket Fish Company, 151
NASA Ames Research Center, 208
National Society of Colonial Dames
    of America, 76
Nativity scene, 253
Nature Company, The, 106
Navy's birthday, 248
Near Escapes, 113
Necklace of Lights, 177

Neptune Beach, 175
New Asia, 53
New Joe's, 118
New Sunshine Ristorante, 151
New Woey Loy Goey Cafe, 54
Night Tour at the Zoo, 102
Niles Canyon Railway Museum, 180
Nob Hill tour, 114
Nobel Prize winners, 165, 171
Noddy, Tom, 93
*Norma Jean the Termite Queen*, 3
North Beach Pizza, 54
North Beach tour, 114
North China, 55
*Nutcracker, The*, 254

**O**

Oakland Harbor boat tours, 185
Oakland Museum, 173, 239
Oakland Zoo, 180
Ocean, 55
Ocean City, 56
Ocean Park Motel, 124
Oceanic Society, 112
Octagon House, 76
Old Borges Ranch, 181
Old Mill Park, 226
Old Mint, 77
Old St. Hilary's Church, 223
Old Uncle Gaylord's Ice Cream Parlor, 56, 152
O'Neill, Eugene, 164
On Ning Tong Co., 71
opera, 49, 80, 161, 249
Operatic Lip Synching contest, 249
Orchid Show, 238
Organ Pops Series, 170
organs, 73, 93, 97, 170, 198
Ortman's Ice Cream Parlor, 152
O Sole Mio, 56
Oxfam, 260

**P**

Pacific Film Archive, 169
Pacific Heights, 128
    walking tours, 76, 114
Pacific Locomotive Association, 180
pagoda, 100
painted ladies, 77
Palace of Fine Arts, 80, 92
Palo Alto auxiliary of Children's Hospital
    Stanford, 189
Palo Alto Children's Theatre, 203
Palo Alto Duck Pond, 206
Palo Alto Junior Museum, 203
Palo Marin Trail, 220
Panama-Pacific Exposition, 92
Pane e Cioccolata, 148
parades, 109, 169, 237, 238, 247, 248, 249, 254
Paradise Beach, 228
Paramount Theatre, 170
parcourse, 102
Park Grill, 123
Park Hyatt San Francisco, 122
Pasand, 57, 152, 198, 216
Patterson Home, 163
Peace Pagoda, 106
Pelican Inn, The, 216
Penguin Island, 102
Penny Carnival, 79

Pescadero Marsh Natural Preserve, 205
Pescadero State Beach, 205
Peter and the Wolf, 81
Peterson and Alsford General Store, 194
pets, 111, 171
Petting Corral, 84
Phineas T. Barnacle, The, 63
Picante Taqueria & Cantina, 153
pick your own produce, 181
Pickle Family Circus, 80
Pier 39, 109
Pine Brook Inn, 198
Ping-Pong, 216
Pioneer Log Cabin, 101
Pizza & Pipes, 198
Pizza Hut, 233
Pizza Time Theatre, 232
planetariums, 91, 171, 184
Plasterer, Eiffel, 93
playgrounds, 97, 102, 174, 175, 177, 179, 181,
    198, 205, 223, 226
Plearn, 153
Pleasanton Cheese Factory, 162
poinsettia display, 98
Point Bonita Lighthouse, 225
Point Reyes Lighthouse, 227
Point Reyes National Seashore, 220, 226
Polk, Willis, 206
Polly Ann Ice Cream, 57
Pomponio State Beach, 205
pony rides, 182
Port of Oakland, 185
Port of San Francisco, 89
Portals of the Past, 102
Portsmouth Square Garage, 16
Pot Sticker, The, 57, 199
Prairie Crawl, 179
Prayerbook Cross, 102
Preservation Fair, 177
Presidio Museum tour, 114
Primate Discovery Center, 102
Prince Albert, 249
Prince of Angels, 75
Pritikin, Robert, 127
produce, pick your own, 181
pub, 216
puppet show, 175
puppet store, 110
puzzles, 110

**Q**

Quadrangle, 208
Queen Victoria, 249

**R**

racing car courses, 207
Rainbow Falls, 102
Rapids Waterslide, The, 182
Red Egg and Ginger Party, 65
redwood groves, 101, 165, 219, 226, 243
Redwood Memorial Grove, 101
Redwood Room, 251
Redwood Valley Railway, 183
*Regional Parks Log*, 184
Renaissance Pleasure Faire, 244
rent-a-pet, 171
revolving door, 121
rhododendron dells, 101, 165
Rice Table, The, 217
Richards, Peter, 93

Richardson Bay Audubon Center &
    Sanctuary, 227
Richmond Plunge, 186
riding lessons, 98
rifle range, 205
Ripley's Believe It or Not! Museum, 94
Robison's Exclusively for Pets, 111
rodeo, 248
Rodeo Beach, 225
Rodin, 81
    Sculpture Garden, 208
roller coasters, 207
    simulated, 110
roller skating, 96
rose gardens, 101, 175
Rose Hill Cemetery, 164
Rotary Natural Science Center, 177
Roundabout, 91
Round The Rock tour, 68
Royal Pacific Motor Inn, 123
Ruby Sailing Yacht, 112
Rusty Pelican, 153, 199

**S**
sabre tooth tiger, 167
Sailboat House, 177
sake tasting, 186
Salmagundi, 58
Sam's Anchor Cafe, 217
Sam Wo, 58
sand castle contests, 176, 242
San Francisco Ballet, 254
San Francisco Children's Art Center, 235
San Francisco Children's Opera, 80
San Francisco Convention and Visitors Bureau, 4
San Francisco County Fair Flower Show, 244
San Francisco Craft & Folk Art Museum, 83
San Francisco Experience, The, 109
San Francisco Fair, 249
San Francisco Fire Department Museum, 94
    tour, 114
San Francisco International Film Festival, 238
San Francisco International Hostel, 128
San Francisco International Toy Museum, 84
San Francisco Maritime National
    Historical Park, 85
San Francisco Museum of Modern Art, 83
San Francisco Mycological Society, 253
San Francisco Orchid Society, 238
San Francisco School of Cooking, 20, 233
San Francisco Symphony Family Concerts, 81
San Francisco Zoo, 102
San Gregorio State Beach, 205
Sanppo, 59
Sanrio, 111
Santa Parade, 254
Santini's Restaurant, 199
Sapporo-ya Ramen, 52
Sarducci, Father Guido, 243
Satellite Gallery, 119
Sausalito, 230
Say Cheese, 66
Schoemaker, Lucas, 20
Schroeder, Pat, 18
Schuyler's Ice Cream Cafe, 148
science classes, 84
Scottish broom flower, 215
Scott's Seafood Grill & Bar, 59, 154, 200
sculpture gardens, 174, 208

Sea Fox wheelhouse, 88
Seafood & Beverage Co, The, 63
Seal Rocks, 63, 71
Seamen's Memorial Cruise, 89
Sears, 59
Segal, George, 82
seismograph, 84, 167, 171
Senator Chambers (macaw), 128
Shadi, Sundar, 253
Shadow Box, 92
Shadow Cliffs Regional Recreation Area, 182
Shakespeare Garden, 100
Shakey's Pizza Parlor, 234
Sheraton at Fisherman's Wharf, 126
ships, 85-89
S. Holmes Esq. Public House and
    Drinking Salon, 118
Shorebird Nature Center, 182
Siam Cuisine, 155
Sid and Caesar (macaws), 29
Simon, Paul, 127
simulated earthquake, 110
Sixth Army, 243
Skates, 156
Sky Whirl, 207
Skyfari, 181
Slide Ranch, 227
Smith Family Farm, 181
Smurf Woods, 207
something special, 228
Space Maze, 224
Spenger's Fish Grotto, 156
Spreckels Lake, 102
Spring Festival, 68
sprint cars, 207
Sproul Plaza, 166
S.S. Jeremiah O'Brien, 84, 89
Stagecoach Restaurant, 200
Stanford University campus, 208
Stanford University Museum of Art, 208
Stanyan Park Hotel, 124
Station House Cafe, 218
STBS, 81
Stein, David, 93
Steinhart Aquarium, 91
Stern Grove Midsummer Music Festival, 242
St. Francis Fountain, 60
St. Francis, The Westin, 121
Stinson Beach, 228
St. Michael, 75
Stow Lake Boathouse, 101
Stoyanof's, 66
St. Patrick's Day Parade, 238
Strawberry Canyon, 165
Strawberry Hill tour, 101
Streamliner train ride, 181
street performers, 105, 106, 109, 245
Stroud, Robert "Birdman of Alcatraz", 68
Strybing Arboretum, 101
Subterranean, 148
Such A Business, 5, 110
Sugar Plum parties, 254
Sukay concert, 247
Sunset Magazine Garden, 208
Superior Trading Co., 71
surfers, 200
Sutro, Adolph, 71
Sutro Baths, 71
Swallow, The, 173

Sweden House Bakery, 222
Sweet Things, 220
Sweet Zoo, 106
Swensen's Ice Cream Parlor, 110
swimming pools, hotel, 118, 126
    public, 186

**T**

Taco Bell, 200
Tactile Dome, 92
taiko drum performances, 109, 249
Taiwan, 61, 157
Takara Sake USA, 186
Tao House, 164
Taqueria Mexican Grill, 219
Taqueria Vera Cruz, 45
taxis, 5
tea ceremonies, 109
Teddy Bear Film Festival and Parade, 169
teddy bears, 105, 106, 169
Teddy's, 116
Telegraph Avenue, 186
Templeton, Gary, 170
tennis courts, 102, 175, 223
Terwilliger, Elizabeth, 228
Terwilliger Nature Education Center, 228, 235
T.G.I. Friday's, 61, 201
Thank Santa, 175
Theatre on the Square, 120
Thinker, The, 81
Tiburon Paintbrush, 223
tidepools, 205, 206
Tilden Nature Area, 182
Tin How Temple, 71
TJ's Gingerbread House, 158
Tommaso's, 61
Tong Palace, 42
Tony Roma's, 219
Tony's Seafood, 219
toy museum, 84
Transcontinental Railroad, 180
Travelodge at the Wharf, 126
Tray of Togetherness, 70
Treasure Island Museum, 94
Trolley Festival, 244
Tung Fong, 63
Twain, Mark, 5
Twin Peaks, 84
Twin Pines Park, 198

**U**

U.C. Theatre, 170
Underground Mining Museum, 164
Underwater Adventure Tunnel, 224
Union Square tour, 114
Union Square Christmas window displays, 255
Union Street, 111
    Spring Festival, 243
University Art Museum, 173
University of California, Berkeley campus, 165
Upstairs at the Cliff House, 63
US Army Corps of Engineers Bay Model
    Visitor Center, 88, 230
*USS Pampanito*, 84, 85
U-2 spy plane, 208

**V**

Vaillancourt Fountain, 122
vegetarian restaurant, 36
Victoria Pastry, 47
Victorian London, 249
Victorian Tea, 164
Victor's, 121
Villa Florence, 121
Village Fair, 230
Village Green, The, 201
Visitor Information Center, San Francisco, 4
Vivande Porta Via, 66

**W**

Waiters on Wheels, 19
Waiter's Race, 243
walking beam steam engine, 86
Walnut Creek Model Railroad Society, 186
*Wapama*, 88
Water Ski & Boat Show, 178
waterslides, 182
Wave Organ, 93
Wax Museum, The, 95
Weibel Vineyards, 187
West End tour, 102
Westin St. Francis Hotel, 121, 256
Whale Center, 112
Whale-of-a-Time-World playground, 179
whale-watching tours, 112
White Elephant Sale, 239
Whittier Mansion, 77
Wild California exhibit, 90
wildflowers, 173, 223
Wildflower Show, 173
Wildlife Center, The, 230
Williams, Robin, 243
William Detzel Carving Company, 102
windmill, 102
wind tunnel, 208
wine tasting, 184, 187
Winter Lodge, The, 209, 236
wishing bridge, 98
Wolfe, Thomas, 3
Woodminster Amphitheater, 170
Woodpecker Nature Trail, 226
Woolworth Co., F.W., 111

**X**

x-rated cookies, 70

**Y**

Yan Can/Charlotte Combe Int'l Cooking
    School, 20
*Yankee Clipper*, 207
Yank Sing, 64
Yet Wah, 7, 65, 158, 202, 220
Yoshi's, 159
Young Performers Theatre, 81, 234
Yujean's Modern Cuisine of China, 159

**Z**

Zachary's Chicago Pizza, 160
Zarro & Zephyr (llamas), 221
Zebra Zephyr tram ride, 102
Zoo Run, 102
Zoofari, 181

# SAN FRANCISCO NEIGHBORHOODS INDEX: FOR CLUSTERED SIGHTSEEING

## CHINATOWN

Attractions:
Chinese Culture Center, 68
Chinese temples, 71
fortune cookie factories, 70
herb shops, 71

Restaurants:
Far East Cafe, 33
Hong Kong Tea House, 38
New Asia, 53
New Woey Loy Goey Cafe, 54
Ocean City, 56
The Pot Sticker, 57
Sam Wo, 58
Taiwan, 61
Tung Fong, 63

## CIVIC CENTER

Attractions:
City Hall tour, 114
San Francisco Children's Opera, 80
San Francisco Museum of Modern Art, 83
San Francisco Symphony Family Concerts, 81

Restaurants:
Max's Opera Cafe, 49
Salmagundi, 58

## DOWNTOWN/UNION SQUARE

Attractions:
F.A.O. Schwarz, 110
F.W. Woolworth Co., 111
Greater Tuna, 79
Kinderzimmer, 111
Macy's Electronics Department, 111
Robison's Exclusively for Pets, 111
STBS, 81
Sanrio, 111
Union Square tour, 114
Visitor Information Center, 4
cable car ride, 114

Restaurants:
The Bread & Honey Tea Room, 26
The Compass Rose, 30
French Room, 33
The Magic Pan, 47
Mama's, 48
Salmagundi, 58
Sears, 59

## FISHERMAN'S WHARF

Attractions:
Alcatraz Island, 68
The American Carousel Museum, 93
The Cannery, 105
Cost Plus Imports, 105
Ghirardelli Square, 106
Guinness Museum of World Records, 94
Ripley's Believe It or Not! Museum, 94
San Francisco International Toy Museum, 84
San Francisco Maritime National Historical Park, 85
San Francisco School of Cooking, 20
*USS Pampanito*, 85
The Wax Museum, 95

Restaurants:
Compadres Mexican Bar & Grill, 29
Ghirardelli Chocolate Manufactory, 34
The Magic Pan, 47
T.G.I. Friday's, 61

## FORT MASON CENTER

Attractions:
Book Bay, 239
The Mexican Museum, 82
Museo Italo-Americano, 83
*S.S. Jeremiah O'Brien*, 89
San Francisco Craft & Folk Art Museum, 83
Young Performers Theatre, 81

Restaurants:
Greens, 36

## THE MISSION

Attractions:
Mission Dolores, 77

Restaurants:
El Faro, 65
La Rondalla, 43
La Taqueria, 44
La Victoria Bakery and Grocery, 60
St. Francis Fountain, 60

## NORTH BEACH

Attractions:
Beach Blanket Babylon, 78
North Beach tour, 114

Restaurants:
Basque Hotel, 25
Caffe Roma, 27
Calzone's, 27
Capp's Corner, 28
Little Joe's, 45
Mama's, 48
North Beach Pizza, 54
Tommaso's, 61

## UNION STREET

Attractions:
Allyne Park, 77
Octagon House, 76

Restaurants:
Doidge's Kitchen, 30
La Cuchina, 43
Mai's Vietnamese Restaurant, 47
Pasand, 57

# CATEGORICAL INDEX
San Francisco locations appear in boldface type.

## TEN GREAT THINGS TO DO WITH KIDS IN SAN FRANCISCO

**Alcatraz Island, 68**
**Beach Blanket Babylon matinee, 78**
**California Academy of Sciences, 89**
**Exploratorium, 92**
**F.A.O. Schwarz, 110**
**Far East Cafe, 33**
**Ghirardelli Chocolate Manufactory, 34**
**Golden Gate Park, 96**
**Mission Dolores, 77**
**San Francisco Zoo, 102**

## WHERE TO GET GREAT SOUVENIRS OF SAN FRANCISCO

**Basic Brown Bear Factory & Store, 105**
**Esprit Factory Outlet, 105**
**Fantasia, 32**
**F.A.O. Schwarz, 110**
**F.W. Woolworth Co., 111**
**Goosebumps, 106**
**Hard Rock Cafe, 37**
**Hornblower Dining Yachts, 39**
**The Kite Shop, 106**
**Music Tracks, 110**
**Octagon House, 76**
**Old Mint, 77**

## THE ULTIMATE CALIFORNIA EXPERIENCE: EARTHQUAKE

Earthquake Trail, 226
Seismograph:
   **Josephine D. Randall Junior Museum, 84**
   Lawrence Hall of Science, 171
   Geology Department, U.C. Berkeley, 167
Simulated Earthquake:
   **California Academy of Sciences, 89**
   **The San Francisco Experience, 109**
**Vaillancourt Fountain, 122**

## WINNERS WITH TEENS

**Alcatraz Island, 68**
**Beach Blanket Babylon, 78**
**Candlelight Fort Tours, 73**
**Chamber of Horrors, 95**
CLIO Awards, 245
**Esprit Factory Outlet, 105**
**factory outlets, 106**
**Fort Funston, 96**
**Funtasia, 109**
**Giant Camera Obscura, 71**
Great America, 207
**Greater Tuna, 79**
**Guinness Museum of World Records, 94**
**Hard Rock Cafe, 37**
**Hotel Diva, 118**
*The Hunchback of Notre Dame*, 75
**Laserium, 91**

Macy's Electronics Department, 111
**Mels Drive-In, 50**
**Musee Mecanique, 71**
**Music Tracks, 110**
NASA Ames Research Center, 208
**Ripley's Believe It or Not! Museum, 94**
*Ruby* Sailing Yacht, 112
**San Francisco Museum of Modern Art, 83**
**Tactile Dome, 92**
*USS Pampanito*, 85

## RESTAURANTS WITH GREAT VIEWS

The Castaway, 190
**Compadres Mexican Bar & Grill, 29**
**Eagle Cafe, 31**
Galaxy Sandwich Shop, 171
**Greens, 36**
Guaymas, 213
**Hornblower Dining Yachts, 39**
L.J. Quinn's Lighthouse, 149
**The Magic Pan, 47**
Miramar Beach Inn, 197
**Mission Rock Resort, 53**
Nantucket Fish Company, 151
Rusty Pelican, 153
Sam's Anchor Cafe, 217
Scott's Seafood Grill & Bar, 154
Skates, 156
Sweden House Bakery, 222
Taco Bell, 200
**Upstairs at the Cliff House, 63**

## GREAT OUTDOOR DINING

Berkeley Thai House, 13
**Cafe de Young, 83**
Chevy's, 136
Guaymas, 213
Late for the Train, 196
L.J. Quinn's Lighthouse, 149
Sam's Anchor Cafe, 217
Sweden House Bakery, 222

## 100% NON-SMOKING RESTAURANTS

Allied Arts Guild Restaurant, 189
Bubba's Diner, 211
Fatapple's, 140
Gramma's, 143
**Greens, 36**
Hobee's, 144
**Hornblower Dining Yachts, 39**
Late for the Train, 196
Station House Cafe, 218
**The Village Green, 201**
Yujean's Modern Cuisine of China, 159
Zachary's Chicago Pizza, 160

## BEST SUNDAY BRUNCH SPOTS

The Castaway, 190
Claremont Resort Pavilion Room, 137
Compadres Mexican Bar & Grill, 29
Danville Hotel Restaurant & Saloon, 139
Gramma's, 143
Greens, 36
Hornblower Dining Yachts, 39
La Cuchina, 43
Late for the Train, 196
Miramar Beach Inn, 197
Pine Brook Inn, 198
Rusty Pelican, 153
Skates, 156
Stagecoach Restaurant, 200

## DIM SUM SPOTS

Hong Kong Tea House, 38
Jade Villa, 146
King of China Restaurant, 42
Kow Loon Pastry, 15
New Asia, 53
Ocean City, 56
Tong Palace, 42
Tung Fong, 63
Yank Sing, 64

## RESTAURANTS WITH TAKE-OUT DELIVERY SERVICE

Cadillac Bar, 26
Chef Chu's, 191
Max's Diner, 49
North Beach Pizza, 54
Tony Roma's, 219

## COFFEEHOUSES

Blue Danube Coffee House, 48
Caffe Roma, 27
The Med, 186

## FAMILY-STYLE ITALIAN RESTAURANTS

Basque Hotel, 25
Bertola's, 132
Capp's Corner, 28
Dan's Place, 191

## ICE CREAM

Edy's, 139
Farrell's, 232
Fenton's Creamery, 141
Fudge Alley, 143
Ghirardelli Chocolate Manufactory, 34
The Ice Creamery, 145
KQED Old Fashioned Ice Cream Social
  & Tasting, 245
Old Uncle Gaylord's Ice Cream Parlor, 56
Ortman's Ice Cream Parlor, 152
Polly Ann Ice Cream, 57
Schuyler's Ice Cream Cafe, 148
St. Francis Fountain, 60
Swensen's Ice Cream Parlor, 110

## TAQUERIAS

Cactus Taqueria, 134
El Faro, 65
La Taqueria, 44
Picante Taqueria & Cantina, 153
Taqueria Mexican Grill, 219
Taqueria Vera Cruz, 45

## GREAT PICNIC SITES

Angel Island State Park, 95
Audubon Canyon Ranch, 224
Berkeley Shakespeare Festival, 167
Botanical Garden, U.C. Berkeley, 165
Campanile, 165
Concord Pavilion, 167
Coyote Point Park, 205
Dunsmuir House and Gardens, 176
llunch with a llama, 220
Marin French Cheese Company, 221
McKegney Green, 224
Mountain Lake Park, 102
Mountain Play, 240
Old Mill Park, 226
Palace of Fine Arts, 92
Point Reyes National Seashore, 226
Stern Grove Midsummer Music Festival, 242
Stow Lake, 101
Strybing Arboretum, 101

## TEA TIME

The Bread & Honey Tea Room, 26
Christmas Carol Tea, 251
The Compass Rose, 30
Four Seasons Clift Hotel, 117
Japanese Tea Garden and Teahouse, 98
The Pelican Inn, 216
Victorian Tea, 164
The Village Green, 201

## GREAT FREEBIES

Adventure Playground, 174
Alexander Lindsay Junior Museum, 171
Audubon Canyon Ranch, 224
Cable Car Museum, 93
Children's Playground, 97
Crab Cove Visitor Center, 175
Fourth of July Fireworks and Festivities, 243
James Fitzgerald Marine Reserve, 206
Josephine D. Randall Junior Museum, 84
Make-A-Circus, 79
Marin Headlands, 225
Maritime Museum, 85
Mission San Jose de Guadalupe, 164
Muir Woods National Monument, 226
NASA Ames Research Center, 208
Oakland Harbor boat tours, 185
Oakland Museum, 173
Old Borges Ranch, 181
Old Mint, 77
Palo Alto Duck Pond, 206
Palo Alto Junior Museum, 203
Point Reyes National Seashore, 226
Shorebird Nature Center, 182
Stern Grove Midsummer Music Festival, 242
Treasure Island Museum, 94
Wave Organ, 93

## ON THE CHEAP

Alameda Penny Market, 184
The American Carousel Museum, 93
Bay Area Discovery Museum, 223
Bertola's, 132
Brennan's, 133
Brothers Delicatessen and Restaurant, 190
Casa de Eva, 135
Chabot Observatory and Planetarium, 184
Children's Fairyland U.S.A., 175
Coit Tower, 72
Eagle Cafe, 31
F.W. Woolworth Co., 111
factory outlets, 106
Fuddruckers, 142
Golden Gate Park, 96
Hobee's, 144
John Muir National Historic Site, 164
La Taqueria, 44 (and any other taqueria)
Le Croissant, 215
Mai's Vietnamese Restaurant, 47
The Mexican Museum, 82
Mifune, 51
Mission Dolores, 77
Mission Rock Resort, 53
Muriel's Doll House Museum, 173
New Woey Loy Goey Cafe, 54
North Beach Pizza, 54
Ocean City, 56 (and any other dim sum spot)
STBS, 81
San Francisco International Toy Museum, 84
San Francisco Maritime National Historical
    Park, 85
Sears, 59
St. Francis Fountain, 60
Tilden Nature Area, 182

## THE BIG SPLURGE

Beach Blanket Babylon, 78
Claremont Resort Pavilion Room, 137
F.A.O. Schwarz, 110
French Room, Clift Hotel, 33
Great America, 207
Greater Tuna, 79
Hornblower Dining Yachts, 39
House of Prime Rib, 39
Marine World Africa USA, 178
Scott's Seafood Grill & Bar, 154
TJ's Gingerbread House, 158

## THE GOLDEN GATE NATIONAL RECREATION AREA

*This recreation area encompasses 72,815 acres in San Francisco and Marin counties. There are maritime parks, beaches, historic sites, and over 100 miles of trails. The following sites are part of the G.G.N.R.A.:*

Alcatraz Island, 68
Angel Island State Park, 95
Aquatic Park, 96
Baker Beach, 96
China Beach, 96
Cliff House, 63
    Visitors Center, 71
Fort Funston, 96
Fort Mason Center, 275
Fort Point National Historic Site, 73
Marin Headlands, 225
Muir Woods National Monument, 226
*S.S. Jeremiah O'Brien*, 89
San Francisco Maritime National
    Historical Park, 85
Stinson Beach, 228

## TRAIN RIDES

Ardenwood Historic Farm, 163
Niles Canyon Railway Museum, 180
Oakland Zoo, 180
Redwood Valley Railway, 183

## TRADITIONAL THANKSGIVING DINNERS

*Often it is a relative bargain to go out for this elaborate dinner. If you have a large group, it's less expensive and probably more fun to prepare dinner at home. But if there are just two or three of you, it's definitely cheaper and easier to eat out. Here are the places which prepare a traditional feast for your pleasure:*

The Castaway, 190
Danville Hotel Restaurant & Saloon, 139
Gramma's, 143
Heidi Pies, 195
Hornblower Dining Yachts, 39
Larry Blake's, 148
Mels Drive-In, 50
Pine Brook Inn, 198
T.G.I. Friday's, 201

*For listings in the following three categories, always call to verify that their policy of being open on these holidays has not changed.*

## ATTRACTIONS OPEN ON THANKSGIVING DAY

Black Diamond Mines Regional Preserve, 164
**Blue and Gold Fleet Bay Tours, 112**
**California Academy of Sciences, 89**
California Marine Mammal Center, 229
**Cliff House Visitors Center, 71**
**Conservatory of Flowers, 98**
**Japanese Tea Garden and Teahouse, 98**
Malibu Castle, 207
Marin Headlands, 225
**San Francisco Maritime National**
    **Historical Park, 85**
**Stow Lake Boathouse, 101**
**Strybing Arboretum, 101**
The Winter Lodge, 209

## ATTRACTIONS OPEN ON CHRISTMAS DAY

Black Diamond Mines Regional Preserve, 164
**California Academy of Sciences, 89**
California Marine Mammal Center, 229
**Conservatory of Flowers, 98**
**Japanese Tea Garden and Teahouse, 98**
Malibu Castle, 207
Muir Woods National Monument, 226
**Ripley's Believe It or Not! Museum, 94**
**Strybing Arboretum, 101**

## ATTRACTIONS OPEN ON NEW YEAR'S DAY

Berkeley Iceland, 184
Black Diamond Mines Regional Preserve, 164
**Blue and Gold Fleet Bay Tours, 112**
**California Academy of Sciences, 89**
California Marine Mammal Center, 229
Children's Fairyland U.S.A., 175
**Conservatory of Flowers, 98**
**Exploratorium, 92**
**Japanese Tea Garden and Teahouse, 98**
Malibu Castle, 207
Marin Headlands, 225
Marine World Africa USA, 178
**Mission Dolores, 77**
Muir Woods National Monument, 226
Oakland Zoo, 180
**Ripley's Believe It or Not! Museum, 94**
**Stow Lake Boathouse, 101**
**Strybing Arboretum, 101**
The Winter Lodge, 209

## CREDITS:
Typesetting, layout, and cover design: Betsy Joyce
Maps: John Parsons and Mark Williams, Eureka Cartography
Printing: McNaughton-Gunn
Computer wizardry: Gene Meyers

### Illustrations:
pages 6, 7, 8, 10, 17: Hideo Yoshida
pages 12, 39, 58, 70, 135, 141, 218, 231, 266: Deborah M. Cotter

### Photos:
cover: David Weintraub, San Francisco Convention & Visitors Bureau;
page 1: Victoria Station;
page 4: Carl Wilmington, San Francisco Convention & Visitors Bureau;
pages 9, 15, 26, 34, 35, 62, 145, 192, 259: Katy Greene;
pages 38, 207: Great America;
page 46: Chronicle Books;
page 69: Robert Stinnel, Red & White Fleet;
page 72: Herb Bettin, San Francisco Convention & Visitors Bureau;
pages 74, 97, 99, 125, 237: San Francisco Convention & Visitors Bureau;
page 76: Haas-Lilienthal House;
page 78: Ron Scherl, Steve Silver Productions;
page 79: Mason Street Theatre;
page 80: Make-A-Circus;
pages 86, 87: San Francisco Maritime National Historical Park;
page 90: California Academy of Sciences;
page 91: S. Middleton, California Academy of Sciences;
page 92: Nancy Rodger, Exploratorium;
page 100: San Francisco Recreation and Park Department;
page 103: Michael Shay, San Francisco Zoological Society;
page 104: San Francisco Zoological Society;
page 107: Ghirardelli Square;
page 108: Hanford Associates;
page 109: Edelman Public Relations;
page 117: John Sutton, Chancellor Hotel;
page 119: Hotel Diva;
page 122: Park Hyatt San Francisco;
page 127: The Mansion Hotel;
pages 128, 242: Golden Gate Council of American Youth Hostels;
page 149: Valerio, Victoria Station;
pages 163, 183: East Bay Regional Parks District;
page 166: California Alumni Association;
page 169: Jon Winet, Pacific Film Archive;
page 172: Saxon Donnelly, Lawrence Hall of Science;
page 176: Dunsmuir Registration Program;
pages 178, 179: Marine World Africa USA;
page 180: East Bay Zoological Society;
page 185: Port of Oakland;
pages 204, 241: California State Department of Parks and Recreation;
page 229: Jane Oka, California Marine Mammal Center;
page 240: George Olson, Dudell & Associates;
page 245: Paladino Agency;
page 246: KQED;
page 247: Alameda Naval Air Station Public Affairs Office;
page 248: Terry Pimsleur & Co.;
page 250: Jack Wodell Associates;
page 252: Carole Terwilliger Meyers;
page 255: Arne Folkedal, San Francisco Ballet;
page 281: Meyers Family photo album.

# About The Author

Carole Terwilliger Meyers, a native San Franciscan, holds a B.A. degree in anthropology from San Francisco State University and an elementary teaching credential from Fresno State College.

Currently she is a columnist for the *San Francisco Examiner* and a contributing editor to *Parents' Press*. In the past she has been a columnist for *California* magazine, the *San Jose Mercury News*, and *California Travel Report* magazine, as well as an editor for both *Goodlife* magazine and the San Francisco Bay Area *ASPO (Lamaze Natural Childbirth) Newsletter*. Her articles have appeared in *Family Circle, New Choices, San Francisco Focus, Image,* and *SF* magazines as well as numerous other magazines and newspapers.

Ms. Meyers resides in Berkeley with her husband and two children.

# Books Available from
## *The Family Travel Guides Catalogue . . .*

### WEEKEND ADVENTURES FOR CITY-WEARY PEOPLE: OVERNIGHT TRIPS IN NORTHERN CALIFORNIA
*(4th ed.) Meyers. 304pp; 6x9; b&w photos, maps.* **$11.95.** The vacation riches of northern California outside the San Francisco Bay Area are detailed—including the Gold Rush country, ski resorts, and family camps. It covers where to stay, where to eat, and what to do and also provides appropriate information for families—such as the availability of highchairs, booster seats, and cribs. Don't leave home without it.

### THE CABLE CAR AND THE DRAGON
*Caen. 40pp; 9x8; color illus; hardcover.* **$9.95.** Written by San Francisco's favorite newspaper columnist, this delightful story takes place one foggy evening when a bored cable car and an equally bored dragon from the Chinese New Year's parade get together for some fun on the city's famous hills. Read it to your child before, during, and after your trip. It's sure to become a beloved memento.

### KIDDING AROUND SAN FRANCISCO
*Zibart. 63pp; 7x9; b&w photos, b&w and color illus, maps.* **$9.95.** Written especially for children, this easy-to-read book gives information on the city's history and sightseeing highlights. Child-friendly restaurants, stores of interest to young shoppers, and a calendar of special events are also included. Recommended for ages 8+.

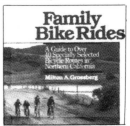

### FAMILY BIKE RIDES: A GUIDE TO OVER 40 SPECIALLY SELECTED BICYCLE ROUTES IN NORTHERN CALIFORNIA
*Grossberg. 112pp; 9x8; b&w photos, maps.* **$7.95.** Detailed descriptions of bike routes include sightseeing suggestions and maps, plus such valuable information as where to park your bike safely and where to stop for refreshments. All routes are short, level, scenic, and off main roads.

### KIDS COOKING: A VERY SLIGHTLY MESSY MANUAL
*Editors of Klutz Press. 88pp; 6x9; color illus; spiral binding.* **$11.95.** The recipes in this built-for-abuse book have all been approved by a panel of "vegetable-leery taste-testers." Recipes included range from Tuna Wiggle to Darrell's "Forget-the-Cookies-Just-Give-Me-That-Batter" Chocolate Chip Cookie Recipe. A set of sturdy color-coded plastic measuring spoons is included.

### SCIENCE EXPERIMENTS YOU CAN EAT
*Cobb. 128pp; 6x8; b&w illus.* **$4.95.** What makes popcorn pop? How does jelly jell? Why does bread rise? Experiment in your kitchen with these 39 easy and delicious science experiments and then eat the results!

### SAN FRANCISCO FAMILY FUN
*Meyers. 296pp; 6x9; b&w photos and illus, maps.* **$12.95.**

# Order Form

*Please print:*                                           Date _____

Name _____

Street Address _____ Apt. # _____
                    (necessary for UPS delivery)

City/State/Zip _____

Mailing Address (if different) _____

Phone (day) _____ (evening) _____

| Title | Page # | Quantity | Price |
|-------|--------|----------|-------|
| _____ | _____ | _____ | _____ |
| _____ | _____ | _____ | _____ |
| _____ | _____ | _____ | _____ |
| _____ | _____ | _____ | _____ |
| _____ | _____ | _____ | _____ |
| _____ | _____ | _____ | _____ |

Subtotal _____

| SHIPPING CHARGES | | | |
|---|---|---|---|
| | Continental U.S (UPS grnd) (UPS air) | Alaska/Hawaii (postal (UPS air) grnd) | Canada (UPS grnd) |
| Under $25 | $3.00 $8.00 | $4.00 $8.00 | $8.00 |
| $25-$50 | $4.00 $9.00 | $5.00 $12.00 | $9.00 |
| over $50 | $5.00 $10.00 | $7.00 $15.00 | $10.00 |
| All shipments are insured. UPS air prices are for 2nd Day Service. | | | |

California residents
add $7\frac{1}{4}$% sales tax _____

shipping and handling _____

TOTAL _____

Method of Payment:  □ MasterCard    **VISA** □ VISA    □ Check

Card Number:                                          Expiration date:

☐☐☐☐ ☐☐☐☐ ☐☐☐☐ ☐☐☐☐        ☐☐   ☐☐
                                                      mo.   yr.

Signature _____

**Enclose check or money order payable to Carousel Press.**

All payments must be in U.S. dollars.

Send to:
**CAROUSEL PRESS**
*The Family Travel Guides Catalogue*
**Order Dept. S**
**P.O. Box 6061**
**Albany, CA 94706**
**(415) 527-5849**

283

# Feedback

One of the pleasures of being a critic is having your opinion heard. Here is your chance to play critic. Let me know what you've disliked (or liked) about your visit to San Francisco. Get it off your chest. Tell me about the bad service, noisy rooms, etc. I promise to read everything and to investigate legitimate complaints.

This is also your chance to let me know if any of my descriptions have become obsolete. Things do change.

And please keep me informed about your discoveries of new places that you think belong in the next edition of *San Francisco Family Fun.*

Sincerely,
Carole Terwilliger Meyers
c/o Carousel Press, P.O. Box 6061, Albany, CA 94706

Your Name _____

Address _____

City, State, Zip _____

Telephone (      ) _____


Listing Name _____

Address _____

City, State, Zip _____

Telephone (      ) _____

Describe your annoyance or discovery:

_____

_____

_____

_____

_____

_____

_____

_____